READINGS IN INDUSTRIAL ECONOMICS

edited by

CHARLES K. ROWLEY

DAVID DALE PROFESSOR OF ECONOMICS

THE UNIVERSITY OF NEWCASTLE UPON TYNE

VOLUME ONE

THEORETICAL FOUNDATIONS

Macmillan

First published 1972 by
THE MACMILLAN PRESS LTD
London and Basingstoke
Associated companies in New York Toronto
Dublin Melbourne Johannesburg and Madras

SBN 333 10951 1 (hard cover)
333 10957 0 (paper cover)

Printed in Great Britain by
RICHARD CLAY (THE CHAUCER PRESS) LTD
Bungay, Suffolk

Contents

Contents

Preface

Industrial economics only too frequently is treated as a descriptive, institutional, even anti-theoretical discipline to which the lesser able and the under-motivated students of economics are directed as a substitute for a vocational course in business studies. It is the principal objective of these *Readings in Industrial Economics* to counteract this impression and to present the discipline as intellectually stimulating and theoretically based, designed to make use of advanced micro-economic theory in the analysis of important problems of public policy. The introductions to both volumes emphasise the need both for a clearly formulated methodology as a basis for positive and normative analysis, and for reaching out to the testing of hypotheses from a really sound theoretical foundation – an approach which has suffered much in recent years owing to the widespread misuse of standard econometric techniques.

It is usual to justify collections of articles as a means of supplementing standard textbooks in the discipline and of avoiding log-jams in the undergraduate and postgraduate libraries. In this case, there is a more fundamental justification, namely that there is no textbook in industrial economics currently available suitable for advanced undergraduate and postgraduate students. Such a textbook has been commissioned by Macmillan and is presently under preparation by Michael A. Crew of the University of Southampton, and myself. Publication is scheduled for 1973. In the meantime, these volumes provide a foretaste of my thinking in the field and should serve for many years to come as a useful, if not an essential, supplement to our textbook.

I am deeply indebted to all the authors and publishers who so willingly co-operated in giving their permission for their material to be reprinted. Specific acknowledgements and identifications of the original sources are to be found at the beginning of each contribution, whilst a short biography of authors is to be found at the end of each volume. In addition, I should like to thank all my students, undergraduate and postgraduate, who attended my courses in industrial economics during 1967–70 at the University of Kent at Canterbury and who contributed so much to my understanding of the subject. I am deeply grateful also to those of my colleagues and friends who directed my attention to the more fruitful aspects of industrial economics, and most especially to R. A. Cooper, M. A. Crew, H. G. Johnson, Michael Jones-Lee, A. T. Peacock, E. G. West and Jack Wiseman. Most of all, however, I should like to thank my wife Marjorie, without whose help and encouragement these volumes would never have seen the light of day.

CHARLES K. ROWLEY

Department of Economics and Related Studies,
University of York

Introduction

Industrial economics does not really exist as a distinct entity within the subject-matter of economics, and this has always posed problems for those whose duty it is to teach such courses within the framework of a wider programme in economics and related studies. For at its most extensive, industrial economics encompasses the whole of price theory – the very heartland of micro-economics – whilst in its most restrictive (and unproductive) form it is treated as a dull, descriptive, even anti-theoretical course of studies, designed to dissuade the brighter undergraduate or postgraduate student from ever taking up economics as a professional career and treated by the less able as an adequate if unstimulating substitute for a vocational course in business studies.

After a number of years' experience in teaching industrial economics, I am more than ever convinced that the narrow, descriptive approach is at once a complete waste of time and a frustration of ability, but that there is yet a worth-while programme of study in industrial economics which develops out of basic micro-economic theory without simply plagiarising the latter course of study. It is the principal purpose of these volumes of readings to present a viable and an intellectually stimulating course in industrial economics which makes use of recent theoretical developments in the analysis of important problems in public policy. The moderately advanced mathematical content of certain of the contributions serves to indicate the increasing scientific rigour of this branch of economics. The emphasis in both volumes upon theoretical rather than empirical analysis reflects my own prejudice in favour of reaching out to the testing of hypotheses from a really sound theoretical foundation, an approach and emphasis which is justified in some detail later in this introduction.

The Subject-matter of Industrial Economics

Conventional courses in micro-economic theory [2] centre attention upon three main areas of study, namely (i) welfare economics, (ii) resource allocation and (iii) distribution. Industrial economics draws upon the foundations provided by the first two of these, moderating the basic theory as necessary for the analysis of specific problems in public policy. It is indeed the public policy orientation of industrial economics – as it is with public finance and social economics, to instance but two equivalent cases – which stakes its claim to a separate consideration in the teaching of economics.

In a sense, my views on the subject-matter of industrial economics are fully reflected in the contributions reprinted in these volumes and there is little more that needs to be said. But some explanation may yet be useful concerning (i) those included contributions which are not universally regarded as part of industrial economics, and (ii) those topics which are usually dealt with but which find no reflection in these volumes.

Within the former category must fall most of the contents of Part Two of Volume 1, concerning models of market organisation. A strong case can be made that this forms an integral part of basic micro-economic theory, and as such should be treated as an existing foundation for the study of industrial economics and not as a component part of the subject. In practice, however, there can be little doubt that courses in microeconomic theory do not do justice to this important topic, at least from the specific viewpoint of industrial economics. The articles reprinted in this volume are chosen precisely because they are directly relevant for the public policy aspects of industrial economics, as will become very apparent in Volume 2.

Within the former category also must fall most of the contents of Part One of Volume 2 concerning the welfare economics of market failure. In this case, my defence is much stronger, resting as it does upon the public policy emphasis of industrial economics. Public policy discussion in the absence of a firm basis in welfare economics is barren and, perhaps worse, encounters all the dangers of value statements being interpreted as scientific prescriptions by those responsible for policy implementation.

Within the second category of omissions falls a wide range of topics – testament to the catholic definition of industrial economics. There is no discussion of cost and demand conditions in these volumes, principally because these are areas so central to micro-economic theory, but they often do feature in industrial economics courses. There is no discussion of the economics of advertising, save that implicit in monopolistic competition theory. There is no real discussion of the economics of vertical integration or of diversification, which are certainly well-beaten paths in industrial economics. There is no discussion of spatial economics, despite the important public policy implications of industrial location, principally because this topic is now centrally relevant to regional and urban economics. There is no discussion of the capital market and the finance of enterprise, principally because this is the heartland of business finance. Most controversially, there is little reference to public enterprise, as the subtitle of Volume 2 is designed to emphasise, principally because this is now a substantive area in its own right, with a vast literature that could not be fairly reflected in these volumes [11]. For the most part, industrial economics, as reflected in these volumes, centres attention upon the relationship between government and private enterprise as examined from a theoretical viewpoint in the light of a clearly formulated methodology.

A Methodology of Positive Economics

For the most part, the methodology which pervades Volume 1, and which was used as an important criterion in the selection of these contributions, is that first clearly exposited by Milton Friedman and published in 1953 [3]. The essence of Friedman's contribution is that the validity of economic theory is in no manner dependent upon the realism of its premises or assumptions, and indeed that excessive preoccupation with such matters is actually harmful to the development of economics as a science:

> This widely held view is fundamentally wrong and productive of much mischief. Far from providing an easier means for sifting valid from invalid hypotheses, it only confuses the issue, promotes misunderstanding about the significance of empirical evidence for economic theory, produces a misdirection of much intellectual effort devoted to the development of positive economics, and

*

impedes the attainment of consensus on tentative hypotheses in positive economics. ([3] p. 14)

Friedman defined positive science in terms of prediction, and suggested therefore that the only relevant test of the validity of economic theory was a comparison of its predictions with experience. The theory should be rejected if its predictions were contradicted more frequently than the predictions of the best alternative theory, whilst theories which had survived many opportunities for contradiction might be utilised with some confidence. From this viewpoint many of the preceding debates, for instance that concerning the validity of profit maximisation in the theory of the firm which had been conducted within the framework of realism of assumptions, appeared to be entirely beside the point. Not surprisingly, therefore, Friedman's methodology encountered initial resistance from substantial sections of the economics profession. In the ensuing debate, a number of important questions were raised concerning the precise implications of accepting the predictive test [5].

In the first place, it became clear that if a theory was to be judged not directly by its postulates but indirectly by its implications or predictions, then there would always have to be a clear statement of the precise implications or predictions on which the theory was to be assessed. For in the absence of such a statement every negative test could be rejected merely by redefining the offending implication as an 'innocuous' postulate, and in such circumstances the theory might not be refutable at all. Such a theory would hardly make a contribution to economic science as defined by Friedman.

Secondly, it was quickly recognised that the predictive test would be much more difficult to exercise in economic science than in, say, physics, because controlled experiments for the most part could not be utilised. It might be much more difficult therefore to disqualify an economic theory by reference to the predictive test than by examining the realism of its premises, and this could provide an undeserved protection for the *status quo*. In any event, it would be essential to outline fairly precisely the conditions under which the test could be said to have refuted the theory. Whether or not such precision is possible given the present state of econometrics is itself a debatable question. If the tests themselves could not effectively distinguish between alternative theories, could not a case be made for paying some attention to the plausibility of the theory and in particular to the realism of that theory's premises?

Thirdly, it was readily apparent that many different economic theories might throw up identical predictions at least concerning specific areas of economic concern. On what basis could these theories be evaluated? Friedman invoked two additional criteria to take account of this problem, namely (i) simplicity and (ii) fruitfulness. On the assumption that economic science is concerned to predict a lot with a little, the principle of Occam's razor would seem to determine that the more complex theories should give way to their simpler counterpart. But not all economists would accept the underlying premise involved. The assumption that economic science prefers general to less general theories wherever possible is less controversial, but the question remains as to the price payable for generality. What is the precise trade-off to be applied between predictive success, simplicity and generality? This remains a troublesome question for those who create and evaluate economic theories within the broad ground rules of Friedman's methodology. At this point, hunch, instinct, feel – call it what you like – must play an indispensable role, however repugnant this may seem to those who look for a scientific heaven in this imperfect world.

Furthermore, although it is clearly possible that theories based upon unrealistic assumptions may turn out to be predictively successful – and there are some excellent examples of this in the natural sciences – there is no necessary reason to suppose that predictively successful theories must be descriptively false in their assumptions, especially when the semantic distinction is upheld between abstraction on the one hand and falsity (or unrealism) on the other. Nature is not always so perverse, even in economic science. For this reason alone many economists would argue that a close relationship should be maintained between reality and the assumptions of a theory, always provided that predictive success is not thereby diminished, even at a high cost in terms of loss of simplicity and generality.

More fundamentally, however, Friedman's methodology is rejected in its entirety by a large number of economists who deny the exclusive association between science and prediction, who view truth as indivisible, and who emphasise the explanatory and descriptive as well as the predictive properties of economics, to say nothing of those economic theorists who view economics primarily as a complicated game of mental chess. There is no basis in principle for considering these viewpoints as inferior to that expressed by Friedman.

Nevertheless, Friedman's methodology has been applied – though not exclusively – in selecting the contributions to be reprinted in this volume, and some explanation is required as to why this approach has been adopted. Three important justifications can be advanced. First, the predictive emphasis is in my view the most useful approach in terms of practical policy. For what is it that households, firms and governments really want to know from the economist? They are hardly interested in the detailed costing systems of the firm or even whether decisions are motivated by profit maximisation or by variations in the sex-drive of senior executives. They are much more directly concerned to know how the firm's price/output behaviour will respond to changes in important economic variables, viz. wage rates, the price of raw materials, excise duties, lump-sum taxes and the like. This is precisely the kind of issue that the predictive test is designed to resolve.

Secondly, the approach can be defended in terms of the insight it offers into the working of the economic system. For in my view, the most original contributions to the economics of industrial organisation in the field of positive analysis have sprung in recent years from the writing of economists who are influenced, at least in part, by the Friedman methodology. The reader can judge for himself the justice of this claim on the basis of the contributions reprinted in this volume.

Thirdly, the approach can be defended in terms of the scientific rigour necessitated by the Friedman methodology. Theories must be precisely formulated and all relevant restrictions must be placed upon the postulated relationships if their comparative static properties are to be evaluated. This will become crystal-clear in reading the present volume. No such precision is required for theories which are not exposed to such stringent analysis. Those who are acquainted with the loosely formulated 'full-cost' theories of the firm postulated by Hall, Hitch and Andrews will know exactly what I mean. I do not mean to raise formal precision to the height of the gods. But much wasteful controversy is inevitable where theories are ill-specified and inadequately evaluated.

A Review of Contributions

Part One of this volume is devoted to an analysis of recent theories of the firm and, if space restrictions had not predominated, would have been introduced by the survey of that subject presented to the American Economic Association in December 1966 by Fritz Machlup in his Presidential Address. Machlup, of course, is renowned as one of the staunchest defenders of marginalism in the theory of the firm [8] in the face of a sustained onslaught from 'full-cost' and other critics (notably Richard Lester [7]) during the immediate post-war period at a time before the Friedman methodology had been advanced. His 1966 survey paper revisits the battlefield and re-examines the issues that were at stake with the benefit of hindsight. Although Machlup is fully aware of and not unsympathetic towards the Friedman methodology, he has never fully embraced it, at least within the context of the theory of the firm. Certainly, Machlup has continued to defend marginalism as a theoretical construct which must not be confused with the apparent behaviour of the firm as an empirical concept – a confusion he labels as the fallacy of misplaced concreteness. In this respect, he must be closely identified with the Friedman methodology. But much of his defence of marginalism is based upon the firm's desire to survive in market conditions which are assumed to be competitive. And while the logic of this analysis cannot be denied – or the implications exaggerated – this defence is *not* in line with the Friedman methodology, as T. Koopmans, writing within a different context, has emphasised:

> Here a postulate about individual behavior is made more plausible by reference to the adverse effect of, and hence penalty for, departures from the postulated behavior. . . . But if this is the basis for our belief in profit maximization, then we should postulate that basis itself and not the profit maximization which it implies in certain circumstances. ([5] p. 140)

Machlup too has stressed the subjective nature of the marginalist concept, emphasising that objective tests of firm behaviour, conducted with all the benefit of hindsight, cannot be used as conclusive proof in an uncertain world that the decisions themselves were not motivated by marginalist principles at the time they were introduced. There is of course much truth in this viewpoint, always provided that the extension of marginalism within a subjective and total utility framework does not render the marginalist theory irrefutable. Machlup himself is far too skilful a theorist to fall into that trap; but others are less skilful and/or less scrupulous in their manipulation of economic theory. Certainly, Machlup's careful survey of the theory of the firm and his consideration and cautious claims for the marginalist postulate merit a careful reading and stand out as an exercise in true scholarship in a profession which is increasingly impatient of and intolerant towards the caution and hesitancy which such scholarship almost invariably requires.

The first contribution, by G. C. Archibald, is also concerned with the maximising approach, but strikes a more technical and a much more restricted note. Archibald is concerned to analyse just why the qualitative content of maximising theories is so limited, i.e. why it is so frequently impossible to obtain predictions with unambiguous signs in response to shifts in specified economic variables. He argues convincingly that the principal reason underlying this problem is the widespread inapplicability of the theorem of conjugate pairs, which simply means that a change in a single parameter shifts more than one condition of equilibrium (i.e. more than one schedule or curve within the theory). In such circumstances, a great deal may depend upon the precise magnitude of shift and change in slope of the several schedules in determining the direction of change of the variables under consideration – a factor which Archibald makes play with in his critique of monopolistic competition theory (printed later in this volume). Archibald clearly demonstrates the importance of careful specification of the cross-partial derivatives in any but the simplest theories of the firm if unambiguous qualitative predictions are to be obtained. If this appears to the reader to be cheating, it should be remembered that such activities are standard practice in the natural sciences.

The second contribution, by André Gabor and I. F. Pearce, does not follow the Friedman methodology (it was written before Friedman's essay was published), but is notable for its replacement of profit maximisation by maximisation of the rate of return on capital – an adjustment which is defended on grounds of plausibility at least in competitive markets. By assuming that the remuneration of the entrepreneur is a cost and that the firm operates in the interests of the owners of the money capital – a reversal of the traditional assumptions –

Gabor and Pearce presented an elegant theory of the firm with important differences from traditional theory at least with respect to optimum firm size and output rate under given cost and demand conditions. The Gabor–Pearce contribution to the theory of the firm has not received the recognition which it undoubtedly deserves. Further work within their framework is evidently possible, especially in exploring the comparative statics of the theory.

The third contribution, by W. J. Baumol, demonstrates that the standard techniques of marginal analysis and mathematical programming are fully applicable to decision problems in the theory of the firm even when the profit maximisation postulate is jettisoned. Baumol evaluated the comparative statics properties of a growth-maximising theory of the firm initially under purely competitive conditions and subsequently under oligopolistic conditions. Baumol demonstrated that the growth maximiser's sales, advertising outlay and growth rate would be larger than that of the profit maximiser, and that the growth maximiser's price/output decisions might be expected to vary in response to changes in fixed costs. He perhaps failed to draw sufficient attention to the fact that where maximum profit attainable was equal only to the minimum profit constraint, the implications and predictions of growth-maximising theories are equivalent to those of profit-maximising theories of the firm. In all other circumstances, however, the two theories offer alternative price/output responses to the imposition of lump-sum taxes, with important inferences for welfare economics, and thus are capable of evaluation by reference to the predictive test.

Baumol's important contribution to the theory of the firm was taken up and further developed by John Williamson in an article which comprises the fourth contribution to this volume. Williamson fully accepted the Friedman methodology and – ignoring the issue of plausibility – proceeded to construct a permanent growth model of the firm designed to derive the differences in behaviour that would follow from the objectives of maximising profits, maximising growth and maximising (discounted) sales. Williamson effectively demonstrated that important behavioural differences would arise as between the alternative basic postulates, in all market conditions save those in which profitability at best was the minimum sum necessary to prevent take-over. He quite correctly refrained from discussing the conditions required in the real capital market for his results to be valid.

One of the most insightful of all recent contributions to the theory of the firm, however, is that by O. E. Williamson in which he substituted a multivariable management utility function for the profit maximisation postulate. Williamson's theory focused attention upon the self-seeking behaviour of corporate management in companies characterised by separation between ownership and control and operating in markets where competitive conditions typically are not severe. Williamson regarded management utility as dependent primarily upon (i) salaries and other forms of monetary compensation together with the number and quality of staff who report to management, (ii) the extent to which management is able to direct the investment of the firm's resources (discretionary investment expenditure), and (iii) the type and amount of perquisites such as expense accounts, lavishly furnished offices and distracting secretaries received by management in excess of the amounts strictly necessary for the firm's operations. Since staff expenditures – which are assumed directly to influence demand – are shown to be greater in Williamson's theory than would be the case in profit maximisation equilibrium, Williamson's theory implies that the equilibrium rate of output will be in excess of that implied by standard theory. Actual profit will be less than the maximum profit available, whilst reported profit will be less than actual profit. Shop-floor labour is treated throughout as a fully co-operative factor input, employed efficiently by the firm at any output rate selected by the management. Like Baumol's theory, Williamson's management discretion theory predicts a negative output-rate response to any increase in fixed costs, e.g. a lump-sum tax imposition.

In my view, the weakness of all the theories of the firm reprinted in this volume is their inability to predict the inefficient use of shop-floor labour, which is surely one of the most pervasive features of the modern industrial economy. Recent contributions by Harvey Leibenstein [6] have emphasised this problem within the context of X-efficiency. A recent paper [1] develops an 'X-theory' of the firm in which the profit maximisation postulate of neo-classical theory is retained but in which the assumption of cost efficiency is relaxed to allow for labour non-cooperation with the objectives of the equity shareholders. In many respects, the comparative static implications of this theory correspond closely with those of O. E. Williamson's management model.

The theories so far discussed in this introduction are all derived more or less explicitly upon an assumption of perfect knowledge. In terms of the Friedman methodology this is quite acceptable, always provided that predictive success is not thereby sacrificed. But in the absence of an uncertainty postulate it is difficult – though not impossible – to predict the kind of adaptive search behaviour by the firm which is such a characteristic of modern business behaviour. The sixth contribution reprinted in this volume, by R. M. Cyert and M. I. Kamien, introduced a theory of adaptive behaviour based upon behavioural rules which the firm is presumed to follow when confronted by uncertainty. Cyert and Kamien developed their theory on the basis of the satisficing concepts contributed to behavioural science by Herbert Simon and R. A. Gordon, and used the technique of dynamic programming to evaluate the implications of their contribution. There is clearly great scope for additional work in this field of economic analysis.

Part Two of the volume is devoted to an analysis of those models of market organisation which are especially relevant for further work in industrial economics. Once again, the emphasis upon predictive properties proved to be an important criterion governing the selection of the reprinted contributions. Perhaps appropriately, therefore, the first contribution in this section and the seventh in the volume is by a leading exponent of the Friedman methodology, G. J. Stigler, and concerns perfect competition, which is certainly the most extensively utilised model of market organisation in contemporary economic theory. Stigler surveyed the historical development of perfect competition, commencing with the rivalrous concept of the classical economists, tracing the impact of the mathematical school (Cournot, Jevons, Edgeworth and Pareto) in formalising the model, and the subsequent reversion to the classical approach imposed by Marshall, and concluding with the complete formulation of the model by J. B. Clark and F. H. Knight. Stigler defended perfect competition against the charge that it was unrealistic by invoking the criteria of generality and predictive utility. He argued that perfect competition had defeated its newer rivals in the decisive area – the day-to-day work of the economic theorist. Whether or not this is so is open to debate. The reader may perhaps judge for himself the validity of this viewpoint by comparing the perfect competitive model with the rival models outlined and discussed subsequently in this volume.

The eighth contribution, also by G. J. Stigler, is a somewhat devastating critique of the still influential model of monopolistic competition advanced by E. Chamberlin during the 1930s. Stigler's criticisms were directed at two main levels, namely (i) at the implications of the uniformity and symmetry assumptions, established by Chamberlin, for the assumption of product differentiation which is central to the model, and (ii) at the methodology by which Chamberlin claimed relevance for his contribution, which laid considerable stress upon realism of assumptions. Stigler did not deny the logic of Chamberlin's analysis for the many-firm industry producing a single (technological) product under uniformity and symmetry conditions but with a falling demand curve for each firm. But he contended that the predictions of this standard model of monopolistic competition differed only trivially from those of competitive theory, largely because the underlying conditions could be achieved only where the demand elasticities for the products of individual firms were very high. He asked that the model of monopolistic competition should be evaluated not by reference to the plausibility of its assumptions but rather by resort to the predictive test.

The ninth contribution, by G. C. Archibald, picked up the gauntlet thrown down by Stigler and simultaneously attempted to evaluate the model of monopolistic competition by its predictions and to chide the 'Chicago' critics for their failure to examine the predictions rather than the assumptions of the model, and in particular for their failure to point out that Chamberlin had never specified what observable, testable predictions could be obtained from his model. Following a thorough analytical evaluation, Archibald claimed that Chamberlin's model yielded no qualitative comparative static predictions and that this was the consequence of a general defect, namely the incomplete specification of the demand relationships within the group. He recommended that further work was required in order to put into the model sufficient content for it to yield significant predictions, but he emphasised that the model was unlikely to prove fruitful at least in the existing state of knowledge concerning techniques of observation. The tenth, eleventh and twelfth contributions present the ensuing debate between Archibald and Chicago – as represented by G. J. Stigler and Milton Friedman – in which I consider that honours were more or less even. The debate makes worth-while reading for those who are fired or enraged by the Friedman methodology and who wish to gain an insight into the nature of professional controversy in contemporary economic science.

The thirteenth contribution, by Josef Hadar, takes the debate on the model of monopolistic competition into a yet further stage by suggesting a way in which the comparative static properties of the model could be rendered determinate, namely by making more specific the assumption about the nature of the effect of advertising on the demand function. On this basis, Hadar investigated the comparative statics of the model mainly with respect to an excise tax and the price of advertising, and demonstrated that the effects of these shift parameters on the levels of output and advertising were always determinate. Once again, it should be emphasised that there is nothing unscientific in placing sufficient restrictions upon a model so that determinate qualitative (or indeed quantitative) predictions can be obtained. For in the last analysis the validity of the model still rests upon the conformity or otherwise of those predictions with evidence drawn from the real world.

The fourteenth contribution, by Josef Hadar and Claude Hillinger, presents a model of imperfect competition in which each firm is assumed to have no knowledge about its demand function other than that it is downward-sloping. In this way, Hadar and Hillinger introduced recent developments in the economics of information into the theory of imperfect competition, demonstrating the possibility of constructing a meaningful and non-empty theory on this basis. In particular, the model was shown to yield a number of determinate predictions following shifts in a tax parameter. The authors clearly indicated that the behaviour of firms would differ in imperfectly competitive markets characterised by knowledge and ignorance respectively of their demand functions. On this basis, the model stakes a claim as a substantive contribution to the theory of market organisation.

The fifteenth contribution, by W. J. Baumol, switches attention away from markets composed of many sellers and presents a model of oligopoly based upon the sales revenue maximisation postulate subject to a minimum profit constraint. Baumol demonstrated that the profit-maximising output rate would usually be smaller than the output rate which achieved either an unconstrained or a constrained sales revenue maximum. Nevertheless, even in the sales-maximising firm, Baumol demonstrated that *relatively* unprofitable inputs and outputs would be avoided, whatever the level of outlay and total revenue. Moreover, once advertising was introduced as an instrument variable, Baumol demonstrated that the sales revenue maximum must always be constrained by the minimum profit requirement, and that sales revenue maximisers normally would advertise more than profit maximisers. Baumol demonstrated that the sales revenue maximiser would react to an increase in fixed costs by lowering output rate and/or advertising expenditures. Once again, this result is at odds with the predictions of standard oligopoly theory. Additionally, Baumol's theory offers some explanation for the pervasive existence in oligopolistic markets of non-price competition, since this presents one method of competing which does not lower sales revenue (but rather raises unit production costs). The principal weakness of Baumol's contribution is the failure to specify the determinants of the minimum profit constraint – a weakness which was remedied in his growth-maximising model discussed earlier in this introduction.

The final contribution, by Mancur Olson and David McFarland, represents an attempt (not to my mind entirely successful) to restore the concepts of 'pure monopoly' and of 'industry' to the central place in the economics of market organisation which they had once held, until the theoretical contributions of Edward Chamberlin in the field of monopolistic competition had torpedoed them by emphasising the universality of substitutability among products. Olson and McFarland argued that excess emphasis upon measures of cross-elasticity of demand in market analysis (the fetish of the post-Chamberlin era) had led directly to the comparative neglect of the two most important factors which distinguished in practical terms the various types of market organisation, namely (i) the number of firms in the market, and (ii) the closeness or remoteness of substitutability between the products of the different firms that comprised the market. They further contended that the concept of 'industry' in pure competition (which is widely accepted in the economics literature) was based upon assumptions which were exactly paralleled by those required for the concept of industry in monopolistic competition and for the concept of pure monopoly.

Be this as it may. It still seems to me that cross-elasticity of demand remains the most appropriate measure (at least in theory) for determining the market for a product, and thereby for defining the number of firms in that market. At the empirical level, therefore, the case argued by Olson and McFarland is not convincing. But in so far as theories of market organisation are viewed as theoretical constructs to be evaluated rather by reference to their comparative static properties than (in some sense) by reference to the realism of their assumptions, then the case for the restoration of 'pure monopoly' to a central place in market analysis can certainly be supported.

Conclusions

The reader may well ask himself why, in a volume such as this which is devoted to the study of theories of the firm and of market behaviour, there is so little reference to an area which has received a great deal of attention in recent years, namely the analysis of markets composed of only a few rival firms each acutely aware of the likely reaction of its competitors to any strategy that it might decide to implement. In particular, there is little reference to oligopolistic competition and no reference at all to game theory in this volume. There are two reasons for this important omission.

First, theories of oligopolistic competition have so far failed to make much headway from the viewpoint of comparative statics predictions at any worth-while level of generality, whatever their merits from the viewpoint of realism of assumptions. In itself this is a telling justification for omitting such theories from a volume such as this which places so much emphasis upon the predictive approach.

Secondly, considerations of space have prevented the inclusion of a number of papers on oligopoly theory which (while eschewing the predictive approach) are worthy of serious consideration in the literature of industrial economics. I would refer particularly in this respect to the important survey article by Franco Modigliani [9], to the little referred-to but significant article by Sir Roy Harrod [4] which emphasised the importance of new entry considerations in analysing Chamberlin's theory of monopolistic competition, and to the article by Dale Osborne [10] which reviews the role of new entry within the context of the theory of limit pricing. These articles, though omitted from this volume, are warmly recommended for the scholarship and insight which they offer to the student of industrial economics.

REFERENCES

[1] M. A. CREW, M. JONES-LEE and C. K. ROWLEY, 'X-Theory versus Management Discretion Theory', *Southern Economic Journal* (Oct 1971).

[2] C. E. FERGUSON, *Microeconomic Theory* (Irwin, 1969).

[3] M. FRIEDMAN, *Essays in Positive Economics* (Chicago U.P., 1953) chap. 1.

[4] Sir ROY HARROD, 'Increasing Returns', reprinted in R. Kuenne (ed.), *Monopolistic Competition Theory: Studies in Impact* (Wiley, 1967).

[5] T. C. KOOPMANS, *Three Essays on the State of Economic Science* (McGraw-Hill, 1957).

[6] H. LEIBENSTEIN, 'Allocative Efficiency *vs.* X-Efficiency', *American Economic Review* (June 1966) 392–415.

[7] R. A. LESTER, 'Shortcomings of Marginal Analysis for Wage–Employment Problems', *American Economic Review* (Mar 1946).

[8] F. MACHLUP, 'Marginal Analysis and Empirical Research', *American Economic Review* (Sept 1946).

[9] F. MODIGLIANI, 'New Developments on the Oligopoly Front', *Journal of Political Economy* (June 1958).

[10] D. K. OSBORNE, 'The Role of Entry in Oligopoly Theory', *Journal of Political Economy* (Aug 1964).

[11] R. TURVEY (ed.), 'Public Enterprise', in *Penguin Modern Economics* (Penguin Books, 1968).

PART ONE

Theories of the Firm

1 The Qualitative Content of Maximizing Models[1]

G. C. Archibald

1. Introduction

It seems unfortunately to be the case that the general qualitative content of maximizing models is small, if not trivial. By 'general' here is meant explicitly 'knowing or assuming no more than that sufficient conditions for an extreme solution are satisfied'.[2] This is enough, as Samuelson showed,[3] to prove the basic theorem of conjugate pairs; but, unfortunately, the case of conjugate pairs appears to be the only case in which an unambiguous qualitative prediction can be obtained, and yet not be empirically a very important case. A good deal of attention has been given in recent years to cases that are not conjugate pairs; and surprise and disappointment are often expressed at the discovery that the conventional – or 'general' – allowance of qualitative information is not sufficient for an unambiguously signed prediction to be obtained. Thus one object of this paper is to gather together some of these cases, and to show that the reason for the lack of qualitative content

[1] I owe an enormous long-term debt to my colleagues in the Staff Seminar on Methodology, Measurement, and Testing in Economics at the London School of Economics, and to Kelvin Lancaster in particular. My immediate debt is to Hugh W. Folk, with whom I have had the privilege of discussing each stage during the writing of this paper. I am also grateful to him and to Dipak Banerjee, Peter B. Kenen, and Sidney Winter for comments on an earlier draft.

[2] For discussion of the conditions for qualitative content in models whose equilibrium conditions are not obtained from a maximization assumption see K. J. Lancaster, 'The Scope of Quantitative Economics', *Review of Economic Studies*, XXIX 2; and his 'Partitionable Systems and Qualitative Economics', *Review of Economic Studies*, XXXI 1; and W. M. Gorman, 'More Scope for Qualitative Economics', *Review of Economic Studies*, XXXI 1.

[3] Paul A. Samuelson, *Foundations of Economic Analysis* (Cambridge, Mass., 1947).

Reprinted from *Journal of Political Economy*, LXXIII (Feb 1965) 27–36, by kind permission of the author and of the University of Chicago Press.

is the same, that the theorem of conjugate pairs cannot be used, while another object is to set out systematically what can be got from the theorem, and to offer some assessment.

It is clear that the basic work is Samuelson's; but he himself was apparently uncertain of the scope of the theorem (as will be seen below), and could not, in any case, have anticipated its application to postwar theoretical developments, such as 'second best' and certain cases in imperfect competition.

A variable and a parameter in a given system are said to be a conjugate pair if the parameter appears only in the equation which determines the equilibrium value of that variable and in no other equation. When that parameter is shifted, we may say that one 'curve' is shifted, while adjustment is completed by shifting *along* the other 'curves' of the system. Of the assumption that conjugate pairs exist, Samuelson wrote:

> Let us examine more closely the nature of our hypothesis . . . that each parameter shifts but one condition of equilibrium, leaving all others unchanged. In the first place this does not mean that a change in the ith parameter results in a change in the ith variable alone. On the contrary, a change in any parameter will typically result in a change in all variables. Our hypothesis merely says that this must come about through a shift in but one schedule with movements along the remaining schedules.
>
> *As I shall later argue, the assumption of this hypothesis does not involve any serious loss of generality and still includes the vast majority (in fact, it is hard to find exceptions) of relationships continued in current economic theory.*[4] [My italics.]

Samuelson was, however, clear that this was not the end of the matter. A few pages later he wrote: 'It must not be thought, however, that the assumption of our equilibrium as the solution of a maximum problem is the "open sesame" to the successful unambiguous determination of all possible questions which we may ask. For it is extremely easy to specify simple and important problems which cannot be answered even qualitatively without further knowledge.'[5] This seems to leave the scope and importance of conjugate pairs rather undecided. The purpose of this paper is to collect some of the unanswerable problems in a systematic way, and to show that the necessary assumption for conjugate pairs leads only to the relatively trivial result that all derived demand curves slope down, and supply curves in

[4] Paul A. Samuelson, op cit., p. 33.   [5] Ibid., p. 41.

perfect competition slope up, while in a substantial number of cases of interest, which have much occupied economists, the assumption cannot be made, with disastrous results for general qualitative theory.

2. The Theorem of Conjugate Pairs

Samuelson proved the familiar theorem of conjugate pairs,[6] and supplied it to several cases. He did not, however, say very much about its limitations. The first step is therefore to restate the theorem in order to obtain a clear statement of the necessary assumptions. We shall find that, in the general case, the direction of changes in the variables in response to a parameter change can *only* be determined for conjugate pairs, which turn out to be, practically speaking, rather uninteresting.

The assumed behavior is that the economic unit maximizes some objective function U (with continuous first and second derivatives) subject to some constraint F, where the arguments of the functions are the variables $x_1, \ldots, x_n$ and some parameter a, selected as a shift parameter (there is in general some set of parameters, but we may suppress all but one without loss of generality).

In order that the Lagrangian function

$$V = U + \lambda F \qquad (2.1)$$

be at a maximum, it is necessary that

$$V_{x_i} = U_{x_i} + \lambda F_{x_i} = 0$$

and $\qquad\qquad V_\lambda = F = 0 \quad (i = 1, \ldots, n). \qquad (2.2)$

Sufficient conditions for equations (2.2) to be a true maximum are that the bordered Hessian

$$H = \left| \begin{array}{c|c} V_{ij} & F_i \\ \hline F_i & 0 \end{array} \right|$$

evaluated at this point be negative definite, that is, that $H(-1)^n > 0$ and the principal minors alternate in sign. (Where there is no room for ambiguity, partial derivatives V_{x_i} will be written V_i.) The system is 'solved' if the variables can

6 Paul A. Samuelson, op cit., pp. 30–9.

be expressed as functions of the parameters in the neighborhood of equilibrium, that is, by forming the n equations

$$x_i = f^i(a) \quad (i = 1, \ldots, n). \tag{2.3}$$

The task of qualitative comparative statics (the qualitative calculus) is to find, where possible, the signs of the partial derivatives $f_a{}^i$, in order that directions of change in the variables in response to a parameter change may be predicted ($dx_i = f_a{}^i da$; the n expressions dx_i/da will be referred to as the solution vector).

The assumption that extremum conditions are satisfied is *alone* sufficient to obtain an unambiguous sign for one (and only one) element dx_i/da of the solution vector if and only if the following conditions are satisfied: (i) (obviously) the sign of V_{ia} is known;[7] (ii) (the conjugate-pair assumption) $V_{ja} = 0$ for all $j \neq i$, and $F_a = 0$.

That these conditions are sufficient means that the derivative of a variable with respect to its conjugate parameter is signed in the general case in which we do not have information about the signs or relative magnitudes of the off-diagonal elements (V_{ij}, $i \neq j$) of the Hessian other than that they are consistent with second-order conditions. What is particularly important, however, is that they are necessary as well as sufficient. Note particularly the following:

(i) The two conditions given above are not sufficient to sign any other element dx/da of the solution vector without further information, usually of a quantitative or semi-quantitative nature.

(ii) If the conditions that $V_{ja} = 0$ for all $j \neq i$ and/or $F_a = 0$ are violated, not even dx_i/da is qualitatively signed.

This may be interpreted: So long as we adhere to the 'general' assumption that the second-order cross-partial derivatives of V are non-zero (which is the case if we assume U_{ij} and/or

---

[7] If this condition is violated (because V_{ia} is unsigned, that is, either V_{ia} and/or F_{ia} are unsigned, or have opposite signs), obviously not even the conjugate pair can be signed. This is what may happen when a shift parameter is introduced into a monopolist's demand function or the supply function of a monopsonist (see H. W. Folk and J. N. Wolfe, 'A Generalisation of the Hicks–Slutsky Theory with Some Applications to Consumer Behaviour as a Learning Process', *Econometrica*, xxx 3).

F_{ij} to be non-zero), and we have no further information about these cross-partials, then we can never sign more than one element of the solution vector when a parameter is shifted, and that only if we can find a parameter that appears in only one of equations (2.2). If it appears in the ith equation and nowhere else, we may describe x_i and the parameter a as a conjugate pair. Thus it turns out that even conjugate pairs depend on a particular restriction on the functional forms of U and F: that there exists a parameter that appears in only one of the equilibrium equations, V_i, V_λ. This restriction requires as much empirical justification as the restriction that some V_{ij}'s are zero (or stand in some known relationship to each other). Just how these restrictions have been used in existing theory will emerge as we proceed.

For proof, we differentiate equations (2.2) totally with respect to all variables and the parameter in question. This gives $n + 1$ simultaneous linear equations, which may be solved by Cramer's method. The equations may be written

$$\left[\begin{array}{c|c} V_{ij} & F_i \\ \hline F_i & 0 \end{array}\right] \cdot \left|\begin{array}{c} dx_1 \\ \vdots \\ dx_n \\ d\lambda \end{array}\right| = -\left|\begin{array}{c} a_1 \\ \vdots \\ a_n \\ a_{n+1} \end{array}\right| da \tag{2.4}$$

where the column vector $|a|$ is composed of the elements of V_{ia}, the partial derivatives of equation (2.2) with respect to a. Write H_{ij} for the cofactor of the ijth element in H. Then if $a_i < 0$ and all $a_{j \neq i} = 0$ ($i, j = 1, \ldots, n + 1$),

$$\frac{dx_i}{da} = -a_i \frac{H_{ii}}{H} < 0$$

because H_{ii} is a principal minor of H and therefore of opposite sign.

We see that the conditions are necessary as follows: (1) $dx_j/da = -a_i(H_{ij}/H)$ is unsigned since H_{ij} is unsigned. (2) Let any element of $|a|$, say a_k, be non-zero as well as a_i. Then (without consideration of the sign of a_k)

$$\frac{dx_i}{da} = -a_i \frac{H_{ii}}{H} + a_k \frac{H_{ki}}{H}$$

and

$$\frac{dx_k}{da} = a_k \frac{H_{kk}}{H} - a_i \frac{H_{ik}}{H}.$$

H_{ik} $(= H_{ki})$ is unsigned, so both dx_i/da and dx_k/da are unsigned. Further,

$$\frac{dx_j}{aa} = -a_i \frac{H_{ij}}{H} + a_k \frac{H_{kj}}{H} \quad \text{(for all } j \neq i \text{ or } k),$$

which is unsigned. Hence no element of the solution vector is signed. If this is true when two elements of $|a|$ are non-zero, it is true, *a fortiori*, when more than two are non-zero.

Some applications (to welfare economics and the theory of the firm) will be discussed below. The immediately obvious and best known application is to the theory of consumer demand: the slope of the demand curve cannot be obtained 'in general' because the condition that all $a_{j \neq 1} = 0$ is violated. Each price is an argument of the constraint as well as the relevant partial derivative of V, so that there are two non-zero elements in $|a|$, yielding the familiar substitution and income terms.

At this point it is convenient to ask what further qualitative information of a fairly general nature we might reasonably assume in order to give our theory a little more empirical content. One obvious candidate is to assume that cross-partial derivatives are zero, so that the off-diagonal elements of H are zero (except, of course, the border). This certainly increases the number of signed elements in the solution vector, but in rather embarrassing ways. In consumer theory, with a linear constraint, the off-diagonal elements are zero if the utility function is of the strongly independent or additive variety, so that it may be written

$$U(x_1, \ldots, x_n) = \sum_{i=1}^{n} u^i(x_i).$$

The embarrassing result is that, in this case, there can be no inferior goods and no gross complements, except in one (apparently very peculiar) case.[8] In monopolistic competition it is particularly tempting to try to add to the meager qualitative content of the maximizing model by assuming cross-partial derivatives to be zero. In one case, at least, putting an intrusive

---

[8] H. A. John Green, 'Direct Additivity and Consumers' Behaviour', *Oxford Economic Papers*, XIII 2, and references cited therein. The peculiar case is explored by Green. Stability conditions do not require that all u_{ii} are negative, but only that $(n - 1)$ of them are. If the marginal utility of exactly one good is constant or increasing, which is permissible, then that good is normal, and the remainder are inferior! Furthermore, all other goods are either complements or unrelated to each other.

cross-partial equal to zero leads to the embarrassing result that the equilibrium output of a firm is not altered by a change in an excise tax on that output.[9] Giving it the sign that appears 'reasonable', we avoid this embarrassment, but at the price of having no qualitative prediction about the direction of change in advertising.

This naturally raises the possibility of adding to the empirical content of our models by assuming cross-partial derivatives, and so on, to have the signs that appear 'reasonable' when we can obtain signs in the solution vector by this means. The difficulty is that empirical content gained in this way is largely illusory. Suppose a theory yields a prediction of the sort 'if a and b, then c', where a is some observable event (say, a change in a parameter), c is the observable result (change in a variable), and b is not independently observed (b is, for example, the condition that a cross-partial has a given sign). If we observe not-c, we can rescue the theory merely by saying, 'Ah, well, we made the wrong guess about b.' In this sort of situation, indeed, we can always 'rig up' the unobserved bits to make the theory predict as we wish, but, by so doing, we render the theory unfalsifiable.[10]

Before going on, one further introductory point should be clarified: there may be some information about maximands or constraints, beyond what is necessary for extremum conditions to be satisfied, that the reader would consider 'qualitative' (for example, that a production function was homogeneous). Where such additional information is available, more 'qualitative' predictions may well be obtained than follow from conjugate pairs alone. Nothing that is said here should be read as denying the proposition that, if more is known, more is known: on the contrary, the burden of the argument is that more must be known if worthwhile predictions are to be obtained. For the purposes of this paper we mean by 'general

[9] See my 'Profit Maximising and Non-Price Competition', *Economica* xxxi 211. Write the demand function facing the firm as $v = f(p, x)$, where v is the quantity of advertising, p is product price, and x the amount taken. The cross-partial in question is f_{xp}.

[10] Except perhaps in one case. Suppose that we have 'rigged' b to be consistent with c (or not-c, as the case may be). If the theory yields some other prediction (a) in which b plays a similar role, then we may obtain some potential falsifiability by requiring consistency. On the general question of untested subsidiary assumptions see Andreas G. Papandreou, 'Theory Construction and Empirical Meaning in Economics', *American Economic Review, Papers and Proceedings*, LII 2.

qualitative content' the content that follows merely from the assumption that extremum conditions are satisfied. On the wisdom and fruitfulness of assuming more without independent empirical evidence see the preceding paragraph.

3. Examples: Second Best

Lipsey and Lancaster remarked, in 'The General Theory of Second Best',[11] that many writers had discovered particular examples of the problem, but had not realized that it was general. We may go a step further: The impossibility of piecemeal welfare economics is only a particular case of failing to satisfy the second necessary condition of the theorem of conjugate pairs.

That this has apparently not been noticed already is perhaps due to the fact that 'second best' is not generally thought of as a problem in comparative statics. It may, however, be easily put into this familiar form. Assume that there are at least two constraints preventing the fulfilment of the Paretian optimum conditions in two or more markets, that at least one constraint is immovable, while the other may be varied by policy, and that the constrained maximum (second best optimum) has been found. Let the parameter of the policy constraint be k_g – a tax rate, tariff, or whatever. Then piecemeal welfare economics becomes the usual qualitative calculus operation: trying to predict the sign of dU/dk_g in order to discover in which direction k_g should be varied. At the general qualitative level of analysis this is impossible.

This may be seen more clearly if we consider the way in which the parameters appear in the constraints. We maximize U subject to several constraints: the production frontier, and two or more non-Paretian conditions. The question is: How should these be written? If the only immovable constraint is one constant inequality k_i between price and marginal cost in the ith industry, then, as McManus pointed out, a Paretian optimum may be achieved, given the full-employment assumption, by adopting the same k in all other industries.[12] Lancaster

[11] R. G. Lipsey and K. J. Lancaster, 'The General Theory of Second Best', *Review of Economic Studies*, XXIV 1.

[12] M. McManus, 'Comments on the General Theory of Second Best', *Review of Economic Studies*, XXVI 3.

and Lipsey replied that, if the ith industry were in the hands of a monopolist, he would not 'hold still';[13] his profit-maximizing k_i would be a function of all other k's. They alternatively wrote the constraint as[14]

$$\frac{U_i}{U_n} = k_i \frac{F_i^{\,p}}{F_n^{\,p}} \tag{3.1}$$

where U is the maximand, F^p the production constraint, and the nth industry is chosen as numéraire. McManus also pointed out that the choice of n was not arbitrary: the nth industry must be perfectly competitive.[15] For present purposes, we may by-pass these problems. If the Paretian optimum is achieved by maximizing

$$V = U + \lambda F^p \tag{3.2}$$

the additional constraints may be written in the form

$$F^i(V_i, k_i) = 0 \tag{3.3}$$

or even more generally

$$F^i(V_i, V_j, k_i, k_j) = 0 \quad (j = 1, \ldots, i-1, i+1, \ldots, n). \tag{3.4}$$

Now a second-best optimum is achieved when U is maximized subject to F^p, one or more constraints $F_i^{\,i}$ (in the form of equations (3.3) or (3.4)) and one particular constraint F^g of the same form, and containing the policy parameter k_g. The problem is to predict the sign of dU/dk_g (it is immaterial whether k_g is originally unity or not. If it is, the sign of dU/dk_g tells us whether utility is increased by a subsidy or a tax in the gth industry. If it is not, the sign of dU/dk_g tells us whether k, should be nearer to or further from unity). The difficulty is simply that

$$\frac{dU}{dk_g} = \sum_{i=1}^{n} U_i \frac{dx_i}{dk_g}. \tag{3.5}$$

To sign equation (3.5) without further information, the necessary and sufficient conditions are that all $U_i(dx_i/dk_g)$'s have the same sign. The fact is that not a single one of them can be

13 K. J. Lancaster and R. G. Lipsey, 'McManus on Second Best', *Review of Economic Studies*, XXVI 3.

14 Lipsey and Lancaster, op. cit.

15 McManus, op. cit.

signed if we maintain the general assumption that all $V_{ij} \neq 0$ but are of unknown magnitude. As can be seen from the conditions for conjugate pairs, not even dx_g/dk_g can be signed because the parameter k_g must appear in *at least* two equations of the equilibrium set, namely,

$$V_g = 0 \quad \text{and} \quad F^g = 0 \qquad (3.6)$$

(if the constraints have the form of equation (3.4) or if some k's are functions of other k's, k_g will appear in more than two equations). Thus there are at least two non-zero elements in the $|a|$ vector, and not a single element of the right-hand side of equation (3.5) can be signed without further information.[16]

A general comment on welfare economics may be added here. What Arrow did was to prove that successful anarchy is impossible, that is, that the 'irreducible element of coercion' in government *is* inescapable. (Arrow's volume[17] might well be published as the Technical Appendix to Mill's *Essay on Liberty*!) Thus society has to have a government (to prevent some undesired individual or combination from imposing his/their welfare function on the community). But government cannot be costless. Hence a government has to raise taxes. Hence, except perhaps in the uninteresting case of a poll tax, there must exist at least one unavoidable departure from the Paretian optimum conditions. Hence all welfare economics of any possible real-world relevance inescapably deals in second-best problems. But there is a more important conclusion still: so far as the case for *laissez-faire* and perfect competition rests on the argument that this insures fulfilment of the Paretian optimum conditions, it is, even in the absence of external effects, an invalid application of piecemeal welfare economics. The existence of a government (necessary to police perfect competition) insures that there will be at least one market in which the optimum conditions are not satisfied, since policing in-

[16] I am indebted to Professor Peter Pashigian for showing me an unpublished paper in which he imposes sufficient restrictions on F^p to sign not only dU/dk_g, but all the other derivatives dU/dk_j ($j = i, \ldots, n - 2$; one k must be immovable). This he does by assuming that there are intermediate products such that the output of each final good is a function of the input of capital, labor, and one intermediate product only, a 'vertical-chain' assumption which provides a convenient batch of zeros. Consideration of this result materially advanced my own understanding of the problem.

[17] Kenneth J. Arrow, *Social Choice and Individual Values* ('Cowles Commission Monographs', No. 12, 1951).

volves taxing: *ergo* there is no presumption in favor of satisfying the Paretian conditions in the remaining markets: *ergo* there is no welfare presumption in favor of *laissez-faire* plus perfect competition.[18]

4. Examples: The Theory of the Firm

We may first consider the general case of a multiproduct, multiplant, multimarket firm that may vary quantities, qualities, prices, selling outlays, etc. The essential assumption is that there exists a well-defined demand surface (or, in the discriminating case, surfaces). The problem is, as usual, to maximize U subject to one or more market constraints F. U is commonly taken to be identical with $R - C$, but it may be remarked that there is no particular reason why the utility function should be cardinal: any monotonic increasing function of $R - C$ would serve perfectly well as the maximand.

Assuming that there are m independent markets $(m \geq 1)$, we may write

$$V = \sum_{i=1}^{m} R^i - \sum_{i=1}^{k} C^i + \lambda_1 F^1 + \ldots + \lambda_m F^m \qquad (4.1)$$

where there are k (≥ 1) additive elements of the cost function. This means that there may be more than one plant with costs of production independent of each other, or that there may be selling outlays which are independent of the quantity or quality of some or all outputs. Let the arguments of the functions of equation (4.1) be elements of the vector $x = x_1,$ $x_2, \ldots, x_n,$ and some parameters which will not be specified yet, where $n \geq 2m$ (there is at least a price and output for each market; if quality and advertising variables are admitted,

---

18 We may also consider the currently fashionable studies of optimal growth paths. In these studies an objective function (for example, utility as a function of the present value of the future income stream) is maximized subject to some constraint or constraints determined by technology, factor endowments, savings ratios, etc. It is fashionable to solve the problem by finding the conditions for U_{max}, or by proving that a solution exists, and to let it go at that. But the discovery of equilibrium conditions is not the end of analysis: we want to know something about the 'comparative static' solution vector as well. It is clear that the conditions for these models to have comparative content are those stated in section 2 above, and that, in general, these conditions will not be satisfied by qualitative considerations. (It is clear that the comparative technique is not confined to static models, nor are its limitations.)

$n > 2m$). We have some restrictions on the way in which the elements of x may appear in the arguments of the functions:

1. If any x_i is an argument of any C^i, it is an argument of at least one R^i (no input is used, or output made, which does not contribute to revenue).
2. The set of arguments of any R^i is identical with that of the ith market constraint F^i.
3. There exists one argument of every R^i that is not an argument of any C^i (production costs are independent of market prices).
4. A special restriction: the same argument of R^i is not an argument of any R^j (the markets are independent).

We have the usual first- and second-order conditions, so we may proceed immediately to comparative statics. If we shift some parameter a, we obtain equation (4.2):

$$\begin{bmatrix} V_{ij} & [F_i^1][F_i^2]\ldots[F_i^m] \\ \hline \{F_i^1\} & \\ \{F_i^2\} & \\ \cdot & 0 \\ \cdot & \\ \cdot & \\ \{F_i^m\} & \end{bmatrix} \cdot \begin{vmatrix} dx_1 \\ dx_2 \\ \vdots \\ dx_n \\ d\lambda_1 \\ d\lambda_2 \\ \vdots \\ d\lambda_m \end{vmatrix} = - \begin{vmatrix} a_1 \\ \cdot \\ \cdot \\ \cdot \\ \cdot \\ \cdot \\ \cdot \\ a_{n+m} \end{vmatrix} da \qquad (4.2)$$

where brackets denote a column vector and braces a row vector. We may at once apply conjugate pairs: if and only if a is an argument of one and only one element of V_i, say the ith, so that all $a_{j \neq i} = 0$, then if $a_i < 0$,

$$\frac{dx_i}{da} = - a_i \frac{H_{ii}}{H} < 0. \qquad (4.3)$$

How can this condition be satisfied, and what does it mean? First, a must not be an argument of any R^i, since, by restriction 2 above, it will then be an argument of F^i, and there will be at least two non-zero elements of $|a|$ (*a fortiori*, a must not be an argument of two or more revenue functions). Second, then, a must be an argument of a cost function, and in such a fashion that it is an argument of only one partial derivative of C. This limits a to being a factor price or a specific tax on one output. Thus the theorem of conjugate pairs tells us that all derived demand curves slope down, including the 'demand' for any particular output whose 'price' has risen (a 'demand' derived from maximization of U). This, I submit, is a pretty trivial result; but unless we can impose some more restrictions it is the only one we are going to get.

Before considering possible restrictions, however, we may clear up some other points. What happens if a is an argument of more than one C^i? The answer is that the condition that only one element of V_{ia} be non-zero still stands. This means that if a wage rate affects more than one element of the x-vector (more than one output; or the cost of quality as well as quantity) the conditions for conjugate pairs are not satisfied. As a particular case, we have no signs by conjugate pairs if a specific tax is imposed on all outputs and/or in all markets. What, then, happens if a is an *ad valorem* tax in one market, say the ith? The answer is, of course, that a appears in all the derivatives $R_i{}^i$, so that there are as many non-zero elements in $|a|$ as there are arguments in R^i, and no element of the solution vector is signed.

One further consequence of this analysis may be pointed out: in general, the effects on price or prices of parameter changes are unpredicted. Even in the conjugate pairs case, where dx_i/da is signed, dp_i/da is an 'off-diagonal', and so unsigned; in no other case is any element of the solution vector signed at all. Our sole result, that derived demands slope down, is meager indeed!

We must now ask if any of the restrictions on the functional forms discussed above lead to any elements of V_{ij} being zero, and, if so, if there can be enough zeros to sign any H_{ij}. The first two restrictions are plainly no help at all. Consider the third. This excludes prices from the cost functions. But, by restriction 2, any price is an argument of an R^i and an F^i, so this is no help. Now consider restriction 4, which looks more helpful. In the simplest case of price discrimination (two markets, one product, no quality variable, no advertising) we have, as is well known, qualitative content (the reader may verify for himself that the Hessian is a 6×6 containing 18 zeros). The introduction of quality or advertising variables robs the single-market case of qualitative content, and the addition of extra markets will not restore qualitative content to a model that lacks it.[19]

It may now be a relief to turn to perfect competition, where we expect rather more qualitative content. The object of this section is to clarify very briefly the relationship between qualitative content and the particular restrictions imposed on the functions in this case. First, consider the restrictions in the general case discussed in equation (4.1) above. The first and third obviously apply to perfect competition, *mutatis mutandis*. The fourth is irrelevant. The second, however, is altered. Let $R = px$. Now if we take the fixed price for our constraint $(F = p - p_0 = 0)$, x is an argument of R but not of F. If, on the other hand, we take the production function as the constraint $F = x - f(x_1, x_2) = 0$ (where x_1, x_2 are inputs), then p is an argument of R but not of F. The result, of course, is to enlarge the set of parameters with respect to which only one of the equilibrium equations yields a non-zero partial derivative, and to increase the number of zeros in the Hessian.

Let us first take the production function as the constraint, forming the equation

$$V = px - p_1 x_1 - p_2 x_2 - \lambda[x - f(x_1, x_2)] \qquad (4.4)$$

(where p_1 and p_2 are the factor prices). The relevant bordered Hessian is (after interchange of the last two columns and the last two rows)

$$H = \begin{vmatrix} \lambda f_{11} & \lambda f_{12} & f_1 & 0 \\ \lambda f_{21} & \lambda f_{22} & f_2 & 0 \\ f_1 & f_2 & 0 & 1 \\ 0 & 0 & 1 & 0 \end{vmatrix} > 0 \qquad (4.5)$$

This contains $(n \times n) = 16$ elements and 6 zeros, or $(n - 1)!$ This is sufficient to sign every cofactor provided that the signs of the non-zero elements are known. The only one in doubt is f_{12}, which is not signed by the convexity condition (necessary in this case for cost minimization because the factor-price constraint is linear) which only requires that the indicated principal minor be negative. Thus if f_{12} is signed, all the elements of every solution vector are signed so long as there is only one non-zero element in the $|a|$ vector. This condition is, however, the rather special one that changes in p_1 or p_2 induce no changes in p, and vice versa, which cannot be maintained for industry-wide changes.

We may alternatively use the market constraint $F = p - p_0 = 0$, where p_0 is the market price, and form the equation

$$V = pf(x_1, x_2) - p_1x_1 - p_2x_2 + \lambda(p - p_0). \qquad (4.6)$$

The bordered Hessian is

$$H = \begin{vmatrix} 0 & f_1 & f_2 & 1 \\ f_1 & pf_{11} & pf_{12} & 0 \\ f_2 & pf_{21} & pf_{22} & 0 \\ 1 & 0 & 0 & 0 \end{vmatrix} \qquad (4.7)$$

which again contains $6 = (n - 1)!$ zeros.

As a last illustration of the consequences of not requiring identical sets of arguments in F and R, consider

$$V = px - C(x) + \lambda(p - p_0) \qquad (4.8)$$

where

$$H = \begin{vmatrix} 0 & 1 & 1 \\ 1 & -C'' & 0 \\ 1 & 0 & 0 \end{vmatrix} = \begin{vmatrix} 1 & 1 & 1 \\ 0 & -C'' & 1 \\ 0 & 0 & 1 \end{vmatrix} \qquad (4.9)$$

which is triangular.

The situation may be summed up as follows: The assumption that maximum conditions are satisfied is sufficient to tell us that derived demand curves slope down, that other demand curves do unless income effects offset substitution effects, and apparently not much else (except in the special case of perfect competition where we obviously obtain upward-sloping short-run supply curves).

2 A New Approach to the Theory of the Firm

André Gabor and I. F. Pearce

If the volume of current writing on the subject can be accepted as evidence, it is clear that economists are becoming increasingly concerned by the fact that business men do not use or even understand the jargon of marginalism, despite the fact that it would seem to be in their interests to operate their firms according to the rule 'marginal costs equals marginal revenue determines optimum output'. Most attempts so far made to explain this phenomenon have followed one or the other of two lines. Either it is argued that the rules of thumb developed by the business man achieve at least approximately the same result as would the strict application of marginal theory, or that short-period difficulties which are assumed away by the theorist render the operation of the rule impossible or undesirable.

It is the purpose of this paper to follow the less usual course of attempting to show that it is the marginal theory which is wrong (at least in the long period and as long as the firm is not conscious of monopoly power) and that, in consequence, any attempt to investigate business behaviour entirely within the framework of such a theory can only be misleading.

Traditional expositions of the theory of the firm do not draw any clear distinction between the two essential functions of the entrepreneur: (*a*) the provision of money capital, and (*b*) management. Money capital is treated, in many cases only implicitly, just as any other factor of production. A charge for money capital (equal to its opportunity cost) is supposed to be included in the cost curve, and the firm is assumed to operate so as to maximize a residue which accrues to the entrepreneur. All that is required to show up the weakness of marginal theory is a simple reversal of this; i.e. to charge the remuneration of the

Reprinted from *Oxford Economic Papers*, IV 3 (Oct 1952) 252–65, by kind permission of the authors and of the Clarendon Press.

entrepreneur as a cost and to assume that the firm operates in the interests of the owners of the money capital employed. The firm is an investment and the entrepreneur an investor.

We do not wish at this stage to argue too much from empirical evidence. Our concern is primarily to try to clear the ground for a fresh approach by showing up the limitations of marginal theory even on the most rigorous assumptions. It does seem proper, however, to point out that the new viewpoint on which our argument rests is justified by accountancy practice. Directors' salaries are always charged as a cost and the residual profit is distributed to ordinary shareholders. Any accountant who is not familiar with economic literature would be astonished by the suggestion that the salary of the managing director should be regarded as profit whilst the dividend is really a cost, even in the case where the managing director himself holds all of the ordinary shares.

Looked at from this point of view it is easy to see that an additional and obviously unjustified assumption is required to make marginal theory valid. If a firm can earn something more than the normal rate of profit on the money capital it controls, then it will be argued by the marginalist that output should be expanded until the marginal rate of return is equal to the normal rate of profit. *But this assumes that the abnormally high rate of profit cannot be earned anywhere except in the firm in question.* Such an assumption is clearly only applicable in the case of monopoly; for, if any firm in a competitive industry can earn more than the normal rate of profit, then this must be because that industry is out of equilibrium and hence all firms in it can earn more than normal profits. There is no incentive to extend a firm's operations beyond the point where maximum profit rate is earned; for any money capital which the entrepreneur may have, or can acquire, can more profitably be used in some other firm in the same industry, which can also be designed to earn the maximum profit rate. A simple arithmetical example will illustrate the possibility. A firm in a competitive industry finds that it can earn a maximum rate of return of 10 per cent when its capital is £1,000, whilst the normal rate of profit is 5 per cent only. Suppose that if output were doubled, following the investment of a further £1,000 of capital (borrowed at the normal profit rate 5 per cent), then the marginal rate of return would be reduced to 5 per cent because of the operation of decreasing

*

returns to scale. Suppose further that, as a result, the average rate of return at the higher output would be reduced to 9 per cent. It is true that by expanding output to the MC = MR point, the ordinary shareholders can improve upon their original rate. They could earn £90 on their own £1,000 plus £90 on the borrowed capital for which they must pay £50 in interest to the preference shareholders: i.e. £130 total dividends would be available for distribution, or 13 per cent as against the original 10 per cent. But if the borrowed £1,000 were used to set up a new firm exactly like the first it could earn the full 10 per cent; for it need not be expanded into the region of decreasing returns to scale. In this case the original shareholders could gain even more. Earnings of the original £1,000 could be raised to 15 per cent. We have ignored, of course, the fact that the commodity price is likely to be fractionally lower as a result of increased output. But this is justified since the fall in price is to be expected in both cases, and in neither will it affect the *ex ante* calculations of the firm.

The principle is indeed a simple one. It means that, on the plausible assumption that the requirement of money capital is proportional to total cost over the range near to optimum output, the best-sized firm remains the best-sized firm whatever happens to the price of the commodity or the market rate of profit. The terms on which the entrepreneur raises money do not matter either, for the fact that capital can be borrowed at something less than the rate of profit which it is expected it will earn will not affect the way in which it will be used.

In order to give precision to these ideas, it is now proposed to restate the problem more formally, fully setting out all our assumptions and showing how the maximum profit rate equilibrium may be determined. The four main types of objection to our views which we have encountered will also be considered and, we believe, effectively countered.

We distinguish two types of factors, defined in accordance with the method whereby their reward is determined. Contracting factors offer their services at an agreed price whilst controlling factors receive a residue. It follows that the aim of the firm will be always to serve the interests of the controlling factors. The latter will naturally approve of such a policy, whilst the former will support it on the ground that it strengthens their bargaining position if they can point to increased profits when recontracting in respect of their own services.

The analysis which follows assumes money capital alone to be the controlling factor. In other words, price/output policy will be that which would be approved by ordinary shareholders if the issues were clearly put to them. For convenience of exposition only, we assume all capital to be share capital. But, as will be argued at length later, in the riskless situation here analysed the proportion of share capital to loan capital will have no effect whatsoever on firm size under competitive conditions.

We define cost as payments to contracting factors (including payments to management) and profit as the balance of revenue remaining after costs have been met. *Normal profits or opportunity costs of capital are not accepted as part of cost.* Normal profit is a useful concept in economic analysis and of course enters into social cost; it is inviting circular argument, however, to employ it in an analysis which purports to show how it is itself determined.

For the present we concern ourselves only with the long period in which all factors are presumed to be variable. The average cost curve is assumed to be U-shaped; the usual argument of increasing returns due to specialization and later decreasing returns following difficulties of co-ordination being accepted. We do not consider these two premisses, i.e. variable factors and a U-shaped cost curve, to be mutually exclusive[1] since we have defined factors only as money capital plus all those goods and services whose suppliers contract with the firm to provide them at a fixed price. Thus on our definitions 'opportunity for specialization' under the guise of some generic term such as 'organization' is not looked on as a factor of production claiming a reward. Management itself is a variable factor hired like any other kind of labour. The firm is presumed to have full knowledge of prices and technical possibilities at all levels of output. To attribute a productivity to a factor 'organization' is to confuse the technical possibilities inherent in the nature of the physical things used with the skill of an individual in finding them out. An important conclusion which follows from all these assumptions is that all cost curves under the

[1] See E. H. Chamberlin, 'Proportionality, Divisibility, and Economies of Scale', *Quarterly Journal of Economics* (Feb 1948).

strictest conditions of perfect competition as usually defined are identical.[2] It seems to us more logical to accept this and to attribute differences which occur in practice to lack of knowledge, to short-period difficulties, or to non-homogeneous factors which we have ruled out. To assume full knowledge and at the same time differences in entrepreneurial ability is to perpetuate the confusion referred to above.

Money capital requirement is assumed to vary with output. We consider only the case where capital requirement increases with increased output as this would seem to be the only case likely to be economically significant. No other restriction is for the moment imposed on the shape of the money capital function. The output which will give the maximum rate of return may be formally determined as follows.

Writing total revenue as a function $R(x)$ of the output x, total cost as $C(x)$, and the total capital requirement as $F(x)$, we have to maximize

$$\frac{R(x) - C(x)}{F(x)}.$$

The required condition is, of course,

$$\frac{F(x)}{F'(x)} = \frac{R(x) - C(x)}{R'(x) - C'(x)},$$

that is to say, the log slope of the total profits curve must equal the log slope of the curve of capital requirement; i.e. the elasticities of the two curves are equal.

Clearly, this is not the marginal cost equals marginal revenue criterion, for $R'(x) = C'(x)$ is not in general the same thing as

$$\frac{F(x)}{F'(x)} = \frac{R(x) - C(x)}{R'(x) - C'(x)}.$$

Fig. 2.1 illustrates this diagrammatically. To determine the maximum profit rate output it is necessary to find some output x_1 such that tangents to the total profit and total capital curves at that output cut the x-axis at the same point. It will be noted

[2] It should be pointed out here, however, that our conclusions regarding the inapplicability of marginal theory under competition do not rest on what amounts to an assumption of identical cost curves. But the question of the imputation of economic rents to contracting factors which are non-homogeneous raises difficulties which are beyond the scope of this paper and which we hope to consider in a later paper.

that as long as $F(x)$ is an increasing function of x then x_1 will be less than x_2, the point where marginal cost equals marginal revenue. This result is quite general and would hold even if the total revenue curve were not a linear function of x as in the case of perfect competition.

A special case is of interest. If it could be assumed that over the range of output near to the maximum profit rate point the proportion in which factors are used remains unchanged[3] and

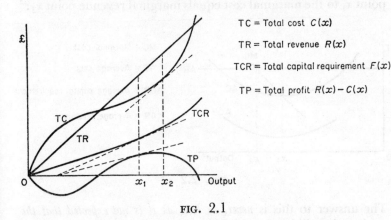

TC = Total cost $C(x)$

TR = Total revenue $R(x)$

TCR = Total capital requirement $F(x)$

TP = Total profit $R(x) - C(x)$

FIG. 2.1

the curve of capital requirement is in consequence approximately proportional to the total cost curve, the equilibrium point can be identified much more simply. We can write $F(x) = \lambda C(x)$ and under perfect competition $R(x) = Px$ (where P is the constant price of the product). As a result the condition for maximum profit rate reduces to $\dfrac{C(x)}{x} = C'(x)$, i.e. minimum average cost.

This is much more easily seen if all the curves are translated into average terms as in Fig. 2.2. By assumption, average capital requirement is at a minimum when average cost is at a minimum, i.e. when price minus average cost is at a maximum. Hence the rate of return on capital will be greatest at minimum

---

[3] Consideration of the problem of the choice of proportions in which factors of production should be used lies outside the scope of this paper. It should be noted, however, that where the aim of the firm is to maximize the rate of return on money capital rather than total profits, the choice of correct factor proportions depends on the expected rate of profit, and not on some objective 'normal profit' rate. Thus the cost curve itself becomes dependent on the demand curve.

average cost. In fact, the business man would achieve his purpose (if this were to maximize the rate of return on capital) by maximizing the mark-up rate, the difference between average cost, and the price he can charge for his product. Furthermore, in this case, the output which gives maximum profit rate is independent of the price of the product.

The question now at issue is: In what circumstances will the firm wish to push its output beyond the maximum profit rate point x_1 to the marginal cost equals marginal revenue point x_2?[4]

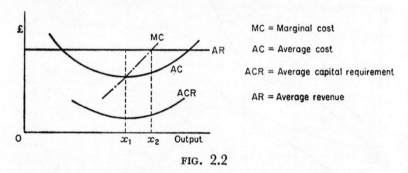

FIG. 2.2

The answer to this is *never, as long as it is not expected that the market price will be affected by the quantity produced.* For as we have already argued, if the profit rate at x_1 is greater than the normal profit rate, so that there is a general incentive to enter the industry, then by definition that high rate (higher than the rate at x_2) can be earned by setting up a new firm in the same industry identical with that under consideration, or by becoming an ordinary shareholder in such a firm.

The present writers have found that most economists to whom these ideas have been put are quite prepared to accept the premises upon which the conclusions rest, but that objections are immediately made which amount to one or some combination of the following four types.

Firstly, it is suggested that the firm which believes it can earn more than normal profits will immediately borrow sufficient money capital to extend output to the marginal cost equals

[4] If the market price equals minimum average cost, x_1 and x_2 will of course coincide, but the reader is reminded that our $C(x)$ function does not include any element of 'normal' or other kind of profit, hence $x_1 = x_2$ would leave no residue for the remuneration of capital and production would not normally take place at all. This point is discussed at length on pp. 25–7 below.

marginal revenue level, the rate of interest on the borrowed money being charged as a cost. It will be noted that this suggested level of output need not be either x_1 or x_2 in Fig. 2.1. This is because the cost curve must be adjusted so as to include the appropriate interest charge. The answer to this argument has been given already, of course, in the numerical example on p. 20. There is no reason to suppose that a firm would wish to use capital in such a way as to earn a lower average rate than the maximum possible (apparently) just because some proportion of it has been borrowed at an even lower rate. Clearly it will be more profitable for whoever is responsible for investing the new capital in real equipment to arrange for the organization of a number of firms producing at maximum profit rate than to extend output of a single firm into the region of decreasing returns.

The second and third types of criticisms made may be taken together. These stem from the objection that we have not included the transfer cost or 'opportunity cost' of money capital in our definition of cost. If we do so, it is held, then maximum profit rate and marginal cost equals marginal revenue amount to the same thing. Group 2 critics wish to add to the cost curve a charge for capital at a rate equal to *the maximum it is possible to earn in the firm under consideration*. Such a suggestion would never be made were it not for the preconceived notion that somehow or other the two criteria, maximum profit rate and marginal cost equals marginal revenue, *ought* to amount to the same thing. It is true that if we assume a fixed rate of remuneration for all factors except one whose price per unit is defined to be the maximum it can possibly earn, then the average cost curve can never lie below the average revenue curve but must touch it at one point; i.e. it must be tangential. And if the two curves are tangential at any output, then the marginal values at that level of output must be equal; i.e. marginal cost equals marginal revenue. The concepts are so defined as to make it impossible for the proposition ever to be false. We could, of course, accept these definitions if we wished; but if we did, it would not be difficult to explain the business man's lack of interest in them. For to make use of the MC equals MR criterion, he would have to determine his optimum output by the maximum profit rate method in order to determine the maximum profit rate possible in order to know how much to add to his cost curve as a charge for capital in order to determine the optimum output (already determined) by the MC equals MR criterion!

Moreover, and this is probably more important from the point of view of the logic of the argument, it should be noted that we cannot accept the maximum rate definition of transfer cost in the case of monopoly; for this would give (by the MC equals MR criterion) maximum profit rate as the optimum output just as it does under competition. And as we shall see, this is *not always* the best output where there is monopoly. Hence it would be necessary to introduce inconsistent definitions.

The third group of critics accept 'normal profit' as a definition of the transfer cost of capital. It is then argued that under competition only normal profits can be earned in the long run, so that when the industry is in equilibrium, marginal cost equals marginal revenue will be the same thing as maximum profit rate. But if normal profit is less than the maximum rate it is possible to earn (as it must be when new firms are being tempted into the industry), then the criterion MC equals MR does not give the maximum profit rate output. One can hardly expect the business man to be content with a criterion which will only do when the industry is in equilibrium, even if he were in a position to determine whether it is or not.

On this point we have encountered the more subtle suggestion that in the long run business men never *expect* to earn more than normal profit, and will choose the firm size accordingly. Presumably they are tempted to organize new firms by the prospect of being able to earn abnormally high profits for a short period only, after which they will be content with normal profit. If this were true, and if one took care to plan the firm's size on the basis of the long-run expected price for the commodity (by definition lower than the prevailing price), then, if one's expectations prove to be correct, the marginal criterion would give the same output as maximum profit rate.[5] But why bother with all this when the maximum profit rate criterion itself will give the correct output quite independently of any 'ifs' or expectations?

The maximum profit rate equilibrium is quite independent

---

[5] Again on the assumption that total capital requirement is proportional to total cost over the relevant range.

of the transfer cost of capital whatever it may be and can be determined without reference to any such concept; x_1 remains the best output whatever the charge for capital. Charging for capital reduces the total profits curve by an amount proportional to the capital requirement curve; that is, a tangent to the new profits curve at x_1 will cut the x-axis at the same point as the tangent to the old. Moreover, in the special case illustrated in Fig. 2.2, the best output is independent of the price of the product (except in so far as this may render a change in factor proportions desirable). The optimum size firm, in fact, remains the optimum size firm, however much the industry may be in disequilibrium. Reference to Fig. 2.2 will make these points clearer. The inclusion of a charge for capital raises average and marginal cost curves together, without affecting the value of x at which they intersect. Again, changing the price of the product still leaves x as the point of maximum profit margin.

The fourth and last type of objection turns on the question of what is meant by a 'firm'. Our 'firm', it is suggested, has become something which approximates much more closely to what is usually referred to in economic literature as a plant. If, it is argued, we identify the firm, say, with its name, Bloggs & Co., then a large number of plants each producing at maximum profit rate can be looked on as giving constant returns to total firm size and that Bloggs & Co. will simply want to go on adding plants until marginal cost (equals average cost) is equal to marginal revenue. This again seems to us to be yet another attempt to make the answer at least look right. How many plants to build is quite a different question from how big should each plant be. And it is the second of these which the firm in a competitive industry must face. The first question cannot even be envisaged unless there is consciousness of monopoly power; for constant costs and constant commodity price gives an infinite output or none at all. It is just conceivable that Bloggs & Co. may vaguely wish that it were in control of a very large number of plants in certain circumstances, but this can only be an imprecise idea as long as the demand curve to the industry is not known. The practical question will be: What size shall the next plant be? The question of how many plants to plan can be rationally considered only if there is consciousness of the way in which increased output will affect the price of the product; and even in this case there is no reason to suppose that the individual *plants* will be planned at any other than maximum profit rate size.

It should be pointed out here that our arguments are not really new. It will at once be recognized by those familiar with the relevant literature that the foregoing is, in effect, no more than a static exposition of a problem much discussed in quasi-dynamic terms in connexion with the theory of investment. In this field, in contrast to the complete unanimity with which the theory of the firm has been accepted, it is interesting to note that there has been disagreement as to the probable aims of the 'entrepreneur'.[6]

It is instructive to speculate upon the causes of this disagreement and to this end it is useful to remind ourselves once again of some of the fundamental assumptions of traditional cost analysis. The theory of the firm is built around the entrepreneur – so much so, indeed, that the firm is *defined* (usually only by implication) as that organization controlled by the entrepreneur. Money capital is treated just as any other factor and, following the usual particular equilibrium assumptions, is presumed to be freely available at a given fixed rate of interest. But this is not all; this fixed rate is taken to be the maximum rate that capital can earn anywhere *other* than in the firm under consideration. And this, moreover, is supposed to hold even for an industry in disequilibrium when there is a tendency for new firms to enter. It seems to us that the only case when this will be true is the extreme case where all capital is loan capital, i.e. where money capital ceases to be the controlling factor in our sense.

On the other hand, in developing the theory of investment, attention shifts from the firm and the entrepreneur to the ownership of money. It is in the owner's interests that the investment is made. It is natural therefore to think in terms of applying money to a number of projects and seeking each time to maximize the rate of return, particularly in a situation of disequilibrium where something more than the competitive rate can (apparently) be earned in each of a number of separate investments in the same line. It is not surprising therefore that

---

[6] An excellent survey of what has been written on this subject is given by F. A. Lutz as a prelude to his own observations in a paper entitled 'The Criterion of Maximum Profits in the Theory of Investment', *Quarterly Journal of Economics* (Nov 1945).

some writers have been led to conclude that the investor will seek to maximize the 'internal rate of return' in each case. But if attention is concentrated on one particular investment, and if, at the same time, an objective rate of interest is assumed to exist, it is easy to think of the investor as an entrepreneur and to argue along the accepted cost-theory lines. Thus we find Prof. Samuelson rejecting Prof. Boulding's solution of the problem simply on the ground that '. . . to argue as Mr Boulding does . . . would be just like arguing that in timeless production firms *seek* to produce at minimum average cost, just because under atomistic competition they are forced to do so'.[7] This is of course precisely what we do argue.

In the paper referred to above Mr Lutz comes down heavily in favour of the total profits equilibrium. But it will be noted that objections have been raised to certain of his arguments by Mr C. G. Hildreth, which amount to the same thing as the objection which we have raised to the ordinary theory of the firm.[8] In a recent book[9] Mr Lutz has replied to Mr Hildreth's criticism at length. The points made seem to us to be analogous to those which we have considered in the present paper (pp. 24–7 above).

Turn now to the question of monopoly. It is not proposed to attempt here the notoriously difficult task of defining monopoly with reference to the conditions which give rise to it. We shall simply say that a monopolistic situation exists for any firm –

(*a*) When the *long-period* rate of return on capital of that firm is higher than the competitive rate.

(*b*) When special circumstances make it impossible for other producers to reduce this rate to the competitive level by manufacturing either the product under consideration or a near substitute.

Ceteris paribus, (*a*) cannot be the case unless (*b*) also applies. It is in these circumstances that the theory outlined above may require modification.

Suppose for a moment that a monopoly as here defined is operating entirely with the capital of its owners. As more capital

---

[7] 'Some Aspects of the Pure Theory of Capital', *Quarterly Journal of Economics* (May 1937).

[8] 'A Note on Maximization Criteria', *Quarterly Journal of Economics* (Nov 1946).

[9] F. and V. Lutz, *The Theory of Investment of the Firm* (Princeton U.P., 1951).

is introduced, the rate of return per unit will increase until, as before, it reaches a maximum at the output where the logarithmic slope of the capital dosage curve equals the logarithmic slope of the total profits curve. But if the rate so obtained is greater than the competitive rate, it will not in general be in the interest of the shareholders to limit output to this point. Optimum output will be where the *marginal* rate of return *to each individual shareholder* is equal to the competitive rate.

But this is not by any means the whole of the story. We may divide the field of monopoly at large into three main sections. Firstly, there are certain groups of firms which operate under conditions which have been described as monopolistic competition. Here we direct attention to our condition (*a*) for monopoly on our definition. Whether a firm believes its demand curve to be downward sloping or not, it is reasonable to suppose that it will wish to invest in that size of plant which will maximize the rate of return on capital in the long run. If it is anticipated that as a result of competition the transitional period of high prices will shortly come to an end, the firm will endeavour to adjust its investment at the outset to the final equilibrium price, which will allow only the normal profit rate to be earned. In the general case, such expectations may introduce an element of indeterminateness, but if it can be assumed that in the relevant region capital requirement is at least approximately proportional to cost[10] and that the anticipated shift of the demand curve will not appreciably affect its elasticity, the optimum size can be found at once. This will be the maximum profit rate size, with normal profit rate as the maximum profit rate. Any attempt to determine plant size by the MC = MR criterion would leave the firm with excess capacity in the long run, just as in the case of perfect competition.

The second section consists of truly monopolistic firms comprising many plants. There may be a 'Blogg & Co.' which has, by fair means or foul, acquired control of all the *many* plants in an industry, and which becomes, in consequence, conscious of facing a downward sloping long-period demand curve. The difference between Bloggs & Co. (with many plants) under competition and Bloggs & Co. as a monopolist is that the question 'how many plants' has now become a real question which must be put. But this does not mean that any different

10 Cf. pp. 24–6 above.

answer will be given to the question 'what size will each plant be'. Whatever price is fixed for the product, each individual plant will produce at maximum profit rate size. No different criterion for size is required than that which would be appropriate under competition. The cost curve for the whole organization will appear as a discontinuous horizontal line. Average cost is constant and equal to marginal cost. The effective criterion, therefore, for the determination of the number of plants will be average cost plus normal profits equal to marginal revenue. This may, of course, be put in the form marginal rate of return on capital equal to normal profits. In the many-plant monopoly neither individual plant managers nor management at the centre need interest themselves in the concept of marginal cost, and only management at the centre need consider marginal revenue.

Thirdly, we have the single-plant monopoly, i.e. the case where economies of scale are so great as to make monopoly inevitable. One plant meets the requirements of the whole industry. Here, formally at any rate, the marginal cost equals marginal revenue criterion holds without modification. For, as long as individual shareholders are introducing capital in proportion to their original holdings, the desired output could be determined by including the competitive rate of return as transfer cost, and equating marginal cost so obtained with marginal revenue in the usual way. But even in this case a number of very good arguments can be put forward in favour of a rate of profit *approach* to the problem. The traditional criterion obscures many issues which are live issues in the world of business.

If new ordinary shareholders are to be introduced to effect a proposed expansion, or if each individual is to subscribe new capital *not* in proportion to original holdings, conflict of interest may arise. This is because, for each individual, marginal rate of profit and the competitive rate are not equated at the same output. A simple example will serve to illustrate the point.

Consider a partnership of two individuals. Each receives a share of profits in proportion to capital subscribed. Suppose the capital of the firm is £5,000: £2,000 of *A*'s and £3,000 of *B*'s. Suppose also profit amounts to 6 per cent of the capital per annum and the competitive rate is 2 per cent only. Imagine that the introduction of another £2,000 capital is expected to reduce the rate on the whole to 5 per cent. If A subscribes £800 and B £1,200, there is no conflict of interest. The £800 will earn net 5 per cent less £20 (i.e. 1 per cent on A's original £2,000), which gives a marginal rate of $2\frac{1}{2}$ per cent. Similarly the £1,200 will earn 5 per cent less £30 (1 per cent on £3,000), i.e. $2\frac{1}{2}$ per cent. It is clearly in the interests of both A and B to expand the business. But if the whole of the £2,000 is to be subscribed by B, then A will be the loser. There will be an obvious conflict of interest. If A were to subscribe £667, this sum would earn 5 per cent less £20, i.e. 2 per cent, which is the alternative rate. He would neither gain nor lose. If he subscribes less he is the loser, if more, he gains. If the £2,000 were raised by the introduction of a new partner, both A and B lose. We are led to conclude that in such circumstances shares are likely to be sold at a premium.

The obvious alternative to these various possibilities is of course to raise money by borrowing at the competitive rate. In this case the price so paid becomes a cost in our definition, and best output is where marginal cost equals marginal revenue. In fact the controlling factor has become a fixed factor and the old analysis applies. The result, abstracting from the risk element, will be just as if the financing had been effected by ordinary shares issued in proportion to original holdings. The question of risk, however, cannot be ignored in this instance. It is well known that investors are especially sensitive about the over-issue of fixed interest-bearing securities, the so-called high gearing of the financial structure. There comes a point where it is considered desirable to increase the proportion of ordinary shares, and it is at this point that questions raised by the rate of profit approach become important. Shareholders may not be unanimous in their approval of an issue of share capital if some are unable to take up their quota.

This situation has its analogy in the theory of investment and is in fact referred to by Mr Lutz.[11] Having put forward the argument (which we hold is not valid under competition but which we accept in the case of monopoly) that 'If a firm finances a certain part of its investment with its own capital and the rest by debts, then, so long as a unit of borrowed funds earns more than the interest on it, the difference will swell total profits which go to the owner and also, since the owner's capital

[11] Loc. cit.

is fixed, the profit rate on his capital', he recognizes that for reasons of risk some limit will be imposed on borrowing.

He argues that, provided debts are incurred at all, then total profit maximization is the appropriate criterion, suggesting that the entrepreneur will first decide how much capital is required to produce up to the point where the marginal rate of return is equal to the rate at which it is possible to borrow and then proceed to raise this capital in the predetermined proportions. Of course this will give the traditional equilibrium, for the amount of capital raised by the issue of ordinary shares is carefully calculated so as to ensure that it will. But it begs the whole question of whose interests the entrepreneur (who may represent a group of individuals who intend to found a firm in which they will be ordinary shareholders) is trying to serve. In fact he will not behave this way at all. His aim will be to maximize the return on his own fixed capital and this will affect his choice of firm size. He will take on debts up to the point where his own capital and the borrowed funds make up the predetermined proportion. If now the rate of return on the marginal pound is still well above the interest rate, he will take on a sort of composite pound consisting of share and loan capital in the predetermined proportion. This will continue until the marginal pound earns sufficient just to pay the market rate on that portion which is borrowed and the share capital rate on that portion which is share capital. This criterion does not give the final equilibrium envisaged by Mr Lutz. On the contrary, it can easily be shown to give the same output as the maximum profit rate criterion. It is to meet just such difficulties as this that business men resort to the device of issuing ordinary shares at a premium, a possibility to which Mr Lutz refers only in connexion with the case where all capital is to be share capital.

We conclude that in a very wide field traditional theory is incorrect and that even in those cases where it does apply there are good reasons for favouring at least the approach which is equally appropriate elsewhere.

3 On the Theory of Expansion of the Firm[1]

W. J. Baumol

Economists who have spent time observing the operations of business enterprises come away impressed with the extent of management's occupation with growth. Expansion is a theme which (with some variations) is dinned into the ears of stockholders, is constantly reported in the financial pages and in the journals devoted to business affairs. Indeed, in talking to business executives one may easily come to believe that growth of the firm is the main preoccupation of top management. A stationary optimum would doubtless be abhorrent to the captains of industry, whose main concern is surely not at what size their enterprises should finally settle down (except where sheer size endangers their standing with the administrators of the antitrust laws) but rather, how rapidly to grow.[2]

Although the static theory of the firm is a helpful snapshot description of a system in motion,[3] it is useful also to have an

[1] This paper owes much to the growing literature of the dynamics of the firm. Particularly, I am indebted to Robin Marris for permitting me to read his unpublished manuscript [5] and to Herbert Frazer who wrote his doctoral dissertation on the subject. Highly relevant and stimulating is Edith Penrose [7]. In addition I owe much to the work of Richard E. Quandt ([8] esp. pp. 156–66). I am also very grateful for their comments to A. Heertje, Fritz Machlup, Burton Malkiel, Richard Quandt, Harold Shapiro, and John Williamson. Finally, I must express my great appreciation to the National Science Foundation whose grant helped materially in the completion of this manuscript.

[2] This view is not unrelated to one of Kaldor's well-known arguments. See N. Kaldor [3]. Here the author reminded us that equilibrium of the competitive firm requires some sort of increasing costs to make it unprofitable for the company to expand indefinitely. But under pure competition there seems to be no obvious source of diminishing returns, and hence little reason for *any* scale of operations of the competitive firm to constitute a long-run stationary equilibrium situation.

[3] Thus I am emphatically *not* proposing that the conventional theory of the firm be relegated to the garbage heap or the museum of curious antiquities. Static analysis of a nonstationary phenomenon can be immensely illuminating, and the

Reprinted from *American Economic Review*, LII (Dec 1962) 1078–87, by kind permission of the author and of the American Economic Association.

alternative construction of the kind which is described in this paper – another equilibrium analysis in which the *rate of growth* of output, rather than its *level*, is the variable whose value is determined by optimality considerations.

1. A Simple Growth Equilibrium Model

For simplicity the first model is confined to a case in which input and output prices are fixed (pure competition), and where the production function is linear and homogeneous. Thus I am either dealing only with the period of time before the firm grows so large that the prices become variables which are subject to the influence of the firm, or we must assume that all firms grow together and that in this process no one of them outgrows the others sufficiently to constitute it a significant force in the market. This premise permits me to evade the problem of demand for the expanding outputs of the firm. So long as it operates under conditions of pure competition its demand curves will be perfectly elastic and no marketing problems will affect its plans.[4]

It is assumed that management considers only a very simple growth pattern – a fixed percentage rate of growth, to be continued into the indefinite future. This heroic assumption is adopted to permit a simple characterization of the optimal growth path by means of a single variable, the permanent percentage rate of growth, g.[5]

Finally, it is assumed, at least for the moment, that the

received theory of the firm contains many very helpful results, both from the point of view of the understanding of the workings of the economy and the applied work of the operations researcher. It would be folly to deny ourselves the use of this body of analysis just because its domain of applicability is somewhat limited.

[4] However, if all firms expand simultaneously in this way they may encounter secularly declining prices and problems of Keynesian excess supply. This macroeconomic problem is not discussed here since it merits being considered by itself in some considerable detail. I have elsewhere taken the optimistic position that if all firms expand rapidly enough they will usually create sufficient purchasing power to constitute a market for their products. No doubt many readers will question this hypothesis which appears to be a distant relative of the Say's Law family.

[5] If this premise is not employed and the optimal rate of growth at every future moment of time is left to be determined, we are forced into the morass of the theory of functionals and we cannot escape without at least some recourse to the calculus of variations.

company's objective (which determines the optimal rate of growth of its output) is conventional profit maximization.

It is posited that costs can be divided into two categories: ordinary production and operating costs, and costs which arise only as a result of the expansion process. That is, any costs which would be associated with a given level of output if the output rate were not changing may be classed under output costs; any additional outlays above and beyond the output costs are called expansion costs. Output costs will only be taken into account implicitly, in the net revenue figures. That is, in discussing revenues, net revenue figures, from which output costs have already been deducted, will be employed.

Let R represent the initial net revenue of our firm, g be the rate of growth (which is to be determined), and i be the rate of interest relevant in discounting future revenues. Then, because of the constancy of the prices of all of the firm's inputs and outputs and the linear homogeneity of the production function, net revenues will grow precisely in the same proportion as inputs. Thus, in t periods, the firm's net revenue will be $R(1 + g)^t$, and the discounted present value of that net revenue will be $R[(1 + g)/(1 + i)]^t$. The present value of the expected stream of revenues will therefore be:

$$P = \sum_{t=0}^{\infty} R\left(\frac{1+g}{1+i}\right)^t = R\frac{1}{1 - \frac{1+g}{1+i}} = R\frac{1+i}{i-g} \tag{1}$$

provided only[6] that $g < i$ so that $(1 + g)/(1 + i) < 1$ as is required for convergence of the geometric series (1).

[6] The problems caused for such a model if the rate of growth exceeds the rate of interest are well known. Specifically, the geometric series (1) will then not converge and the present value of the firm's profit stream will no longer be finite. See, e.g., David Durand [2]. However, as Miller and Modigliani have shown, the case $g > i$ is not a serious possibility. They write ([6] fn. 14): 'Although the case of (perpetual) growth rates greater than the discount factor is the much-discussed "growth stock paradox" . . . it has no real economic significance. . . . This will be apparent when one recalls that the discount rate, . . . though treated as a constant in partial equilibrium (relative price) analysis of the kind presented here, is actually a variable from the standpoint of the system as a whole. That is, if the assumption of finite value for all shares did not hold, because for some shares g was (perpetually) greater than i, then i would necessarily rise until an over-all equilibrium in the capital markets had been restored.' (The notation has been changed from the original to that employed in this paper.)

An alternative way of avoiding this problem is to drop the (unrealistic) premise that the horizon is infinite. However, a finite horizon (say one involving 5 periods)

It is perfectly obvious in this situation that we have

$$\frac{\partial P}{\partial g} > 0 \tag{2}$$

that is, the present value of the net revenue stream will grow indefinitely with the rate of expansion g. In fact, P will grow at an increasing rate with g, and its value will exceed any preassigned number as g approaches i, as shown in the net revenue curve, RR' in Fig. 3.1. There is clearly nothing here to place a limit on the rate of expansion of the firm.

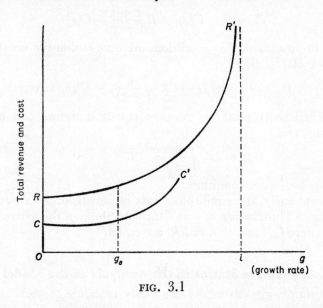

FIG. 3.1

The firm will only be constrained from accelerating its activities without limit by its expansion costs, the present value of which we designate as $C(g)$. The literature is replete with discussions of the administrative costs of growth and there is no point in recapitulating these materials here. It is enough to point out that growth is what strains the firm's entrepreneurial resources and adds to the company's risks, and it may be expected that after some point the resulting increases in costs

---

will yield an expression for total revenue which is somewhat more messy than (1). Though it will be a fifth-degree polynomial, it will have only positive coefficients and so any equilibrium will still be unique. Indeed, the results of the infinite horizon model all seem to continue to hold in the finite horizon case.

will catch up with the marginal revenues derived from more rapid expansion.[7] That is, it may be assumed that the slope of the cost curve CC', which is the graph of the function $C(g)$, will normally be less than that of RR' near the horizontal axis, but that eventually the slope of the former will catch up with and finally exceed that of the latter. (It may be, however, that in some cases the slope of the cost curve will exceed that of the revenue curve throughout the positive quadrant so that the optimal growth rate will be zero negative.)

Specifically, we obtain the growth–profit function:

$$\Pi = P - C(g) = R\frac{1+i}{i-g} - C(g). \tag{3}$$

The profit-maximizing conditions are then (using the notation Π_g for $\partial\Pi/\partial_g$, etc.):

$$\Pi_g = P_g - C'(g) = R\frac{1+i}{(i-g)^2} - C'(g) = 0 \tag{4}$$

(the first-order marginal revenue equals marginal cost condition), and

$$\Pi_{gg} = 2R\frac{1+i}{(i-g)^3} - C''(g) < 0, \tag{5}$$

the second-order condition.

Graphically, the equilibrium rate of growth is given by Og_e in Fig. 3.1, the value of g at which the slope of the expansion cost curve CC' and that of RR' are equal.[8]

2. Comparative Statics in the Analysis of the Model

This simple growth model can easily be made to yield some results in terms of comparative statics. While some of these are

[7] This view of the shape of the cost function can also be defended with the aid of the usual (somewhat shaky) appeal to the second-order maximum conditions. For, given the shape of our revenue function, the cost curve must behave in the manner shown in Fig. 3.1 or there would be no profit-maximizing growth rate.

Note also that C is likely to be a function of other variables in addition to g, i.e., it is apt to depend on the initial absolute level of output – a small firm is likely to find it less costly to expand 10 per cent than does a large company. However, since $C(g)$ is the present value of all expected future costs taken together, initial cost differences may not play a very important role.

[8] We might even envision a long-run zero-profit competitive growth equilibrium in which entry has caused shifting of the curves and produced a zero-profit tangency position at which growth level has settled. There is some question in my mind whether, in a growth model such as this, much relevance can be ascribed to that type of long-run adjustment.

not particularly surprising, they may offer some reassurance that the model does not possess particularly perverse properties, and that it can serve as an instrument of analysis much like the standard stationary equilibrium model.

First, a rise in the interest rate will reduce the present value of the stream of expected revenues, for we have[9] by (1):

$$P_i = R \frac{(i-g)-(1+i)}{(i-g)^2} = -R \frac{1+g}{(i-g)^2} < 0. \qquad (6)$$

Moreover, a rise in the interest rate will reduce the *marginal* revenue yield of increased economic growth, P_g, for we have, differentiating (6) partially with respect to g,

$$P_{ig} = P_{gi} = -R \frac{(i-g)^2 + 2(i-g)(1+g)}{(i-g)^4} < 0 \qquad (7)$$

by our basic assumption $g < i$.

It is now rather simple to prove that (at least in a perfect capital market where some market rate of interest determines the relevant discount factor) a rise in the interest rate will reduce the equilibrium rate of growth of the firm. For differentiating the first-order maximum condition (4) totally and setting $d\Pi_g = 0$ (so that the equilibrium condition continues to hold) we obtain:

$$d\Pi_g = P_{gi}di + \Pi_{gg}dg = 0$$

or

$$\frac{dg}{di} = -\frac{P_{gi}}{\Pi_{gg}} < 0 \qquad (8)$$

by (5) and (7).

Geometrically, this obvious result is a consequence of the fact that a rise in i reduces the slope of the RR' curve in Fig. 3.1

[9] A complication is introduced by the fact that interest payments are among the output costs which have been subtracted from our net revenue figure, R, so that R should no longer be treated as a constant when differentiating with respect to i. This can be taken care of by noting that our assumptions of linear homogeneity and constant price imply that the quantity of money capital employed by the firm should be strictly proportionate with $R(1 + g)^t$. Say it will equal $kR(1 + g)^t$ and therefore incur an annual interest payment, $ikR(1 + g)^t$. In that case we need merely write $R = R^*(1 - ik)$ and make this substitution in our revenue function (1). It may then easily be verified by direct differentiation that the resulting expression for P_i will be slightly more complicated than (6) but that it will still be negative. A similar remark holds for (7) and (8).

throughout its length, as indicated by (7), so that the equilibrium growth level, Og_e, must move to the left.

A somewhat more interesting application arises out of the recent proposals to stimulate business growth by means of appropriate government subsidies.[10] Suppose one is considering two alternative subsidy plans for this purpose. The first plan involves payments (S_{1t}) proportionate with the percentage rate of increase of the firm's output growth:

$$S_{1t} = s_1 g_t = s_1 g.$$

The present value of all such expected future subsidy payments is

$$S_1 = s_1 g \sum_{t=0}^{\infty} \left(\frac{1}{1+i} \right)^t = s_1 g \left(1 + \frac{1}{i} \right). \tag{9}$$

The alternative plan proposes to offer a stream of subsidies (S_{2t}) proportionate to the absolute rate of increase of output:

$$S_{2t} = s_2[R(1+g)^t - R(1+g)^{t-1}] = s_2 g R(1+g)^{t-1}$$

whose capitalized present value is:

$$S_2 = \frac{s_2 g R}{1+g} \sum_{t=1}^{\infty} \left(\frac{1+g}{1+i} \right)^t = \frac{s_2 g R}{1+g} \left[\left\{ \sum_{t=0}^{\infty} \left(\frac{1+g}{1+i} \right)^t \right\} - 1 \right]$$

$$= \frac{s_2 g R}{1+g} \left[\frac{1+i}{i-g} - 1 \right] = \frac{s_2 g R}{1+g} \cdot \frac{1+g}{i-g}$$

or

$$S_2 = \frac{s_2 g R}{i-g}. \tag{10}$$

Adding, in turn, the subsidy expressions (9) and (10) to our basic profit function (3) we obtain the two new profit expressions:

$$\Pi^* = R \frac{1+i}{i-g} - C(g) + s_1 g \left(1 + \frac{1}{i} \right) \tag{11}$$

and

$$\Pi^{**} = R \frac{1+i}{i-g} - C(g) + \frac{s_2 g R}{i-g}. \tag{12}$$

By the same procedure as was employed when the effect of an

interest rate change was examined, we arrive at the respective comparative statics results:

$$\frac{dg}{ds_1} = -\frac{1 + 1/i}{\Pi_{gg}{}^*} > 0 \tag{13}$$

and

$$\frac{dg}{ds_2} = -\frac{iR}{\Pi_{gg}{}^{**}(i - g)^2} > 0 \tag{14}$$

if the second-order conditions $\Pi_{gg}{}^* < 0$ and $\Pi_{gg}{}^{**} < 0$ both hold. Thus both types of subsidy would, indeed, stimulate the growth of the profit-maximizing firm.

We can go beyond this somewhat uninteresting conclusion by asking which of these two types of subsidy will yield more growth per dollar of government outlay. For this purpose we must deal not with s_1 and s_2, the subsidy rates, but with the total subsidy outlays, S_1 and S_2, as given by (9) and (10). From these we obtain:

$$\frac{ds_1}{dS_1} = \frac{1}{g(1 + 1/i)} \tag{15}$$

and

$$\frac{ds_2}{dS_2} = \frac{i - g}{Rg}. \tag{16}$$

Multiplying (13) by (15) and (14) by (16) and writing out the expressions for $\Pi_g{}^*$ and $\Pi_{gg}{}^{**}$ we obtain:

$$\frac{dg}{dS_1} = -\frac{1}{g\Pi_{gg}{}^*} = -\frac{1}{g\left[2R\dfrac{1 + i}{(i - g)^3} - C''(g)\right]} \tag{17}$$

and

$$\frac{dg}{dS_2} = -\frac{i}{g(i - g)\Pi_{gg}{}^{**}}$$
$$= -\frac{i}{g\left[2R\dfrac{1 + i}{(i - g)^3} - C''(g) + \dfrac{2is_2R}{(i - g)^3}\right](i - g)}. \tag{18}$$

Hence subsidy S_2 will yield higher marginal returns than subsidy S_1 if and only if expression (18) exceeds expression (17), i.e. if and only if

$$-\frac{1}{g\Pi_{gg}{}^*} < -\frac{i}{g(i - g)\left[\Pi_{gg}{}^* + \dfrac{2is_2R}{(i - g)^3}\right]}.$$

This requires

$$(i - g) \left[\Pi_{gg}{}^* + \frac{2is_2R}{(i - g)^3} \right] > i\Pi_{gg}{}^*$$

or

$$-g\Pi_{gg}{}^* + (i - g)\frac{2is_2R}{(i - g)^3} > 0$$

and since (because $\Pi_{gg}{}^* < 0$ by the second-order condition) both terms in this last expression are positive, this requirement will always be satisfied. We conclude that in our model a subsidy of the second type will then always yield higher marginal growth returns than does a subsidy of the first type.

It is also noteworthy that a net investment tax credit of the sort originally proposed is essentially equivalent in our model to a growth subsidy proposal of type two. For the investment credit is a subsidy proportionate to the level of net investment. With our linear homogeneous production function, and with constant input prices, the capital–output ratio will be constant so that a subsidy proportionate to investment will automatically be proportionate to the absolute rate of increase in output.

Since so many other considerations must enter any decision among alternative growth stimulation methods there is no point in laboring this discussion further. The case serves, however, to illustrate how meaningful theorems can be derived from the growth equilibrium model of the firm.

3. Profit versus Growth Maximization

The discussion so far has been confined to the case of pure competition and has assumed that the firm's objective is to maximize profit. But larger *oligopolistic* firms may well have a different set of objectives.[11] Specifically, I have suggested that management's goal may well be to maximize 'sales' (total revenue) subject to a profit constraint. Though I remain firmly convinced of the merit of the hypothesis as a static characterization of the current facts of oligopolistic business operation, in the present context – a growth equilibrium analysis – it is desirable to modify the hypothesis in two respects.

First, maximization of *rate of growth* of sales revenue seems a somewhat better approximation to the goals of many manage-

11 See [1] esp. chaps. 6–8.

ment groups in large firms than is maximization of the current *level* of sales. For example, most company publicity materials seem to emphasize the extent to which the firm has 'progressed' rather than the sheer magnitude of its current operations. In my earlier static model I was forced to employ a sales-revenue-level objective as an approximation to a measure of the rate of growth of the firm's scale of operations. A growth equilibrium model now frees me from this necessity.

The second modification deals with the nature of the profit constraint, which in a static model may have seemed to be arbitrarily imposed from the outside – perhaps even a device to avoid explaining what had to be explained, very much like the fixed mark-up of doubtful origin which lies at the heart of the full-cost pricing discussions. A growth analysis enables me to give an explanation of the profit constraint which, I hope, is somewhat less superficial and rather more convincing.

From the point of view of a long-run growth (or sales) maximizer, profit no longer acts as a constraint. Rather, it is an instrumental variable – a means whereby management works towards its goals. Specifically, profits are a means for obtaining capital needed to finance expansion plans. Capital is raised both by direct retention of profits and by the payment of dividends to induce outside investors to provide funds to the company. But, beyond some point, profits compete with sales. For the lower prices and higher marketing outlays which are necessary to promote sales also cut into net earnings. Hence, too high a level of profits will reduce the magnitude of the firm's current operations, while too low a profit level will prevent future growth. The optimal profit stream will be that intermediate stream which is consistent with the largest flow of output (or rate of growth of output) over the firm's lifetime.

Specifically, this optimal profit rate can be described with the aid of a simple model such as the following:[12]

Let

g represent our firm's growth rate,

I be its level of investment as a per cent of the value of current capital assets (the percentage rate of growth of the firm's money capital),

[12] For present purposes there is no need to take explicit account of such decision variables as prices, advertising outlay, etc.; but the model can easily be expanded to do so.

C

Π be the profit rate as a per cent of present equity,[13]
D be the dividend as a per cent of present equity, and
E be the retained earnings as a per cent of present equity
   per unit of time.

The objective then is to maximize:

$$g = f(I, \Pi)$$

subject to[14]

$$I = \phi(\Pi, D) + E$$
$$\Pi \equiv D + E.$$

The first of these equations, the objective function, expresses the competitive relationship between growth and profit
rates, and states that the rate of growth of the firm's operations
varies (directly) with investment, and (after a point) inversely
with the profit rate (as indicated in Fig. 3.1). The next equation, however, shows that the profit rate indirectly assists
growth by providing capital through retained earnings, and by
attracting funds from outside sources at a rate, $\phi\,(\Pi, D)$, which
depends both on the dividend rate and the company's profit
rate. From this system we can then determine the optimal
profit rate, Π, which from our long-run point of view enters
into the constraints just as one of the variables in the system.
Only in a static sales-maximization model, then, does profit
appear as an independent datum arbitrarily given from the
outside – a fixed minimal profit requirement which has somehow to be met by the firm.

Substantive theorems for a (sales) growth maximization
model may be developed which contrast its consequences with

[13] In practice, of course, different profit rates may be optimal at different points
in the company's history. But in the fixed-price constant-returns-to-scale model
which is employed here there is no reason to depart from a single optimal profit
level.

[14] Perhaps, in accord with the Miller–Modigliani view [6] that dividends do not
matter, D should be omitted from the Φ function. Other possible variables that
have been suggested for inclusion as elements which significantly affect the
willingness of the public to supply funds to the firm are $d\Pi/dt$, the rate of growth
of the firm's profit rate, and g, the rate of growth of its output.

It has been suggested that other, partly conventional, constraints are imposed
by the capital market and should be incorporated in a more elaborate version of
the model. These include restrictions on the debt–equity ratio, on the ratio between
current assets and sales, and on the extent of reliance on noninternal financing.

those of profit maximization.[15] However, these propositions are completely analogous with those which I have already developed elsewhere for the case of sales maximization. For example, the growth maximizer's sales, advertising outlay, and (trivially) his growth rate will be larger than those of the profit maximizer and the pricing and output decisions of only the former may be expected to vary in response to changes in fixed costs. Since the logic of these results in our present analysis is exactly the same as it was in the sales maximization model there is no point in repeating the argument here.

I will only suggest what appears to be the most important point, that our discussion has shown the standard apparatus of marginal analysis and mathematical programming to be fully applicable to decision problems even when management's objective is not the venerable profit maximization of economic theory.

REFERENCES

[1] W. J. BAUMOL, *Business Behavior, Value and Growth* (New York, 1959).
[2] D. DURAND, 'Growth Stocks and the Petersburgh Paradox', *Journal of Finance*, XII (Sep 1957) 348–63.
[3] N. KALDOR, 'The Equilibrium of the Firm', *Economic Journal*, XLIV (Mar 1934) 60–76; reprinted in N. Kaldor, *Essays in Value and Distribution* (Glencoe, Ill., 1961).
[4] K. KNORR and W. J. BAUMOL (eds.), *What Price Economic Growth?* (Englewood Cliffs, N.J., 1961).
[5] R. MARRIS, 'The Micro Economics of Managerial Capitalism' (unpublished manuscript).
[6] M. H. MILLER and F. MODIGLIANI, 'Dividend Policy, Growth, and the Valuation of Shares', *Journal of Business*, XXXIV (Oct 1961) 411–33.
[7] EDITH PENROSE, *The Theory of the Growth of the Firm* (London, 1959).
[8] R. E. QUANDT, 'Effects of the Tax-Subsidy Plan', Appendix B in K. Knorr and W. J. Baumol [4].

15 It is sometimes stated or implied that long-run growth and profit maximization must necessarily lead to identical decisions and results (see, e.g. Penrose [7] p. 29). But if, as in our model, it is sales rather than assets whose growth is being maximized, or if, even in the long run, investment in the firm can fall short of or exceed profit earnings, it is extremely easy to find counterexamples. In fact, only in the most unusual circumstances would sales (revenue) growth maximization be achieved by the maximization of profits.

4 Profit, Growth and Sales Maximization [1]

John Williamson

1. Introduction

One of the more discredited concepts in the theory of the firm is that of an 'optimum size' of firm. Empirical evidence has provided no substantiation for the thesis of a long-run U-shaped cost curve and, since firms are not restricted to the sale of a single product or even a particular range of products, there is no more reason to expect profitability to decline with size than there is evidence to suggest that it does. This raises the question as to what does limit the size of a firm. The answer that has been given is that there are important costs entailed in *expanding* the size of a firm and that these expansion costs tend to increase with the firm's rate of growth. This view was first advanced by Edith Penrose [7], has been most fully developed by Robin Marris [5], and has received its most elegant formulation in a paper by Professor Baumol [2] (pp. 34–45 above).

The development of a theory of growth of the firm was a necessary prerequisite to another feature of the last two analyses just cited – the consideration of alternative assumptions about managerial objectives. Only static profit maximization and Baumol's static sales maximization hypothesis [1] (with its seemingly arbitrary minimum profit constraint) can be analysed other than in a growth context. Many economists, the author included, would judge that these are less realistic assumptions than that management wishes to maximize growth or a discounted sum of future sales. Whether they in fact are is an empirical question whose resolution demands a technique for

[1] The author is indebted to William Baumol, Keith Hartley, Alan Peacock and Alan Williams for useful comments on an earlier draft. Responsibility for any errors and opinions expressed is that of the author alone.

Reprinted from *Economica*, n.s. XXXIII, 129 (Feb 1966) 1–16, by kind permission of the author and of Economica Publishing Office.

elucidating the alternative implications of different objectives. The principal purpose of this paper is to construct a model which will permit one to derive the differences in behaviour that would follow from the objectives of maximizing profits, maximizing growth and maximizing (discounted) sales.

The framework in which this is accomplished is that of a permanent growth model of the firm. The model is based upon that presented by Baumol [2], but has been considerably extended. It is developed in section 2, simplified in section 3 and solved in section 4. The basic assumption of a permanent growth model is that unit costs and revenues are independent of the absolute scale involved, although they depend in the traditional ways on the level of the firm's operations relative to its present size. It therefore follows that, if prices and technology are unchanging or altering in appropriately offsetting ways, management is able to make a once-for-all selection of the values of its policy variables. (Where these are not expressed in ratio form, the appropriate value of the variable will increase at a constant proportionate rate over time.) Of course, if at some future date (contrary to the expectations presently held with certainty) there were a change in external circumstances, or a change in management's objectives, or a change in management (perhaps as a result of take-over) with a consequential change in objectives, then the values of these variables would change to new 'permanent' levels.

The (economic) policy variables on which any firm has to reach decisions may conveniently be classified into four categories, though the firm actually has only three degrees of freedom in selecting them. First, there are the decisions on input levels required to satisfy the efficiency conditions – the selection of least-cost input combinations, the optimal distribution of given investment funds among alternative projects, and the optimal distribution of sales effort.[2] Second, there is the other decision that is analysed in traditional price theory, that of the output, price or sales[3] level in the current period; this will be referred to as the output decision. Third, there are the financial decisions embracing the division of profits between

---

[2] This is intended to include the decision as to whether to raise price in order to finance, say, extra advertising, given whatever constraint is imposed by the 'output decision'.

[3] The existence of a demand curve implies that these are equivalent.

dividends and retained earnings, the flotation of new equity and the raising of new capital by bond finance. Fourth, there is the decision as to how much should be spent on expanding the size of the firm – the investment decision.

The present paper is largely confined to a consideration of the output decision, the retention ratio and the flotation of new equity. The reasons for this restriction are as follows. The efficiency conditions are irrelevant to our aims since they will be satisfied by a firm successfully pursuing any of the objectives under investigation (or, for that matter, virtually any other consistent aim apart from an easy life). If the firm sells bonds, it will not be able to increase the ratio of debt to assets (i.e. its 'gearing' or 'leverage') indefinitely because of the added risk involved ([5] p. 206). The extra investment funds that accrue from this source will therefore bear a constant ratio to the funds obtainable from the other two sources, so that inclusion of this complication would not add any qualitatively different conclusions. Finally, the investment decision need not be considered explicitly as it is implied by the net revenue and the financial decisions of the firm – this is the missing degree of freedom.

Given the framework outlined, and in particular the basic assumption of rather stationary external circumstances that is necessary to construct a permanent growth model, only weak additional assumptions are necessary to prove the following results:

A. The growth rate of the firm cannot be increased by resort to additional equity finance.

B. Growth is never limited by lack of finance as such, as postulated by Baumol [2] and Downie [3], but by the fear of take-over, as postulated by Marris [5].

C. A profit or growth maximizer will grow at a positive rate if it is a profitable firm; a sales maximizer need not.

D. It is not possible, as Baumol has claimed [2], to derive the static sales maximization model from the assumption of growth maximization. (It can, however, be derived from a long-run sales maximization assumption.)

E. A profit and growth maximizer would reach the same

output decision, but a sales maximizer would, except in a limiting case, produce more.

F. A profit maximizer would, except in a limiting case, distribute more of its profits than a growth maximizer.

2. Development of the Model

We define the following variables, where lower-case letters denote ratios and capitals denote other variables. Where no time subscript appears, that variable is to be interpreted as applying to time zero. (The time subscript for period zero is included in those equations where variables for other periods appear as well.) Since the rate of interest is assumed constant and the permanent growth context implies that retention ratio and rate of new issue are maintained constant, the variables i, r, and f never carry a time subscript.

(a) Policy variables:

$S =$ value of sales or total revenue; $r =$ retention ratio; $f =$ (permanent) growth rate of equity.

(b) Exogenous variables:

$$k = \frac{value\ of\ firm\ at\ which\ it\ would\ be\ taken\ over}{potential\ maximum\ value\ of\ firm};$$

$i =$ rate of interest.

(c) Variables which are exogenous at time zero but endogenous thereafter:

$K =$ capital; $F =$ equity.

(d) Endogenous variables:

$R =$ net revenue (profits), which consists of total revenue less those costs which the firm would incur to maintain current output if it were not growing; $X \equiv C + I =$ expansion costs (i.e. all other costs incurred by the firm); $I =$ (net) investment, i.e. addition to capital; $C =$ non-investment expansion costs; $M =$ market value of firm; $g =$ future (permanent) growth rate of S_t, R_t, K_t, X_t, I_t, C_t; $m \equiv M/F =$ value of share.

Most of these definitions are self-explanatory. The exceptions are k, which will be explained in section 4, and g, the future permanent growth rate of the firm. This, it should be noted, is an endogenous variable whose value is determined by the particular decisions made regarding the firm's policy variables. In order to assess the generality of the model, it is necessary to investigate briefly the plausibility of the assumption that the six variables listed will all grow at the same rate.

Consider a perfectly competitive firm with an unchanging linear homogenous production function facing constant prices, and assume that the increasing costs of growth arise because the process of expanding management requires existing managers to spend some of their time training new managers and integrating them into the managerial team. Then increasing output by a certain proportion, g, over its present level would increase total revenue, costs and hence net revenue in this same proportion. Moreover, the output expansion would require an equal proportionate increase in the capital stock, since with unchanging technology the firm would wish to maintain the ratio of capital to output found optimal in the present period. A growth of g in the present period requires a certain level of spending on management training, C; an equal proportionate increase in the next period requires an expenditure of $(1 + g)C$, since the unit cost of training managers is maintained constant by the increased stock of existing managers to do the training, but the number needing to be trained increases by the proportion g. In this simple case, therefore, it is easy to show that total revenue, net revenue, the capital stock and the various forms of expansion costs all increase at the same rate g.

Although it cannot be demonstrated in an equally rigorous manner, the implication of recent discussion is that much the same conclusion is likely to apply to a diversified, oligopolistic firm. Suppose that the general level of output prices is constant; then total revenue will expand at the same rate as output provided that the firm is not forced to cut its prices in order to move down existing demand curves. But the virtually unlimited opportunities for diversification remove any such necessity. Net revenue will also expand at this rate, not only if factor prices and technology are constant, but also if they offset one another; this would occur if wages increased at the same rate as productivity rose due to neutral technical progress. It is well known that with neutral technical progress the capital–output ratio is constant, so that the capital stock and therefore investment will also increase at the same rate. No modification of the argument in the previous paragraph is required so far as C is concerned. Consequently, it is not unreasonable to postulate that S, R, K, X, I and C will all increase at the same rate as output if the price level is constant. (If prices were increasing at a constant rate, these variables would all increase at the same rate in real terms but an appropriately magnified rate in money terms.)

The first relationship we shall derive, that between sales and net revenue, comes from the standard theory of the firm. As output expands (in the current period), net and total revenue both increase initially but eventually both reach maxima. Net revenue reaches a maximum first due to positive marginal costs, and the position of maximum total revenue marks the end of the economically interesting output range. The relationship may therefore be summarized as

$$R = R(S) \qquad R'' < 0. \qquad (1)$$

Second, let us analyse expansion costs. By definition, these consist of the cost of adding to the capital stock to keep it in line with the planned greater sales in the following period plus such other costs as the firm must incur in the process of expansion. Assuming a constant capital–output ratio and constant prices, it is evident that $I = gK$. More interesting are the other expansion costs, which were the principal interest of Mrs Penrose's enquiry [7] and have been extensively discussed by Marris [5]. They consist largely of the managerial diseconomies involved in growing fast and the costs of research, development and sales promotion entailed in diversification. The literature on this point may conveniently be summarized for our purposes by the assumptions made about $C(g)$ below, although the last one – that the marginal cost of growth is negligible for very small growth rates – is less firmly founded than the others.

$$X \equiv I + C = gK + C(g) \qquad \begin{aligned} & C' > 0 \\ & C'' > 0 \\ & C(0) \equiv 0 \\ & C'(0) \approx 0. \end{aligned}$$

*

Taking the inverse function of equation (2), one derives

$$g = g(X) \qquad g' > 0, g'' < 0. \tag{3}$$

The statement that growth depends on the amount spent on expansion, but that there are decreasing returns to such expenditure, is actually weaker than the assumptions from which it was derived. As a matter of fact, the latter are needed only in the proof of result C.

The sources from which expansion funds may be obtained are retained earnings and the proceeds of new equity issues. Retained earnings are defined as the product of the retention ratio and net revenue. (Of course, insofar as the tax laws permit some expansion costs to be counted as current costs, the conceptual retention ratio differs from the published ratio of a firm.) The amount raised by floating new equity is the product of the price for which the shares are sold and the number that are sold. The number sold in period 0 is the product of the proportionate increase in the number of shares and the number outstanding at the start of the period, or fF. Their price is computed on the assumption that dividends are paid on existing shares prior to selling the new shares, so that the amount that investors will be willing to pay for the new shares is the price of a share in period 1, m_1, discounted to the present period. It follows that

$$X_0 = rR_0 + \frac{m_1}{1+i}fF_0 = rR_0 + \frac{fM_1}{(1+i)(1+f)}. \tag{4}$$

The market value of the firm is given by the discounted future earnings of the shares at present outstanding.[4] In period t, the firm will earn a net revenue of $(1+g)^t R$, but it will only pay out $(1-r)(1+g)^t R$. Moreover, some of this will accrue to those who purchase new securities issued between time zero and t; only $F/(1+f)^t F$ will accrue to those who own shares at the beginning. Discounting these future earnings and summing yields the market value of the firm as

---

4 This is only one of several possible ways in which the stock-market value of the firm may be computed. It is what Miller and Modigliani [6] term the 'stream of dividends approach' to valuation, and is the simplest one to apply in the present model. The other approaches are logically equivalent since we are implicitly assuming absence of transactions costs, taxes and uncertainty. It may be noted that the permanent growth context permits one to dispense with consideration of undistributed profits or capital stocks.

$$M = \sum_{t=0}^{\infty} \left[\frac{1+g}{(1+f)(1+i)} \right]^{t} (1-r)R$$

$$= \left[\frac{1}{1 - \dfrac{1+g}{(1+f)(1+i)}} \right] (1-r)R$$

$$= \frac{(1-r)(1+f)(1+i)R}{i-g+f+if} \quad (5)$$

provided that $(1+f)(1+i) > 1+g$ so that the geometric series converges. A sufficient condition for this is $i > g$. Although we have listed i as an exogenous variable, there is an overwhelming economic reason for believing that $i > g(R)$; since otherwise a firm which invested slightly less than R would have an infinite valuation by the stock market, the interest rate would be revised upwards by the stock market till this ceased to be true. And it will be shown in section 3 that $i > g(R)$ is a sufficient condition to ensure that $i > g$. It may also be noted that, since $R_1 = (1+g)R_0$ and all other factors in equation (5) are invariant over time, one has

$$M_1 = (1+g)M_0. \quad (6)$$

3. Simplification of the Model

It is interesting to analyse a frequent assumption to the effect that there is an absolute limit to the amount of finance a firm can obtain for expenditure on expansion.[5] The reasoning is that with low pay-out rates any increase in dividends is so effective in raising share prices as to permit a greater augmentation of external finance than the loss of internal finance; and vice versa when pay-out rates are high. Consequently there is a trade-off between external and internal finance and some optimum financial policy which maximizes access to total funds. At this point expansion funds reach an absolute maximum.

To investigate this proposition, one substitutes equations (5) and (6) into (4) to yield

$$X = rR + \frac{(1-r)(1+g)fR}{i-g+f+if}. \quad (7)$$

To find that combination of the firm's financial policy variables

[5] See, for example, Baumol [2] pp. 34–45 above, and Downie [3] p. 66.

which maximizes the finance available for expansion (and therefore its growth rate), one differentiates (7) with respect to r and f.

$$\frac{\partial X}{\partial r} = R + \frac{fR}{(i - g + f + if)^2} \left[(1 - r)(1 + i)(1 + f) \partial g / \partial r \right.$$
$$\left. - (1 + g)(1 - g + f + if) \right]. \quad (8)$$

At $r = 1$, this simplifies to

$$\frac{\partial X}{\partial r} = \frac{(1 + f)(i - g)R}{i - g + f + if} > 0$$

provided that $i > g$. Since the first term in the square brackets in (8) is positive when $r < 1$, it follows that $\partial X / \partial r > 0$ throughout the feasible range of r and irrespective of the value of f.

$$\frac{\partial X}{\partial f} = \frac{(1 - r)R}{(i - g + f + if)^2}$$
$$[(1 + g)(i - g) + f(1 + i)(1 + f) \partial g / \partial f] > 0. \quad (8)$$

Assuming that as $f \to \infty$ the growth rate approaches a finite limiting value g_0, one has, however,

$$\lim_{f \to \infty} X = rR + (1 - r)(1 + g_0)R/(1 + i). \quad (9)$$

One concludes that there is no optimum retention ratio and rate of equity creation which maximize the availability of new finance. An increase in the rate of selling shares will always increase the funds available, though these funds will approach a finite limiting value. Similarly, any increase in the retention ratio will increase the availability of funds.

The maximum funds that would be available through retentions are R. This exceeds the maximum available if new equity is issued, since the value of equation (7) is always less than R provided $r < 1$; and if $r = 1$ then $X = R$ and all funds are raised internally. But when the retention ratio is unity the value of the firm is zero by equation (5). Marris has argued that this is not an economically significant solution ([5] chap. 1), since when a potentially profitable firm is depressed to a low market value it creates the risk of provoking a take-over raid.[6]

[6] Analytically, take-over means that new values of the policy variables are selected, presumably with the aim of raising M. The raiders will make a profit provided that the new value of M exceeds that which existed under the policies of the previous management. (We assume a perfect capital market.)

This indeed seems by far the most powerful reason for believing that firms will be constrained at some determinate point in their desire to grow.

Result A of section 1 was proved in the last paragraph; growth can never be increased by resort to additional equity finance. The significance of this conclusion may be assessed by supposing that the firm has made its investment decision, so that X and therefore g are determined, and its output decision, so that R is specified. Then from equation (7) the rate of equity creation, f, needed to finance X will depend on r by the formula

$$f = \frac{(i - g)(X/R - r)}{(i - g)r + (1 + g) - X/R(1 + i)}.$$

Substituting in (5) and simplifying yields[7]

$$M = (1 + i)(R - X)/(i - g).$$

In other words, we are living in a Miller and Modigliani [6] type of world where, because there are no transactions costs, taxes or uncertainty, the purely financial decisions of the firm have no impact on its value or on the rate of return enjoyed by investors. There is therefore no compelling reason for a firm to choose any particular method of raising finance. However, it is a familiar fact that management prefers to raise finance internally and that new equity issues are comparatively unusual occurrences, and this is presumably explicable in terms of the frictions involved in equity flotation that are ignored in our model. The analysis therefore suggests that the essential rôle of new issues is to finance occasional bursts of abnormal expansion where increasing returns are present rather than permanent, steady growth. In view of the above, it is possible to simplify the analysis of section 4 very considerably by assuming that all finance is raised internally with no loss of generality.

Result B was that the restraint on growth always consists of a fear of take-over rather than that there exists some absolute maximum on the amount of funds the firm could obtain; this proposition was also established above. Although not

---

[7] It may be noted that this bears a close similarity to Baumol's equation (3) (p. 38 above), except that we have provided, by breaking down his $C(g)$ into $\sum \left(\frac{1 + g}{1 + i}\right)^t X$, a rather convincing reason for expecting his second-order conditions to be fulfilled.

immediately obvious, this conclusion is intuitively plausible. Essentially, a firm could always increase its expansion funds at the cost of its present shareholders, either by reducing its dividends or by promising a higher proportion of future dividends to new shareholders, were it not for the power of present shareholders to sell out to a new management which would engage in fewer expansion activities which are so costly as to earn a return below the current rate of interest.

Finally, it may be noted that we have also established that $i > g(R)$ is sufficient to ensure $i > g$. By definition, X cannot exceed R when $f = 0$. And we also established that $r < 1$ implies $X < R$. Consequently, expansion funds cannot exceed net revenue,[8] so that the assumption that the stock market behaves in such a way as to give the firm a finite value ensures that no firm can ever (i.e. even with the aid of new issues) achieve a permanent growth rate as large as the interest rate.

4. A Comparison of Profit, Growth and Sales Maximization

Profit maximization is, of course, interpreted as the desire to maximize the present value of the firm, M. Neither is there any difficulty in interpreting the meaning of growth maximization in the context of a permanent growth model, since total revenue, net revenue, and assets all expand permanently at the same rate g. Slightly less obvious is the appropriate definition of sales maximization, since the total sales of a firm between now and infinity are obviously infinite. But so, of course, are total profits over this period: they are reduced to a well-defined value by the technique of discounting. It seems quite plausible to suppose that managements which derive utility from the size of the undertaking they control will similarly discount future sales. After all, most managers must anticipate retirement or coronary thrombosis in the less than infinitely far distant future, so that it is reasonable to suppose that they will prefer an increase in sales in the present to an equal increase in the future. We therefore assume that management applies a discount rate s to

[8] It should be noted that, if we were to take account of bond finance, the maximum funds available to the firm could exceed R. Consequently, the condition $i > g(R)$ would require strengthening.

future sales, and therefore seeks to maximize a function H of the form

$$H = \sum_{t=0}^{\infty} \left(\frac{1+g}{1+s}\right)^t S = \frac{1+s}{s-g} S \qquad (10)$$

provided that $s > g$ so that the geometric series converges. It must be admitted that there is no particularly convincing reason for believing that $s > g$ analogous to that for assuming $i > g$; if the condition does not hold, presumably management is in a state of bliss. Or perhaps it just satisfices.

(a) Profit maximization

It was shown in section 3 that it is possible to assume that all finance is raised internally without loss of generality. One may therefore set $f = 0$ in equation (5), so that the problem of the profit-maximizing firm is to select S and r so as to maximize

$$M = (1 - r)(1 + i)R/(i - g) \qquad (11)$$

subject to $\qquad g = g(rR) \qquad g' > 0, g'' < 0$
$$R = R(S) \qquad R'' < 0.$$

Now

$$\frac{\partial M}{\partial R} = \frac{(i - g)(1 - r)(1 + i) + (1 - r)(1 + i)R\,\partial g/\partial R}{(i - g)^2} > 0$$

so that the profit-maximizing firm will select that output level S^* that maximizes net revenue (R^*).

One also has

$$\frac{\partial M}{\partial r} = \frac{-(i - g)(1 + i)R + (1 - r)(1 + i)R\,\partial g/\partial r}{(i - g)^2} = 0 \qquad (12)$$

or $\qquad\qquad 1 - r = \dfrac{i - g}{\partial g/\partial r}$

as the first-order condition for a profit-maximizing retention ratio.

This result is most easily interpreted diagrammatically. By substituting R^* into $g = g(rR)$, one obtains a unique relationship between the retention ratio and the growth rate that this permits, and from the signs on the derivatives of g this has the shape shown by $g(rR^*)$ in Fig. 4.1. Intuitively, for a given level of net revenue – which happens to be the maximum possible level since the firm desires to maximize profits – the amount of finance available for expansion is a linear function of the retention ratio, but the assumption of increasing costs of expansion leads to a situation in which the permitted rate of growth increases less than in proportion to the retention ratio.

One may also plot on this diagram a series of curves which reflect the extent to which the objective function of the firm is met, i.e. a set of curves which show all those combinations of *r* and *g* at which the value of the firm would be equal to some particular level of *M*. We shall borrow the term 'iso-valuation

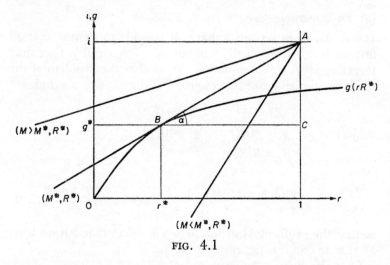

FIG. 4.1

line' from Marris ([5] p. 252) to describe these loci of points at which the value of *M* is constant. Each one is labelled with the value of *M* that it represents when *R* has the value specified after *M*. The iso-valuation lines show a relationship between *g* and *r* and may therefore be derived by rearranging equation (11) to yield

$$g = i - \frac{(1+i)R}{M} + \frac{(1+i)R}{M} r.$$

Hence all of the iso-valuation lines converge on the point *A* at which $r = 1$ and $g = i$, although they do not do anything quite as embarrassing as meet at this point since *M* is undefined when $g = i$. They are all upward-sloping straight lines: higher growth is needed to compensate for reduced dividends if the value of the firm is to remain unchanged. Finally, the less steep is the line – i.e. the higher it appears – the greater is the value of M that it represents.

The object of the profit-maximizing firm is therefore to reach the highest possible iso-valuation line. This occurs in the diagram at B, the point of tangency to $g(rR^*)$. We shall denote the value of the firm at this point by M^*. At B it is evident that $BC = AC/\tan \alpha$,

i.e.
$$1 - r = \frac{i - g}{\partial g/\partial r}$$

which is the first-order condition (12) for a profit-maximizing retention ratio. It is apparent that the assumption of decreasing returns to expansion expenditure reflected in the shape of $g(rR^*)$ ensures that the second-order condition will be satisfied.

There is nothing in the diagram to show that this tangency condition need occur at a positive g. However, the assumptions made about $C(g)$ in equation (2) imply that in the neighbourhood of $g = 0$, we have $gK \approx X = Rr$, so that $\partial g/\partial r \approx R/K$. Now the definition of a profitable firm is one that earns a rate of return on capital employed greater than the rate of interest, so that, if the firm is profitable, $R/K > i$, which implies $\partial g/\partial r > i$ at $g = 0$. At this point, therefore, the left-hand side of (12) exceeds the right-hand side, and reducing this inequality requires a higher r and g. Since it is by definition true that a growth-maximizing firm will grow at least as fast as a profit-maximizing one, this establishes that (profitable) profit and growth maximizers will grow at a positive rate, which was the first part of proposition C.

(b) Growth maximization

It was shown in section 3 that the constraint on a growth maximizer arises from the danger of being taken over. A firm is likely to be taken over when its market value sinks to a low level in comparison with what the new owners could expect to make out of it.[9] The measure that Marris adopts as an indicator of the value of the firm to a take-over raider is the value of its net assets which, in our model, are represented by K. However, a more appropriate norm would seem to be M^*, since it is in

9 For his development of a theory of take-over, on which the present remarks are largely based, see Marris [5] chap. 1.

general reasonable to expect that a new management would not change the total nature of the trading activities in which the firm engages. It will therefore be assumed that management wishes to prevent the stock-market value of the firm falling below a specified proportion, k, of its potential maximum value, in order to safeguard its job security. This proportion k will vary inversely with the efficiency of existing management relative to that which would be provided by the potential raiders; it will tend to vary directly with the extent to which these raiders are themselves 'profit-motivated'. Without some sort of general equilibrium analysis beyond the scope of the present paper, it is necessary to take k as exogenous.

The problem of the growth maximizer is therefore to select S and r so as to maximize $g = g(rR)$

$$\text{subject to} \qquad M \geq kM^* \qquad 0 < k \leq 1$$
$$R = R(S).$$

Since $\partial g/\partial R > 0$, the growth maximizer will select the same output level S^* as the profit maximizer; both will seek the highest possible level of current net revenue.[10] This is the first part of result E; it has the (happy?) consequence that the voluminous literature on pricing policy may be applied without modification to growth-maximizing firms. It also establishes that it is not possible to derive the static sales maximization model from the postulate of growth maximization, as was stated in proposition D.[11]

[10] Intuitively, one might have expected a growth maximizer to keep his initial sales down so as to 'keep the base small'. While this factor would operate in any finite period model (and this constitutes an additional reason for believing that the sales maximization hypothesis may be fruitful), it is inoperative in a permanent growth context since it would involve keeping subsequent sales down correspondingly as well.

[11] Baumol's error arose from a confusion between the firm's current net revenue, R, and what one may term its profitability (the excess of revenue over *all* costs), $R–X$. Specifically, he argued that since faster growth involves lower profits (meaning profitability), the sales level needed to maximize growth would be determined as a compromise between the desire to earn profits to finance expansion and the reduction in profits (here equated to net revenue) caused by this faster growth. But it is clear that a growth maximizer will never be prepared to forgo current net revenue, unless one introduces some quite different postulate such as that future expansion costs will be less if sales are pushed further in the present. (A rationale for this might be the creation of consumer goodwill.) In other words, the unprofitable activities that a growth maximizer engages in are those involved in pushing g beyond g^* and not those arising from pushing S beyond S^*. See above, pp. 53–6.

Since $\partial g / \partial r > 0$ and $\partial M / \partial r < 0$ for values of $r > r^*$, it is obvious that the constraint will be exactly satisfied and r_g, the growth-maximizing retention ratio, will be given by a corner solution. The diagrammatic solution to the problem is shown in Fig. 4.2. If one draws any horizontal from AB to the iso-valuation line (M^*, R^*), and then divides this horizontal in the ratio $1 - k : k$, the iso-valuation line passing through the resulting point is (kM^*, R^*). The intersection of this iso-valuation line with $g(rR^*)$ yields the maximum possible growth rate, g_{max}, which is clearly greater than the profit-maximizing growth rate g^* unless $k = 1$.

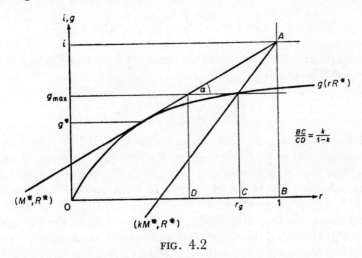

FIG. 4.2

Formally, one derives

$$M = \frac{(1 - r)(1 + i)R^*}{i - g} = \frac{k(1 - r^*)(1 + i)R^*}{i - g^*} = kM^*$$

or

$$\frac{1 - r}{k} = \frac{1 - r^*}{i - g^*}(i - g) = \frac{(i - g)}{\tan \alpha}$$

which is satisfied at g_{max} since $(i - g)/\tan \alpha = BC + CD = BC/k = (1 - r)/k$.

It may be noted that the only case in which the growth maximizer and profit maximizer would distribute the same proportion of their profits is that in which they stand in imminent danger of take-over, i.e. when $k = 1$. This is the result asserted in proposition F.

(c) *Sales maximization*

At the beginning of section 4 we concluded that the problem of the sales maximizer is to select r and S so as to maximize

$$H = \frac{1 + s}{s - g} S \qquad \text{(provided } s > g\text{)} \qquad (10)$$

subject to $M \geq kM^*$, $g = g(rR)$, $R = R(S)$.

Now $\partial H/\partial g > 0$, $\partial g/\partial r > 0$ and $\partial M/\partial r < 0$ imply that the sales maximizer will also exhaust such slack as may be provided by $k < 1$ and exactly satisfy the constraint. It follows that

$$1 - r = \frac{kR^*}{R} \frac{1 - r^*}{i - g^*} (i - g)$$

so that one could construct the relevant iso-valuation line on Fig. 4.2 by making

$$\frac{BC}{CD} = \frac{kR^*/R_s}{1 - kR^*/R_s}$$

if one knew R_s, the sales-maximizing value of R. There is, however, no way of determining R_s from this diagram. If we assume that R_s is known and is less than R^*, then the optimal iso-valuation line (kM^*, R_s) would lie between (kM^*, R^*) and (M^*, R^*). The equilibrium r would occur at the highest inter-section of this line with $g(rR_s)$, which would lie to the right of $g(rR^*)$. However, this diagram does not yield any very interest-ing information for the sales-maximizing case.

Consider instead the way in which g will vary with S, given that the constraint is exactly satisfied. As sales increase to S^*, g will rise to reach a maximum of g_{max} and then start to decline as the 'surplus' is used to finance unprofitable sales rather than unprofitable growth. One therefore obtains a curve with the properties of $g = h(S)$ in Fig. 4.3. An increase in k would reduce the height of this curve throughout its length.

One may also derive a series of iso-H curves by rearranging (10) to read

$$g = s - \frac{1 + s}{H} S.$$

The iso-H curves therefore all approach the point $(S = 0, g = s)$, though they do not actually reach it since H is undefined at this point. They are all downward-sloping straight lines. Higher curves represent larger values of H.

It is obvious that the highest attainable value of H is H_2, where the iso-H curve is tangential to $h(S)$. It is easy to confirm that this is the maximum by differentiating (10) with respect to S to get the first-order condition for the sales-maximizing level of sales S_s, and it is apparent from the diagram that the

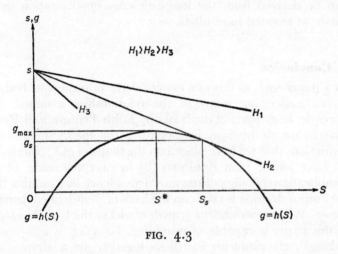

FIG. 4.3

second-order condition will also be satisfied provided the demand curve is monotonic:

$$\frac{\partial H}{\partial S} = \frac{(s - g)(1 + s) + (1 + s)S \, \partial g/\partial S}{(s - g)^2} = 0$$

or

$$s - g + S \frac{\partial g}{\partial S} = 0.$$

It is obvious that this condition is satisfied at $S = S_s$, $g = g_s$. If management's time preference is sufficiently high, i.e. if s is large enough (and k is small enough), it is evident that the sales maximizer, unlike the profit and growth maximizers, will not in fact grow, as is asserted in the second part of result C. It is also evident that $s > g_{max}$ ensures that $S_s > S^*$ unless $k = 1$, when the curve $g = h(S)$ (which is defined to include the stock-market constraint) is compressed to the single point $S = S^*$, $g = g^*$. This was the second part of result E.

Finally, suppose that the sales maximizer were considering

its output decision subject to the constraints that it wished to avoid being taken over and that it wished to grow at g_s. This is logically equivalent to the problem:

$$\text{maximize } S, \text{ subject to } R \geq R_s.$$

This demonstrates that Baumol's static hypothesis, that firms try to maximize sales subject to a minimum profit constraint, can be derived from the long-run sales maximization hypothesis, as asserted in result D.

5. Conclusion

In a paper such as this one cannot delve into the vast body of theory underlying many of the relationships assumed. For example, large parts of the books by Edith Penrose and Robin Marris are devoted to investigating the theory behind the restrictions that we have placed on the shape of $g(X)$. Similarly, we have joined Joan Robinson [8] in sweeping aside all the complications of oligopolistic interdependence by assuming that the output decision is taken on the basis of well-defined demand curves. What a permanent growth model of the type developed in this paper is capable of providing, however, is a means of linking such problems as these together in a simple and systematic way.

We have demonstrated that doing this enables one to establish a number of interesting results, some of which are far from trivial. The most interesting were listed in the Introduction, so that there is no point in repeating them here. The most general conclusion is one that one would hesitate to state explicitly were it not for the suspicion it still seems to engender in certain quarters: that in all cases except where profitability is at best the minimum sum necessary to prevent take-over,[12] the policies the firm pursues will depend on the form of its objectives. Profit, growth and sales maximizers will act differently.

One could easily extend the above analysis to include more general managerial utility functions such as $U(g, M)$ or $U(g, S)$. The former would yield indifference curves tangential to $g(rR^*)$ above r^* in Fig. 4.1, the latter indifference curves tan-

---

[12] Baumol's conclusion in [1] that a sales maximizer who could not only just satisfy his minimum profit constraint would act in the same way as a profit maximizer is, of course, a special case of this result.

gential to some point on the downward-sloping part of $h(S)$ in Fig. 4.3. But no very interesting insights seem to emerge from such a generalization.

Of more interest is the observation that any one of the three objectives is capable of yielding a set of comparative statics theorems. For example, inspection of Figs. 4.1 and 4.2 makes it clear that an increase in the rate of interest would reduce the growth rate and the retention ratio for both profit- and growth-maximizing firms. Changes in the efficiency of the firm or the prices of its factors would have straightforward implications for the position of such curves as $g(rR^*)$ and $h(S)$, which could similarly lead to comparative statics predictions. It does not seem to be possible to predict the effect of a proportional profits tax on the retention ratio without making assumptions additional to those contained in the paper; I suspect that one requires some conditions such as $g''' =$ constant to get a definite solution.

Finally, it is interesting to draw attention to an empirical finding which has caused a certain amount of discomfort in the past but for which we are able to offer a superior explanation to 'systematic irrationality on the part of the investing public' (Miller and Modigliani [6] p. 432), or discount rates that vary with the futurity of the return (Marris [5] p. 221). This is the finding that 'when stock prices are related to current dividends and retained earnings, higher dividend payout is usually associated with higher price–earnings ratios' (Friend and Puckett [4] p. 657). The reason that this has caused dismay is that 'investors should be indifferent if the present value of the additional future returns resulting from earnings retention equals the amount of dividends forgone' (idem.), whereas apparently they are not. But, of course, investors are irrational in preferring dividends only if the present value of the additional future returns actually *does* equal the amount of dividends forgone, and if the firm is a growth (or for that matter a sales) maximizer then it is obvious from Fig. 4.2 that they do not, for the retention ratio is pushed beyond the point at which the value of the firm is maximized. With a great deal of ingenuity Friend and Puckett manage to cast a certain amount of doubt on the conventional findings, but the bulk of the empirical evidence would still seem to indicate that dividends are more highly valued. Since this is consistent with the view that shareholders are rational in seeking to maximize their wealth, and that management rationally seeks objectives other than profit maximization, while any other interpretation assumes that at least one of these parties acts irrationally, one may conclude that there is substantial empirical evidence favouring abandonment of the time-honoured profit maximization assumption.

REFERENCES

[1] W. J. BAUMOL, *Business Behavior, Value and Growth* (New York, 1959).
[2] ——, 'On the Theory of Expansion of the Firm', *American Economic Review* (Dec 1962).
[3] J. DOWNIE, *The Competitive Process* (1958).
[4] I. FRIEND and M. PUCKETT, 'Dividends and Stock Prices', *American Economic Review* (Sep 1964).
[5] R. MARRIS, *The Economic Theory of 'Managerial' Capitalism* (1964).
[6] M. H. MILLER and F. MODIGLIANI, 'Dividend Policy, Growth, and the Valuation of Shares', *Journal of Business* (Oct 1961).
[7] E. PENROSE, *The Theory of the Growth of the Firm* (Oxford, 1959).
[8] J. ROBINSON, *The Economics of Imperfect Competition* (1963).

5 Managerial Discretion Models

O. E. Williamson

The preceding chapters have reviewed the kinds of suggestions for modifying the theory of the firm that have been made in the past fifteen years, examined possible limitations of the profit maximization assumption, and suggested an alternative motivational foundation that would appear to be generally consistent with managerial behavior (broadly conceived). The objective now is to develop a model that is responsive to some of the criticisms of the classical theory of the firm by providing analytical content to the motivational assumptions given in Chapter 3. This involves the construction of utility functions for the firm that make the notion of 'expense preference' explicit. Invoking the assumption of maximizing behavior, equilibrium and comparative statics properties of the models are obtained.

Since the results are best put in perspective by comparing them with those obtained from alternative models – in particular, those of the traditional theory of the firm – parallel operations are performed on two versions of the profit maximizing model. These appear in the following chapter. The first is the usual or single-period profit maximizing model. Next, a discounted or multi-period profit maximization model is constructed. The latter is important both because it avoids the *ad hoc* treatment frequently accorded to long-run profit maximization and because it makes more severe the problem of discriminating between the utility maximizing and profit maximizing hypotheses. That is, certain of the implications of the utility maximization analysis are also obtained from the multi-period profit

Reprinted from O. E. Williamson, *The Economics of Discretionary Behavior: Managerial Objectives in a Theory of the Firm* (Prentice-Hall, 1964) chap. 4, pp. 38–60, by kind permission of the author and of the present publisher, the Markham Publishing Company, Chicago.

maximizing model that do not occur under the usual short-run formulation.

To complete the morphology of models of the business firm, Baumol's sales maximization hypothesis is also examined. A parallel treatment of the equilibrium and comparative statics properties is performed. Again some overlap exists between the implications of this model and those of the managerial discretion models and the profit maximization hypothesis.

1. Managerial Discretion Models of the Business Firm

1.1. *General properties of the models*

Managerial discretion models of the business firm are intended to apply to firms where competitive conditions are not typically severe and where the management may therefore enjoy significant discretion in developing its strategy. The underlying motivational assumptions for these models have been developed in Chapter 3. They require that the firm's preference function be extended to include certain expense components in addition to the usual profit term.

The most fundamental type of expense preference, at least with respect to its effect on comparative statics properties and possibly with respect to its effect on expenditures as well, is the positive preference that managers display toward staff. The implications of introducing staff into the objective function of the firm are examined in the first of the discretion models.

A second variety of expense preference is the desire of managers to spend some portion of actual profit earned on emoluments – on discretionary additions to salary and on corporate personal consumption. The implications of introducing an emoluments term into the firm's preference function are developed in the second of the discretion models.

Emoluments and staff components are both included in the utility function of the firm in the third model. Although profit is included as one of the objectives sought by the management of the firm in each of the three models examined, it is not merely profit *per se* but also the discretion that it provides that makes profit desirable to the management. To make this clear, the descriptive expression 'discretionary profit' is used rather than the more precise expression 'the algebraic difference between reported (after tax) profit and minimum profit demanded' to identify this profit term.

The following terms enter into the analysis:

R = revenue = PX; $\partial^2 R / \partial X\, \partial S \geq 0$

P = price = $P(X, S; E)$; $\partial P / \partial X < 0$; $\partial P / \partial S \geq 0$; $\partial P / \partial E > 0$

X = output

S = staff (in money terms), or (approximately) general administrative and selling expense

E = the condition of the environment (a demand shift parameter)

C = production cost = $C(X)$

M = managerial emoluments

π = actual profit = $R - C - S$

π_R = reported profit = $\pi - M$

π_0 = minimum (after tax) profit demanded

T = taxes, where t = tax rate and $\bar{T}$ = lump-sum tax

$\pi_R - \pi_0 - T$ = discretionary profit

U = the utility function.

1.2. *The staff model*

With staff and discretionary profit entering into the utility function, the firm's objective is taken to be

maximise: $U = U(S, \pi - \pi_0 - T)$

subject to: $\pi \geq \pi_0 + T$.

The constraint can be rewritten as $\pi - \pi_0 - T \geq 0$. Assuming diminishing marginal utility and disallowing corner solutions, it follows that the firm will always choose values of its decision variables that will yield positive utility with respect to each component of its utility function. The second component is $\pi - \pi_0 - T$. If it is always to be positive, then the constraint will always be satisfied as an inequality. Thus the constraint is redundant and the problem can be treated as one of straightforward maximization.[1] Substituting the functional relationships for profits into the expession yields:

maximize: $U = U[S, (1 - t)(R - C - S - \bar{T}) - \pi_0]$.

[1] Although this is a convenience, it is by no means a necessity. Thus, an inequality constrained maximization problem can be handled by making use of the Kuhn–Tucker theorem [4].

The following first-order results are obtained by setting the partial derivatives of U with respect to X and S equal to zero.[2]

$$\frac{\partial R}{\partial X} = \frac{\partial C}{\partial X} \tag{1}$$

$$\frac{\partial R}{\partial S} = \frac{-U_1 + (1 - t)U_2}{(1 - t)U_2}. \tag{2}$$

From equation (1) we observe that the firm makes its production decision in the conventional fashion by equating marginal gross revenue to the marginal costs of production. However, equation (2) reveals that the firm will employ staff in the region where the marginal value product of staff is less than its marginal cost. That is, the firm will operate where $\partial R/\partial S < 1$, whereas the usual short-period profit maximization model would employ staff only to the point where the equality between marginal costs and benefits obtains. Equation (2) can be rewritten as

$$\frac{\partial R}{\partial S} = 1 - \frac{1}{1 - t}\frac{U_1}{U_2}$$

where U_1/U_2 is the marginal rate of substitution between profit and staff. *Ceteris paribus*, an increase in the ratio reflects a shift in tastes in favor of staff. In a profit maximizing organization this ratio is zero.

These relationships are displayed graphically in Fig. 5.1. With staff plotted along the ordinate and output along the abscissa, isoprofit contours are imbedded in the XS plane. These contours are elliptical with major axes running from southwest to northeast.[3] Connecting points of tangency between the isoprofit contours and a series of horizontal lines at successively greater levels of staff traces out the locus $R_x = C_x$ – i.e. the locus of optimal output given the level of staff expense. Similarly the points of tangency between the isoprofit contours and a

---

[2] In these expressions, U_1 is the first partial of the utility function with respect to S and U_2 is the first partial with respect to $(1 - t)(R - C - S - \overline{T}) - \pi_0$.

[3] That this is the correct relationship follows from the assumption that $\partial^2 R/\partial X\,\partial S > 0$. Under this assumption, the effect of increasing staff is to shift the marginal revenue curve of the standard price–quantity demand curve to the right so that necessarily, whatever the shape of the marginal cost of production curve, the optimum output increases as staff increases. To preserve this property in the construction of an isoprofit map on the output–staff plane requires that the isoprofit curves have major axes running from southwest to northeast. See n. 5, p. 73 below, for further discussion of the sign of $\partial^2 R/\partial X\,\partial S$.

series of vertical lines drawn at successively greater levels of output yields the locus $R_s = 1$. Their intersection, K, corresponds to the short-run profit maximization position.

Since the equilibrium relations are $R_x = C_x$ and $R_s < 1$, the utility maximizing firm will take up a position somewhere along the locus $R_x = C_x$ but above the locus $R_s = 1$. Point A in Fig. 5.1 represents such a position. Thus, the utility maximizing firm will choose a larger value of staff, and this will in turn give

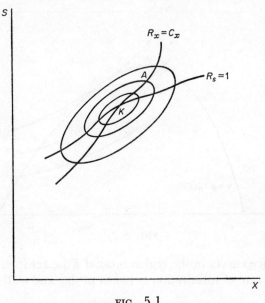

FIG. 5.1

rise to a larger value of output than would be chosen by the firm that maximizes short-run profit.

The locus $R_x = C_x$ specifies the pairs of (X, S) combinations along which the firm that has its utility function augmented to include a staff component will locate. For every value of staff there exists an optimal value of output, say $\hat{X}$, where $\hat{X} = f(S)$. Given the condition of the environment, profit depends on the choice of X and S, that is, $\pi = g(X, S; E)$. If, however, X is chosen optimally, then

$$\pi = g(\hat{X}, S; E) = g[f(S), S; E] = g'(S; E).$$

Thus, profit can be plotted as a function of staff. This is done in Fig. 5.2 with profit along the ordinate and staff along the abscissa. By introducing indifference curves between profit and staff, the equilibrium results can be interpreted somewhat differently. Again, the point K represents the profit maximizing position and A, the point where the tangency between the indifference curves and the profits curve obtains, is the position at which the utility maximizing firm will locate.

Several generalizations suggest themselves immediately. First, for the firm to select the point K requires that the slope of the

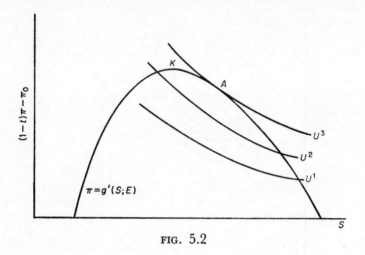

FIG. 5.2

indifference curves in the region around K be zero; that is, the marginal rate of substitution between profits and staff must be zero. Since

$$\text{MRS} = -\frac{d\pi}{dS} = \frac{\partial U/\partial S}{\partial U/\partial \pi}$$

this implies that the marginal utility of staff in the vicinity of K must be zero. Either staff must be 'objectively' valued only for its contribution to profit or the benefits associated with expanding staff must be exhausted before K is reached. If the argument regarding the positive preference for staff is accepted, the first of these can be dismissed and the second represents a limiting condition. Considering the variety of ways in which staff contributes to managerial satisfactions, the zero marginal utility condition seems unlikely to be realized.

A second observation is that if the profit curve is very sharply peaked, the resulting tangency will be one where the value of staff (and output) selected will not be far removed from the profit maximization position. As the profit curve becomes flatter, however, and as the indifference curves become more steeply sloped (i.e. as staff becomes relatively more highly valued), the tangency shifts progressively to the right.

Having established the equilibrium conditions, the comparative statics properties of the model remain to be developed. That is, we want to displace the equilibrium. In particular, we want to find how the system adjusts to a change in the condition of the environment (the demand shift parameter E), a change in the profit tax rate (t), and a lump-sum tax $(\bar{T})$.

It will facilitate the argument to compact the notation and designate each decision variable by $\mathcal{Z}_i$ and each parameter by α_j. Then the function $U(X, S; E, t, \bar{T})$ can be represented as $U(\mathcal{Z}_1, \mathcal{Z}_2; \alpha_1, \alpha_2, \alpha_3)$. The general form[4] for determining the response of the pth decision variable to a change in the kth parameter is:

$$\left(\frac{\partial \mathcal{Z}_p}{\partial \alpha_k}\right)^0 = \frac{-\sum_{i=1}^{2} \dfrac{\partial^2 U}{\partial \mathcal{Z}_i \partial \alpha_k} D_{ip}}{|D|}, \qquad \begin{array}{l} p = 1, 2 \\ k = 1, \dots, 3 \end{array}$$

where D_{ip} is the cofactor of the ith row and the pth column of D and $|D|$ is the determinant of the second partials $\partial^2 U/\partial \mathcal{Z}_i \, \partial \mathcal{Z}_j$. The sign matrix D is

$$D = \begin{vmatrix} - & + \\ + & - \end{vmatrix}$$

Second-order conditions for a maximum require that D be positive.[5]

---

[4] See Samuelson [6] pp. 12–14.

[5] If D is an $n \times n$ matrix, second-order stability conditions for a maximum require that the principal minors alternate in sign beginning with a negative. It might be noted that I assign $\partial^2 U/\partial X \, \partial S$ a positive sign in the D matrix. This follows from my assumption that $\partial^2 R/\partial X \, \partial S$ is positive. From a strictly theoretical standpoint it is not essential that this be positive in order to preserve stability. All that is necessary is that the 2×2 matrix be negative definite. From a practical standpoint, however, it is difficult to imagine how $\partial^2 R/\partial X \, \partial S$ could be anything other than positive (or, as a limiting condition, when the effects of staff on price are exhausted, zero). That is, as output increases, staff unchanged, we would generally expect that the change in gross revenue that would obtain from increasing staff incrementally would be larger than the corresponding change that would occur at lower values of output. This same assumption is made in the profit maximization models examined in the following chapter. If the demand function is multiplicative, $\partial^2 U/\partial X \, \partial S$ will be positive unambiguously.

The signs of the values $\partial^2 U/\partial \mathcal{Z}_i \, \partial \alpha_k$ for $\mathcal{Z}_i = X, S$ and $\alpha_k = E$, t, $\bar{T}$ are as follows:[6]

$$
\left| \frac{\partial^2 U}{\partial \mathcal{Z}_i \, \partial \alpha_k} \right| =
\begin{array}{c|ccc}
 & E & t & \bar{T} \\
X & + & 0 & 0 \\
S & + & +? & -
\end{array}
$$

The comparative statics responses, shown in Table 1, are obtained directly and without difficulty from the sign relationships alone. The direction of adjustment of any particular decision variable to a displacement from equilibrium by an increase in a parameter is found by referring to the row and column entry corresponding to this pair.

TABLE 1

COMPARATIVE STATICS RESPONSES FOR THE STAFF MODEL

		Parameter		
		E	t	$\bar{T}$
	X^0	+	+?	—
Variable	S^0	+	+?	—

direction of adjustment of any particular decision variable to a displacement from equilibrium by an increase in a parameter is found by referring to the row and column entry corresponding to this pair.

That the response to an increase in the profits tax rate is not unambiguous is due to a combination of substitution and income effects. As shown in Appendix 4-A, the net substitution effect of staff to an increase in the profits tax rate is always positive, whereas the 'income' effect is always negative. The gross substitution effect is the combination of these two separate effects

---

[6] Although the sign of $\partial^2 U/\partial X \, \partial E$ is certain to be positive as indicated, I need to appeal to a 'reasonableness' argument to assign a positive sign to $\partial^2 U/\partial S \, \partial E$. The argument, very simply, is that as the environment moves from a buyers' market to a sellers' market (i.e. as E increases), an incremental increase in staff activity yields a larger increase in gross revenue than the same increment would have produced under less favorable environmental conditions. The results are unaffected if $\partial^2 U/\partial S \, \partial E$ is zero but ambiguities develop if $\partial^2 U/\partial S \, \partial E$ is permitted to become negative. In this case, the model has to be specialized and particular demand and cost expressions introduced. These same qualifications with respect to the sign of $\partial^2 U/\partial S \, \partial E$ hold for the profit maximization model examined in the following chapter.

so that its sign depends on their relative magnitudes. As shown in Appendix 4-A, the gross substitution effect will usually be positive although, when the firm encounters adversity and has difficulty in satisfying its minimum profit constraint, the response may be negative. The direction of response of output to a change in the profits tax rate is identical to that of staff. Indeed, it is a derived rather than a direct effect: in the absence of the staff component in the utility function, output would be unchanged.

These income and substitution effects can also be interpreted graphically by an extension of the apparatus used in Fig. 5.2. In the construction of that figure it was shown that

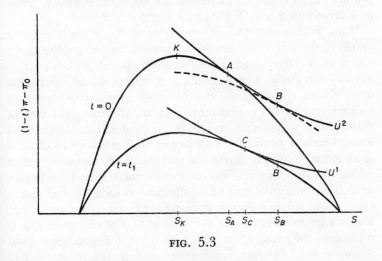

FIG. 5.3

$\pi = g'(S)$. It is likewise true, therefore, that $(1 - t)\pi - \pi_0$ can be expressed as a function of staff, where $(1 - t)\pi - \pi_0$ is discretionary profit (Fig. 5.3).

The profit as a function of staff curves are drawn for a tax rate of $t = 0$ and $t = t_1$, where $t_1 > 0$. At tax rate $t = 0$, the optimum position for the firm occurs at A, where tangency between the profits curve $t = 0$ and the indifference curve U^2 occurs. When the tax rate is increased to t_1, tangency of the resulting profit curve and the indifference curves occurs at C. As drawn, the optimal choice of staff increases ($S_C > S_A$).

The adjustment can be broken up into an income and a substitution effect by introducing a *compensated* tax change. Thus the dashed curve through A is a vertical displacement of the

D

curve $t = t_1$. If the firm were awarded a lump-sum bounty simultaneously with the increase in the profits tax just large enough for it to continue to realize the utility represented by U^2, its profit curve would be the dashed curve shown. Since the slope of the curve t_1 is everywhere less than the corresponding slope of the curve $t = 0$, tangency between the dashed curve and the indifference curves will occur to the right of A. The point designated B represents such a position, and the shift from A to B is the *net substitution effect*. Since profit and staff are substitutes, the net substitution effect is unambiguously positive; that is, when the 'price' of taking satisfaction in the form of profit increases, the compensated tax adjustment always leads to a substitution of staff for profit and $S_B > S_A$.

If the indifference curves were vertical displacements of one another, the curve U^1 would be tangent to the profits curve $t = t_1$ at B'. The vertical displacement condition, however, is not quite realistic. It represents a condition where, given the level of staff, the marginal rate of substitution across successive indifference curves is constant. Instead, the marginal rate of substitution will normally fall as profit declines. That is, at lower levels of profit, the increase in staff required to offset a specified reduction in profit and still maintain the same level of utility becomes larger. Thus the indifference curve U^1 is drawn so that the marginal rate of substitution at each level of staff is everywhere smaller than it is along the indifference curve U^2. Hence tangency occurs not at B' but at C. The shift from B to C represents the *income effect*. Were the vertical displacement condition to hold between indifference curves, the income effect would be zero. In the usual circumstance where the marginal rate of substitution falls as profit declines, the income effect will be negative and $S_C < S_B$.

By postulating that the marginal rate of substitution behaves in this prescribed way instead of permitting it to vary without limitation, I impose a restriction on the utility function that may seem objectionable. I submit, however, that the restriction is perfectly reasonable. It merely guarantees that the staff component in the utility function is not an inferior good. Whereas special assumptions of this sort are unwarranted in the analysis of consumer behavior where the arguments that enter the utility function are deliberately left in an unspecified general form (and hence the possibility of inferior good must be admitted), the components of utility function under study here are fully specified and, hence, the analysis can be bounded appropriately. Indeed, where generality is attained only at the expense of relevance, a specialization of the analysis that removes uninteresting or implausible contingencies is altogether warranted.

Invoking this principle in the present case dictates the following choice: since each of the expenses for which a positive preference has been indicated is surely a normal good, and since leaving the inferior good possibility open merely produces confusion, the inferior good contingency is disallowed. Indeed, Scitovsky's analysis of entrepreneurial behavior is essentially an application of this principle and rests on a stronger specialization of the utility function than the one I employ. In his analysis the marginal rate of substitution, given the level of activity, is constant across successive levels of profit.[7] In the present analysis, this constant marginal rate of substitution relationship represents a limiting condition.

The gross substitution effect is the combination of the net substitution and income effects and thus depends on the relative magnitudes of these two effects. As shown in Appendix 4-A, the gross substitution effect will normally be positive $(S_C > S_A)$, although as adversity is encountered and the firm is hard pressed to satisfy its minimum profit constraint, it may become negligible and could become negative. As long as the firm is enjoying comparative prosperity, however, the gross substitution effect will generally be positive and staff will be increased in response to an increase in the profits tax rate.

The effects of a progressive tax rate can be investigated by letting $T = h(\pi)$ be the profits tax. Then discretionary profit will be $\pi - h(\pi) - \pi_0$, and, since $\pi = g'(S)$, this can be expressed as a function of staff. This is shown in Fig. 5.4, where the responses to a constant and progressive tax rate are examined. Three profit curves are drawn. The top curve represents a zero tax condition. The solid curve below it shows profit under a progressive profits tax. The dashed curve shows profits under a constant profits tax. The progressive tax rate produces a profit curve flatter at the top than does the constant tax rate. Thus tangency between the indifference curves and the profit curve is shifted significantly to the right (at C). Actual profit is given

[7] See *The Economics of Discretionary Behavior*, p. 18, n. 6.

by C' and the distance between C and C' is the amount of tax collected.[8] To summarize, under the progressive profits tax, actual profit is reduced from π_A to $\pi_{C'}$, due to expanding staff from S_A to S_C, and a tax of CC' is collected.

The constant profits rate t_1 is chosen so that tangency between the resulting profit curve and the indifference curves occurs at a point that yields precisely the same amount of tax as was collected under the progressive tax program. Thus the length BB' is the same as CC'. Since the marginal tax rate under the constant profits tax is less than it would be under the progressive

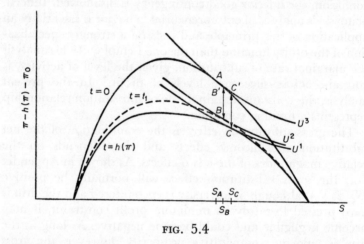

FIG. 5.4

profits tax plan, there is less incentive for the firm to absorb profits and take its satisfactions through staff. Thus $S_B < S_C$, $\pi_B > \pi_C$, and $\pi_{B'} > \pi_{C'}$. These results hold over the entire range of possible progressive versus constant profits tax rates as long as tax collections under both arrangements are required to be equal.

The effects of a lump-sum tax can also be examined with this type of diagram. To increase the lump-sum tax shifts the profit curve vertically downward. If the indifference curves were vertical displacements of one another, tangency would occur at precisely the same level of staff expense. Since, however, the marginal rate of substitution decreases as profit decreases

---

[8] Actual profit is given by C' only when $\pi_0 = 0$. Otherwise actual profit is given by profits at C' plus π_0. However, the value of π_0 in no way affects the general properties of the results.

(given the level of staff), the indifference curves become some-what flatter and tangency obtains at a lower value for staff.

As is well-known (and as is shown in Chapter 5), the short-run profit maximizing firm is entirely unresponsive to both a change in the profits tax rate as well as to the levy of a lump-sum tax. The implications of the utility maximization analysis as contrasted with those of the usual profit maximizing analysis are thus significantly different and appear to be testable.

1.3. *The emoluments model*

An emoluments term is substituted for the staff term that appeared in the preceding model. That is, management is assumed to have a positive taste for discretionary assignments of available funds for salary and perquisites, but has a neutral preference for staff. Thus the objective becomes

$$\text{maximize:} \quad U = U[M, \pi_R - \pi_0 - T]$$
$$\text{subject to:} \quad \pi_R \geq \pi_0 + T.$$

Again the constraint is redundant so that the problem can be handled as one of conventional maximization. Substituting the functional relationships for profits into the expression, the objective is to

$$\text{maximize:} \quad U = U[M, (1 - t)(R - C - S - M - \bar{T}) - \pi_0]$$

First-order conditions for an extremum are obtained by setting the partial derivatives with respect to X, S, and M equal to zero. Thus we obtain

$$\frac{\partial R}{\partial X} = \frac{\partial C}{\partial X} \tag{3}$$

$$\frac{\partial R}{\partial S} = 1 \tag{4}$$

$$U_1 = (1 - t)U_2. \tag{5}$$

From equations (3) and (4) it follows that the firm will adopt a conventional short-run profit maximization position so that *actual* profit will be identical with maximum. That is, the firm will earn profits represented by K in Figs. 5.1 and 5.2. However, equation (5) reveals that the firm will absorb some part of actual profit as emoluments, the amount being dependent on the tax rate. Thus *reported* profit will be less than maximum by the amount withdrawn by the management as rent. Hence, the profits tax is levied against, and dividends are paid out of, earnings that are less than maximum.

The comparative statics properties of the model are found by the same procedure used for the preceding analysis. The sign matrix for the second partials of U is given by

$$D = \begin{vmatrix} - & + & 0 \\ + & - & 0 \\ 0 & 0 & - \end{vmatrix}$$

The signs of the values $\partial^2 U/\partial Z_i\, \partial\alpha_k$ for $Z_i = X,\, S,\, M$ and $\alpha_k = E,\, t,\, \bar{T}$ are

$$\left| \frac{\partial^2 U}{\partial Z_i\, \partial\alpha_k} \right| = \begin{array}{c c c c} & E & t & \bar{T} \\ X & + & 0 & 0 \\ S & + & 0 & 0 \\ M & + & +? & - \end{array}$$

The comparative statics responses can all be obtained from the signs of the partial derivatives of the equilibrium relations as displayed above alone. They are shown in Table 2.

TABLE 2
COMPARATIVE STATICS RESPONSES FOR THE EMOLUMENTS MODEL

		Parameter		
		E	t	$\bar{T}$
	X^0	+	0	0
Variable	S^0	+	0	0
	M^0	+	+?	−

The ambiguity of the response to an increase in the profits tax is again due to counteracting income and substitution effects (Fig. 5.5). The initial (zero tax) equilibrium position is given by A. When a tax of t_1 is levied, the equilibrium position shifts to C. This can be separated into a net substitution and income effect by introducing a compensating variation. The dashed line is drawn parallel to the line $t = t_1$ and is tangent to the indifference curve U^2 (which passes through the initial position) at the point B. Thus the shift from A to B is the net substitution effect and, given the convexity relations shown between profit and emoluments, is always positive. The income effect is given by the shift from B to C. Since, for a given level of emoluments, the marginal rate of substitution between profit and emolu-

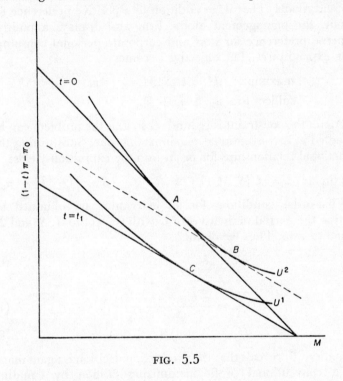

FIG. 5.5

ments declines as profit falls, the income effect will always be negative.

The gross substitution effect will be the combination of these two separate effects and will depend on their relative magnitudes. The argument developed in Appendix 4-A for examining the staff model carries over. Thus, the gross substitution effect can normally be expected to be positive; but as the firm approaches its minimum profit constraint, a reversal may occur.

Again it can be shown that a progressive profit tax encourages more of a substitution of emoluments for profits than would occur under a constant profits tax calculated to produce the same tax receipts. Since the argument exactly parallels that already given in the discussion of the staff model, the proof of this is omitted.

1.4. *The staff and emoluments model*

Staff and emoluments terms are both introduced into the present model. That is, in addition to a positive preference for profit, the management of the firm also displays a positive expense preference for staff and corporate personal consumption expenditures. The objective becomes

$$\text{maximize:} \quad U = U(S, M, \pi_R - \pi_0 - T)$$
$$\text{subject to:} \quad \pi_R \geq \pi_0 + T.$$

Again the constraint is redundant so that the problem can be handled as a conventional maximization one. Substituting the functional relationships for profit into the expression yields:

$$\text{maximize:} \quad U = U[S, M, (1 - t)(R - C - S - M - \bar{T}) - \pi_0].$$

First-order conditions for an extremum are obtained by setting the partial derivatives of U with respect to X, S, and M equal to zero. Thus we obtain[9]

$$\frac{\partial R}{\partial X} = \frac{\partial C}{\partial X} \tag{6}$$

$$\frac{\partial R}{\partial S} = \frac{-U_1 + (1 - t)U_3}{(1 - t)U_3}. \tag{7}$$

$$U_2 = (1 - t)U_3. \tag{8}$$

Equation (6) reveals that the production decision is again made in a conventional profit maximizing fashion by equating marginal gross revenues to the marginal costs of production, and from equation (7) it follows that the staff decision is again made so that the marginal value product of staff is less than its marginal cost ($R_s < 1$). Equation (8) discloses that the firm will absorb some amount of actual profit as emoluments, the amount being dependent on the tax rate.

Although the amount of profit absorbed as emoluments

---

[9] U_1 is the first partial of the utility function with respect to S, U_2 is the first partial with respect to M, and U_3 is the first partial with respect to $(1 - t)$ $(R - C - S - N - \bar{T}) - \pi_0$.

affects the level of discretionary profit, it has no direct influence on productivity. Thus the qualitative properties of the equilibrium of the previous models, as displayed in the figures examined earlier, likewise hold for this model.

Comparative statics properties of the model are obtained in the same way. The sign matrix of the second partials is

$$D = \begin{vmatrix} - & + & 0 \\ + & - & -? \\ 0 & -? & - \end{vmatrix}$$

The signs of the values $\partial^2 U / \partial Z_i \, \partial \alpha_k$ for $Z_i = X, S, M$ and $\alpha_k = E, t, \bar{T}$ are

$$\left| \frac{\partial^2 U}{\partial Z_i \, \partial \alpha_k} \right| = \begin{array}{c c c c} & E & t & \bar{T} \\ X & + & 0 & 0 \\ S & + & +? & - \\ M & + & +? & - \end{array}$$

The sign relationships are not sufficient to derive any of the comparative statics properties for this model. This does not,

TABLE 3

COMPARATIVE STATICS RESPONSES FOR THE STAFF–
EMOLUMENTS MODEL

		Parameter	
	E	t	$\bar{T}$
X^0	$+$	$+?$	$-$
Variable S^0	$+$	$+?$	$-$
M^0	$+$	$+?$	$-$

however, mean that these properties are indeterminate. It only requires that the sign entries in the matrices be replaced by the functional relationships that they represent. Let d_{ij} be the element of the ith row and jth column of D. Then in d_{11} the $(-)$ term is replaced by $U_3(1 - t)(R_{xx} - C_{xx})$, in d_{12} the $(+)$ is replaced by $U_3(1 - t)R_{xs}$, and so forth. Solving the resulting system algebraically substantially eliminates the ambiguities that develop from the sign relationships alone. Thus, by

*

replacing signs by general functional notation, wider scope for
the application of qualitative economics can be claimed than
Lancaster has indicated is possible [5]. This is rigorously
shown in Appendix 4–B.

The comparative statics responses for this version of the
managerial discretion model are shown in Table 3.

Increasing the profits tax rate again gives rise to a somewhat
ambiguous response.[10] The graphical analysis of the preceding
sections reveals the nature of the difficulty. As long as the firm
is earning a moderate profit and the tax rate increase is not so
great as to press the firm to satisfy its minimum constraint, an
increase in staff, emoluments, and output can be expected. This
is particularly likely if the profits tax is progressive. A reversal
of these effects may occur, however, when the firm is experi-
encing difficulty in satisfying its minimum profit constraint.

2. General Significance of the Results

2.1. *Expense preference reviewed*

The argument in the preceding chapters has suggested that, in
the absence of vigorous competition in the product market and
where the separation of ownership from control is substantial,
there is no compelling reason to assume that the firm is operated
so as to maximize profit. On the contrary, such behavior would
appear to require an unusual variety of rationality – and one not
widely found in human affairs – namely, a complete detach-
ment of individual interests from occupational decision making.
A more moderate position has been suggested. Thus I proposed
that where discretion in the decision-making unit exists, this
will ordinarily be exercised in a fashion that reflects the individual interests of the decision makers. After reviewing the
kinds of individual objectives that managers might rationally
pursue it was indicated that, since most of the decision making
in the firm ultimately involves spending, 'expense preference'
would be a useful and meaningful way in which to study the
behavior of the business firm.

[10] The responses of M to a change in each of the parameters are difficult to
derive. After much manipulation, I have derived those for the profits tax and
lump-sum tax unambiguously. The response to a change in the condition of the
environment does not yield to this treatment. Assuming, however, that actual
profit increases as demand increases (which is certainly an innocuous assumption)
emoluments will also be increased as indicated.

Two categories of expense preference were identified and related to the motives of the managers. The first of these is the positive preference for staff. The second is the positive preference for emoluments – discretionary allocations of profit for salary and perquisites. The final preference category that was identified is a profit class which, for descriptive purposes, was called discretionary profit. It has been the purpose of the preceding section of this chapter to examine the implications of such an approach by developing the equilibrium and comparative statics properties of three models which include two or more of these preference components.

2.2. *Casual empiricism as preliminary evidence on the behavior of the business firm*

Since the third model, the staff and emoluments model, incorporates all of the comparative statics responses of the preceding two, attention will be limited to it. With respect to the demand shift parameter E, this managerial model indicates that staff expenditures and output will move directly with the condition of the environment. In the limit, as the condition of the environment becomes progressively worse and the firm is pressed to satisfy its minimum profit constraint, the firm's use of staff converges to its profit maximizing value but everywhere else the firm operates where actual profit is less than maximum due to the positive preference the firm displays toward staff. Thus spending for staff (or, approximately, general administrative and selling expense) should be highly responsive to business conditions. In general this appears to be true. Evidence that supports this is cited in Chapter 6.

In addition to the staff and output expenditures, the managerial discretion model also predicts that spending on emoluments will be responsive to the condition of the environment. Spending for these purposes will increase as conditions improve, whereas a deterioration of the environment will lead to a reversal of these profit absorption activities. Thus salaries as well as expenditures for travel, expense accounts, office improvements, and so forth, should be very much a function of business conditions. Again, this appears to conform to the facts.[11]

An increase in the profits tax rate t assigns a higher penalty

[11] As pointed out in the discussion of Midwest Processing Corporation in Chapter 6, these adjustments may involve some complicated lag relations.

to reporting profits so that an inducement exists to shift out of profit into other varieties of satisfactions. Subject to the earlier qualifications, this is exactly what the discretion model predicts. Thus, spending on both staff and emoluments increases in response to an increase in the profits tax rate. Output also increases due to the connection between optimal staff and optimal output, where an increase in the former leads to an increase in the latter.[12] Our experience with excess profits taxes appears to support this type of spending behavior.

When a lump-sum tax $\bar{T}$ is levied, the utility maximizing firm is no more able to avoid it than is the profit maximizing firm. This does not, however, prevent the former from making an adjustment. Indeed, since the discretion model has the firm operating in a region that is suboptimal from a profit maximizing standpoint, the firm will choose to revise its strategy in order to maintain a balance between its rewards. Thus, since a lump-sum tax reduces reported profit, the firm will reduce its spending for staff (and thus increase actual and, hence, reported profit) and on emoluments (which also increases reported profit). Output will also be reduced and for the same reason as given above, i.e. optimal output depends on the level of staff selected and as staff is reduced, so is optimal output.

It might be noted that the lump-sum tax is really doing triple duty inasmuch as its effect is identical to that of increasing the minimum profit constraint or imposing any sort of fixed charge on the firm. That is, the discretion model predicts that contrary to the traditional theory (but perhaps more in accord with standard business practice), fixed costs do influence the firm's optimum configuration of variable factors.[13] Evidence, albeit of an indirect sort, is gathered on this in Chapter 6.

Although it is not a property that derives from the comparative statics of the model, the fact that a newly installed executive with the assigned objectives of reducing costs can remove staff with ease is an event which is entirely consistent with the managerial discretion model. To explain this only requires that we recognize that the objective of cost reduction is one which implies a low preference for staff. Hence, the manager

[12] In the limit, as S increases and $\partial R/\partial S \to 0$, $\partial^2 \partial R/X\, \partial S \to 0$ and the output response disappears. That an increase in staff leads to an increase in the optimal value of X can be seen from the slope of the locus $R_x = C_x$ in Fig. 5.1. As S continues to increase, the slope of $R_x = C_x$ increases and eventually becomes vertical.

[13] This point has also been made by Baumol ([3] p. 78).

with a lower preference for staff than his predecessor may typically be able to achieve significant reductions in staff without simultaneously impairing performance. Moreover, when these changes in personnel and objectives occur at the top executive levels (particularly at the level of the president), shrinkage of the entire staff structure may be both attempted and achieved.

3. Application to Public Utilities

Since the types of departures from profit maximizing behavior that are said to exist in public utilities (and other regulated industries) appear to be derivable by a direct application of the proposed model, it may be worthwhile to demonstrate the relevance of the model to this class of firms separately. Alchian and Kessel have discussed this kind of behavior previously [1], but they have not attempted to develop their argument in the context of a model. The behavior they describe follows as a logical consequence of the managerial discretion models developed above.

The rates that a public utility is permitted to charge are set at levels which are intended to allow the utility to cover its costs and earn a fair rate of return ([2], p. 1052). Ordinarily, rates are not adjusted continuously as conditions change but are revised only periodically. In the short run, therefore, a utility may earn above or below normal profit, but this is not a situation that will be long continued; profit will eventually be restored to a fair level by rate adjustments.

Since above-normal profit cannot be long continued and since supernormal profit may invite the early attention of the regulatory commissions, the management of a public utility that has other than profit maximizing objectives has an incentive to hold profits at or below some 'safe' level. This tendency to absorb profit is further reinforced by the fact that the penalty for inefficient operations is particularly weak among the regulated monopolies. Not only is there a virtual guarantee that rates will be set so as to cover costs and permit the utility to show earnings sufficient to attract new capital but, in addition, the regulatory commissions have not attempted to control costs. Hence, there is a positive reward for absorbing profits without there being an offsetting penalty to discourage this. This situation is said to be responsible for the conditions of large staff and managerial accommodations among the public utilities.

By inserting a maximum (or 'safe' level) profit constraint into the model, this kind of behavior can be shown to follow as a direct implication. Thus the objective is to

$$\text{maximize:} \quad U = U[S, M, \pi_R - (\pi_0 + T)]$$
$$\text{subject to:} \quad \text{(i)} \quad \pi_R \geq \pi_0 + T$$
$$\text{(ii)} \quad \pi_R \leq \pi_M$$

where π_M = maximum safe level of profits to report.

For the reasons given previously, the minimum profit constraint is redundant but the maximum profit constraint may be encountered. The problem restated using the method of the Lagrangian multiplier becomes

$$\text{maximize:} \quad L(X, S, M, \lambda)$$
$$= U[S, M, (1 - t)(R - C - S - M) - \pi_0]$$
$$- \lambda[(1 - t)(R - C - S - M) - \pi_M]$$

where $(-\lambda)$ is a Lagrangian multiplier.

Setting the partial derivative of L with respect to X, S, M, and λ equal to zero yields:

$$\frac{\partial R}{\partial X} = \frac{\partial C}{\partial X} \tag{9}$$

$$\frac{\partial R}{\partial S} = \frac{-U_1 + (1 - t)(U_3 - \lambda)}{(1 - t)(U_3 - \lambda)} \tag{10}$$

$$U_2 = (1 - t)(U_3 - \lambda) \tag{11}$$

$$(1 - t)(R - C - S - M) \leq \pi_M. \tag{12}$$

When equation (12) is satisfied as an inequality, $\lambda = 0$ and equations (9), (10), and (11) become identical to (6), (7), and (8) obtained previously. When the constraint is encountered, however, λ takes on positive values [4] and the system is further removed from a profit maximization position. This effect can also be seen by perturbating the system with respect to π_M. Assuming that the constraint is binding, it can be shown that $(\partial S/\partial \pi_M)^0 < 0$ and $(\partial M/\partial \pi_M)^0 < 0$ [and $(\partial X/\partial \pi_M)^0 < 0$ due to the connection of optimal output with staff]. Thus, if a binding maximum profit constraint were to be imposed on a firm previously free from such a ceiling, staff and emoluments would be expanded to prevent the firm from violating the constraint and inducing a rate correction. This is precisely the behavior described above.[14]

This type of behavior need not be limited to public utilities, of course. Any firm which, for whatever reason (for example, to discourage anti-trust prosecution), finds itself encountering a maximum or 'safe' level profit constraint could be expected to exhibit this behavior.

4. Conclusion

Managerial discretion models are designed to study behavior in business firms where competition in the product market is not typically severe. In such circumstances the management will usually enjoy significant discretion in operating the firm. Since the last of the three models developed includes the properties of the first, my summary comments will be confined to it.

Among the properties of the model are:

1. The basic behavioral assumption of the model is the same as the basic rationality assumption throughout economics: individuals seek their own self-interest.
2. Under conditions where forces of competition are weak, the model returns implications different from those of the traditional short-run profit maximizing model – implications which it would appear are capable of being tested. These include (*a*) staff expenditures (or, approximately, general administrative and selling expense) may be permitted to absorb significant amounts of resources under conditions of favorable demand but these excesses will tend to disappear in the face of adversity; (*b*) expenditures for emoluments will tend to vary directly with the business cycle; (*c*) staff expenditures will increase if an excess profits tax is imposed; (*d*) the latter will also be true of

[14] Averch and Johnson have also examined the effect of introducing a safe level profit constraint [2]. Their behavioral assumption, however, is different from mine. They assume that the public utility seeks to maximize *profit* subject to regulatory constraint. As a result, they do not obtain any of the expense responses that I do but find instead that the firm will attempt to inflate its rate base by investing in plant beyond the level called for in traditional theory. By expressing output as a function of labor and capital and making the regulatory constraint a maximum rate of return rather than a maximum profit level, it would appear that this investment response (in addition to the expense responses) can also be obtained from the model above.

emoluments; and (*e*) fixed costs will affect the firm's optimum configuration of variable factors.

3. The model preserves (that is, converges to) the results obtained from the profit maximizing hypothesis under conditions of pure competition.

4. Conditions said to be characteristic of public utilities are obtained by straightforward application of the model.[15]

In addition, the model has the property that it subsumes a rather general set of arguments that have been raised, but seldom tested, against the profit maximization hypothesis. Thus, if the discretion model should be disconfirmed in all but an unimportant subset of circumstances, a large number of arguments contradictory to the classical model would be challenged.

REFERENCES

[1] A. A. ALCHIAN and R. A. KESSEL, 'Competition Monopoly and the Pursuit of Pecuniary Gains', *Aspects of Labor Economics* (National Bureau of Economic Research, Princeton, 1962).

[2] H. AVERCH and L. L. JOHNSON, 'Behavior of the Firm under Regulatory Constraint', *American Economic Review*, LII (Dec 1962) 1052–69.

[3] W. J. BAUMOL, *Business Behavior, Value and Growth* (New York, 1959).

[4] H. W. KUHN and C. W. TUCKER, 'Non-linear Programming', *Proceedings of the Second Berkeley Symposium on Mathematical Statistics and Probability* (California U. P., Berkeley, 1951).

[5] K. J. LANCASTER, 'The Scope of Qualitative Economics', *Review of Economic Studies*, XXIX (Jan 1962) 99–123.

[6] P. A. SAMUELSON, *Foundations of Economic Analysis* (Cambridge, Mass., 1947).

[7] O. E. WILLIAMSON, 'Model of Rational Managerial Behavior', R. M. CYERT and J. G. MARCH, *A Behavioral Theory of the Firm* (Prentice–Hall, 1964) chap. 9.

[15] In an earlier version of this analysis I argued that 'the welfare implications of the model are easily obtained and readily translated into policy proposals' ([7] p. 252). As the discussion in Chapter 9 reveals, however, some of the welfare implications are less obvious than I had believed. They require additional assumptions about the character of the functional relationships than are specified here and may require an analysis of some complicated lagged responses.

I have indicated ([7] p. 245, n. 23) that a general preference function that left the relationship between the components unspecified led to the same results as an additive preference function. As shown in Appendices 4-A and 4-B, this is almost, but not completely, accurate. Certain of the cross effects that complicate the analysis of a general preference function are eliminated when the utility function is specified to be additive.

Finally, the comparative statics analysis of the effects of a change in the profits tax rate in [7] fails to mention the offsetting character of the substitution and income effects that are operating (see Appendices 4-A and 4-B for a separation and analysis of these effects).

6 Behavioral Rules and the Theory of the Firm

R. M. Cyert and M. I. Kamien

The neoclassical theory of the firm as synthesized by Samuelson is an example of the use of deductive arguments to arrive at meaningful theorems in economics.[1] Starting with only a few explicit assumptions, a number of interesting theorems and corollaries are derived. The theorems describe a set of optimal decision rules which a profit-maximizing firm should follow to determine its level of outputs and inputs given market price. Failure to follow these rules will not only diminish profit but will make it impossible for the firms to survive under the free entry market conditions assumed. If it does follow them, the firm has no problem of dealing with uncertainty because nothing is uncertain in the model posited.

The received theory of the firm is a useful and significant intellectual contribution. It has enabled economists to explain many kinds of behavior in the world and has, in general, served as a framework for both scientific work and policy recommendations.

Our aim in this paper is to nurture a growing body of work which aims at developing a theory of the firm that will lead to confirmable propositions explaining the behavior of the firm in noncompetitive markets. At the heart of our paper is the judgment that the firm is an adaptive mechanism operated by human beings with limited information-processing capabilities. We propose to look at the firm under conditions which are less restrictive than those of the neoclassical theory. We will relax the assumption of certain knowledge of market environment

[1] P. A. Samuelson, *Foundations of Economic Analysis* (Cambridge, Mass., 1947) pp. 57–89.

Reprinted from A. Phillips and O. E. Williamson (eds.), *Prices: Issues in Theory, Practice, and Public Policy* (University of Pennsylvania Press, 1967) pp. 1–10, by kind permission of the authors and of the University of Pennsylvania Press.

and the internal technological conditions. In the process we hope to provide an explanation for use of behavioral rules (rules of thumb) by firms for pricing and output decisions.

We begin with the proposition that profit is, at the very least, a major objective of the firm. The task is to devise an analytic model which explains how the firm makes its decisions in the face of uncertainty so as to earn profits enabling it to survive and grow. Herbert Simon's work on satisficing and R. A. Gordon's references to satisfactory profits are attempts to develop decision criteria in an environment that more closely resembles the real world than does the classical model.[2]

Behavioral Rules

Without going into the other objectives of the firm and the other obstacles to profit-maximization, it is reasonable to suppose that the firm devises approximate solutions for the attainment of its goals. The approximating procedures are often referred to as behavioral rules. These rules presumably evolve through confrontation with similar situations over time and some experimentation. The firm may discover some simple relationships between the price it sets and sales volume, market share, and profit by trying several different price levels. Or the behavioral rules may be based on customary procedure in the given industry. An example of this might be the mark-up above cost.[3]

Behavioral rules not only serve to approximate the optimal procedure for achieving certain objectives but also help preserve internal stability within the firm. Recognition of the separation of ownership and control in a modern corporation requires that the managers of such a firm be viewed collectively as an organization. We know from organization theory that the internal stability of a decision-making organization is enhanced by the ability to transform decision processes into programmed behavior. Behavioral rules are a form of programmed decision-making.

[2] R. A. Gordon, *Business Leadership in the Large Corporation* (Berkeley, Calif., 1961) and H. A. Simon, 'A Behavioral Model of Rational Choice', *Quarterly Journal of Economics*, LXIV (1955) 99–118, reprinted in H. A. Simon, *Models of Man: Social and Rational* (New York, 1957).

[3] See, for example, R. M. Cyert and J. G. March, *A Behavioral Theory of the Firm* (Englewood Cliffs, N.J., 1963) chap. 7.

Relationship of Behavioral Theory and Dynamics

While the behavioral approach to the theory of the firm appears promising, its achievements to date have been limited. For the most part, this can be attributed to the infancy of the approach. The tools required for better exploitation of the method have not yet been fully developed. Moreover, an economist venturing into this area must acquaint himself with the rudiments of organization theory, while the organization theorist must learn some basic economics.

These difficulties aside, the behavioral theory of the firm lacks most, in terms of completeness, a dynamics (although this may be interpreted as an overstatement, since in the behavioral approach no clear delineation between statics and dynamics has yet been made). Again, if we reflect on the development of classical economic theory, this is not too surprising. Even now the definition of economic dynamics is a somewhat elusive concept. In particular, the accepted definition appears to be 'a system is dynamical if its behavior over time is determined by functional equations in which *variables at different points in time* are involved in an *essential* way'.[4]

But what of dynamics in the behavioral approach? How does time enter in an essential way in the decision-making processes of the firm as conceived in the behavioral theory? We believe it does this in two ways. In the first place, recognition of the future compounds the uncertainties that the firm must presently face. Not only does the firm often lack knowledge of the shape of its present cost and demand functions but it must also contemplate the possibility that these functions might change over time.

Secondly, time enters in an essential way into the behavioral theory approach to the firm through the evolution of its decision rules. The behavioral decision rules ordinarily use past values of the relevant variables for determining the current values of these variables. The rules are altered in the sense of their functional form or exclusion of certain variables and the inclusion of other variables in their stead on the basis of how well these rules perform in meeting the desired objectives. The time element imposes a need for flexibility in the formation of behavioral rules, or, in other words, to allow learning to take

---

[4] Samuelson, op. cit., p. 314.

place. This is not the case, for example, with regard to behavior posited for the suppliers in the naïve cobweb model. The supplier always determines his production level on the basis of last period's prices despite the fact that he may often be ruined by following this rule. The same type of stereotyped behavior is displayed by the competitors in the Cournot duopoly model.

We should in fact expect the firm not only to revise its behavioral rules on the basis of past experience but also to do this at an increasing rate. The learning process itself has to be learned, and we might assume that it improves with experience. This point has not as yet, it seems, been incorporated into the study of behavioral rules. Baumol and Quandt, for example, rely on initially short reaction time or certain values of elasticities of demand and cost in order to obtain stable learning behavioral rules.[5] A more complete analysis would incorporate the notion that the reaction time itself changes over time, presumably getting shorter.

Time enters into the behavioral approach, as the medium through which complete adjustments to the environment take place. This is the distinction in adjustment which necessitates the definitions of a short run and a long run. In the classical theory the short run differs from the long run in that in the latter case the firm is capable of altering all its factors of production, whereas in the former case it cannot. It seems to us, in the light of what has been said above, that the analogous concept in the behavioral approach should be that in the short run the firm cannot cause all decision processes to be of the programmed variety, whereas in the long run it can. An immediate consequence of this definition is that the firm's reaction time to an exogenous change in its environment would be more rapid in the long run than in the short run. Of course, as long as some uncertainty exists, and the future will assure this, reaction time will not become zero but rather approach this limit asymptotically.

Focusing our attention on the definitions of long run and short run proposed above should also enable us to understand and explain economic phenomena which have not been satisfactorily explained by the classical theory. The most prominent of these is the behavior of oligopolistic firms and price move-

[5] W. J. Baumol and R. E. Quandt, 'Rules of Thumb and Optimally Imperfect Decisions', *American Economic Review*, LIV (Mar 1964) 23–46.

ments in such markets. Several attempts have been made to explain the constancy of prices over long periods of time despite changes in technology and input costs. Also, when price changes do take place they are typically initiated by one firm and almost immediately followed by the other firms. The common explanation offered is collusion among these firms. Sometimes, of course, this is the case. However, at other times evidence to support the collusion hypothesis cannot be found, and we must suppose that the goings on are an inherent feature of this type of market organization.

Among the other better-known explanations of the behavior of firms in oligopolistic markets are the kinked demand curve model, the dominant-firm model, and the game theoretic approach. Unfortunately none of these provides a commonly accepted explanation of oligopoly behavior. While the notion of the kinked demand curve is appealing at first glance, it fails to explain the simultaneous increase in prices often observed in actual oligopolistic markets, e.g. the recent advances in steel prices and automobile prices. The firms in the model behave asymmetrically with regard to a change in the price initiated by one of the firms. If any firm lowers prices, the rest will all follow. This is basically a defensive act. On the other hand, firms will not follow a price increase. This behavior appears to be more of an aggressive nature. Putting it another way, the firms appear to regard their relationship to the market as a zero-sum game. They always fail to recognize that higher profits might be obtained by cooperating.

In terms of the dynamics described above, the explanation of the same phenomena might go something like this. At the inception of the industry in which there are many small firms a great deal of learning and formation of behavioral rules has to take place. As the industry progresses through time behavioral rules are developed and refined. Some firms leave the industry because they cannot compete successfully. Consolidations may be the result of learning that economies of scale exist. Over time the remaining firms develop more refined rules. The amount of information shared in common by these firms becomes large. Each can anticipate to a great extent the actions of his competitors and recognize the basis on which a competitor makes a move. Response time decreases. The end result is seemingly simultaneous, since each firm over time becomes like the other firms and is affected in the same way by external changes (e.g. increases in prices of raw materials).

An Illustrative Model

We now return to the main focus of our paper, namely the evolution of behavioral rules.

Some of the arguments set forth above can best be clarified with a simple price-setting model exhibiting the way in which behavioral rules, learning, and time enter into the description of firm behavior. The model we present below is meant to convey the spirit of the methodology we think appropriate for the study of the firm rather than a description of actual behavior.

We posit a firm which sells a single product in a market consisting of many firms selling products of varying degrees of substitutability. In other words, some of the firms are lesser competitors to the firm in question than others. The important feature of this market situation is that the relevant firm does not regard only one or a few rivals directly responsive to its pricing decisions. The responses are instead diffused among its several competitors.

Let us suppose further that the firm's cost function is of the form

$$C(q) = cq \tag{1}$$

where c is a positive constant, and that its demand curve is describable by the equation

$$q = a - bp \tag{2}$$

where $a, b > 0$, providing that its rivals maintain current prices.

Consequently, the firm's profit as a function of price is

$$\pi(p) = (a + bc)p - bp^2 - ca \tag{3}$$

or, lettering $\alpha = -b$, $\beta = (a + bc)$, and $\gamma = -ca$, we can rewrite (3) as

$$\pi(p) = \alpha p^2 + \beta p + \gamma \tag{4}$$

Now

$$\pi'(p) = 2\alpha p - \beta \tag{5}$$

and

$$\pi''(p) = 2\alpha < 0 \tag{6}$$

which indicates that $\pi(p)$ is concave. If the firm knows the values of the parameters α, β, γ, it can determine the optimal price directly by setting $\pi'(p) = 0$. If we designate the optimal price by p^*, then in this instance, $p^* = -\beta/2\alpha$. If the firm knows only that the profit function $\pi(p)$ is unimodal, it can arrive at the optimal price in a series of steps by means of a sequential search procedure. A simple rule such as that to increase (decrease) price by 10 per cent as long as the resulting increment to profit is positive and to stop the first time incremental profit is zero or negative will achieve the desired objective or at least come very close.

Suppose, however, the true increment in profits stemming from a change in price is confounded by extraneous events as, for instance, income fluctuations, price changes in related products not in the given market, and price movements within the industry which are exogenous to the firm under consideration. In this case, neither of the above procedures will necessarily yield p^*. Formally, this situation can be described by incorporating an error term into expression (2), thereby altering (4). Thus (2) becomes

$$q = a - bp + \epsilon \qquad (2')$$

where ϵ represents an error term, and (4) becomes

$$\pi(p) = \alpha p^2 + \beta p + \gamma + \epsilon p. \qquad (4')$$

Then $$\pi'(p) = 2\alpha p + \beta + \epsilon \qquad (5')$$

wherein we implicitly assume that $d\epsilon/dp = 0$. In other words, changes in the error term ϵ are independent of changes in price p.

We also assume that the firm has a point estimate of the parameter α from past experience and that this estimate is considered to be fairly reliable. Moreover, we assume that α remains fixed so that changes in ϵ serve merely to shift expression (5') up and down. The firm now seeks to locate the 'optimal' price. We purposely leave 'optimal' undefined at this point to emphasize, for reasons that will become apparent below, the multiplicity of meanings that can be associated with the term. Finally, we suppose that the firm has no knowledge of the expected value of ϵ. Instead, $E[\epsilon]$ is a random variable. The firm does, however, believe that $E[\epsilon]$ is distributed according to some distribution function $g(\xi)$. By setting price at different levels and observing the outcome, the firm revises its prior distribution function $g(\xi)$ to conform with the new information obtained. In this manner the firm learns and adapts itself to the environment.

To be more specific, let us assume that the firm structures this problem in terms of two decisions, viz.

$$D_1 : p_t = (1 + r)p_{t-1} \qquad (7)$$
$$D_2 : p_t = (1 - r)p_{t-1}$$

where $0 \leqslant r \leqslant 1$.

The firm may raise price by r per cent above last period's price, decision D_1, or lower price by r per cent from last period's price, D_2. We let u_1 denote the probability that decision D_1 will result in a positive increment to profit, and consequently $(1 - u_1)$ is the probability that decision D_1 will result in a decrease in profit. Similarly, we let u_2 denote the probability that decision D_2 will lead to an increase in profit, and therefore that $(1 - u_2)$ is the probability that decision D_2 reduces profit. We further designate an increase in profit, regardless of its magnitude, by 1 and a reduction in profit by -1. It should be noted that the probabilities u_1 and u_2 are taken to be independent of the current price level. The firm does not know these probabilities but does believe that they are generated by the distribution functions $g_1(\xi)$ and $g_2(\xi)$ respectively.

We may envision the firm under these circumstances as, say, making decision D_1, observing the outcome and then updating its prior beliefs regarding $g_1(\xi)$ and $g_2(\xi)$. This behavior could be described by Bayes's formula. In particular, suppose that after τ decisions have been made, k have been of the D_1 type and that the number of times profit increased thereafter was l. On the basis of this information the firm's revised distribution should be, according to Bayes's formula,

$$f_1(\xi \mid k, l) = K_1 \xi^l (1 - \xi)^{k-l} g_1(\xi) \qquad (8)$$

where $f_1(\xi \mid k, l)$ is defined as the probability that u_1 lies between ξ and $\xi + d\xi$ given k and l and where K_1 is a normalizing factor chosen so that

$$\int_0^1 f_1(\xi \mid k, l) \, d\xi = 1.$$

Now, given that τ decisions have been made, net profits have increased j times in all, and decision D_1 has been chosen k

times before with l subsequent successes, we can deduce that decision D_2 must have been chosen $(\tau - k)$ times before and yielded $1/2(\tau + j) - l$ successes. Thus, defining $f_2(\xi \mid \tau, j, k, l)$ as the probability that u_2 lies between ξ and $d\xi$ it follows that

$$f_2(\xi \mid \tau, j, k, l) = K_2 \xi^{1/2(\tau+j)-l}(1 - \xi)^{i-k-1/2(\tau+j)+l} g_2(\xi) \quad (9)$$

where K_2 has a similar interpretation to K_1.

If we further suppose that the firm chooses as its initial distributions the uniform distributions

$$g_1(\xi) = 1 \qquad g_2(\xi) = 1 \qquad 0 \leqslant \xi \leqslant 1$$

then expressions (8) and (9) simplify to

$$f_1(\xi \mid k, l) = K_1 \xi^l (1 - \xi)^{k-l} \tag{8'}$$

and

$$f_2(\xi \mid \tau, j, k, l) = K_2 \xi^{1/2(r+j)-l}(1 - \xi)^{i-k-1/2(\tau+j)+l}. \tag{9'}$$

Let us now turn to the question of what might constitute an optimal method of selecting between D_1 and D_2 at each stage of the process. The first criterion might be to select the decisions in such a way as to maximize the increment to profits over the entire duration of the process. The process terminates when a price has been found such that deviations from this price can only result in a decrease in profit.

In the language of dynamic programming as applied to adaptive control processes we define the optimal value function $V(\tau, j, k, l)$ to be the expected value of the process starting at stage τ (time τ), in the course of which profits have increased j times and where k previous choices of decision D_1 have been followed by l increases in profit. It should be noted that the function V is the firm's subjective expected value rather than the ordinary expected value which would be calculated if the probabilities u_1 and u_2 were known. We also note that t will designate the stage of the process and j the state of our process.

Suppose now that the firm chooses D_1 and that u_1 equals a particular number ξ. Then with probability ξ the result will be 1 (profits will rise) and the process advances to state $(\tau + 1, j + 1, k + 1, l + 1)$. On the other hand, the probability that profits decrease is $(1 - \xi)$ and in this case the process advances to state $(\tau + 1, j - 1, k + 1, l)$. Thus, if $u_1 = \xi$ the future expected value of the process is given by

$$\xi(1 + V(\tau + 1, j + 1, k + 1, l + 1)$$
$$+ (1 - \xi)[-1 + V(\tau + 1, j - 1, k + 1, l)]. \quad (10)$$

But, since the hypothesis that $u_1 = \xi$ is based only on our best information to date, expression (10) must be weighted by the probability that $\xi \leqslant u_1 \leqslant \xi + d\xi$, namely $f_1(\xi \mid k, l)$ and integrated over all ξ. We thereby obtain

$$\int_0^1 \{1 + V(\tau + 1, j + 1, k + 1, l + 1) +$$
$$(1 - \xi)[-1 + V(\tau + 1, j - 1, k + 1, l)]\} f_1(\xi \mid k, l)\, d\xi. \quad (11)$$

But under the special assumptions made regarding the prior distribution $g_1(\xi)$ it turns out that

$$\int_0^1 \xi f_1(\xi \mid k, l) = \frac{l + 1}{k + 2}. \quad (12)$$

By employing arguments analogous to those used in obtaining (11) to the selection of decision D_2 we conclude that

$$V(\tau, j, k, l) = \max$$

$$\begin{cases} D_1 : \left(\dfrac{l + 1}{k + 2}\right)[1 + V(\tau + 1, j + 1, k + 1, l + 1)] + \\ \quad \left(1 - \dfrac{l + 1}{k + 2}\right)[-1 + V(\tau + 1, j - 1, k + 1, l)] \\ \\ D_2 : \left(\dfrac{\frac{1}{2}(i + j) - l + 1}{i - k + 2}\right)[1 + V(\tau + 1, j + 1, k, l)] + \\ \quad \left(1 - \dfrac{\frac{1}{2}(i + j) - l + 1}{i - k + 2}\right)[-1 + V(\tau + 1, j - 1, k, l)]. \end{cases} \quad (13)$$

The natural terminus of the process is the stage T at which $V(T, j, k, l) = -1$. That is, the optimal price will have been reached when the expected value of any further change in price is -1. The immediate question that comes to mind is whether a stage T exists for which $V(T, j, k, l) = -1$. We shall not attempt to establish the existence of such a T rigorously here; intuitively it would seem by virtue of the learning process employed that this stage will exist at least as a limit in probabilities.

Yet, even if this stage exists it will be in the distant future. This natural termination point might, therefore, be undesirable for two reasons. First, the future brings with it additional uncertainty, such as the possibility that the firm's demand function may undergo a drastic change. Second, the required information-storage processing ability for the execution of this process will almost certainly exceed the capability of the firm. Consequently, the firm might instead settle for the achievement of some profit level deemed acceptable for termination of the process. In this case the firm would look not only at the direction of change in profits but at the actual magnitudes as well. Having achieved the desired profit level it would stop adjusting prices.

While the above model is admittedly a member of the simplest variety of adaptive control processes, it does serve to point up several of the points made before. In particular, a firm seeking to maximize profit under uncertainty may pursue short-run behavioral rules which would be construed in the light of a neoclassical interpretation as nonoptimal and yet may in fact be optimal when viewed from the behavioral standpoint. Moreover, our model helps to explain how the distant future, which brings with it greater uncertainties and the inherent computational difficulties in the pursuit of even the simplest optimal adaptive control process, causes the firm to adopt more modest goals than profit-maximization.

A more complete model would incorporate the firm's pursuit of several objectives and the firm's use of variables in addition to profits, such as market share and sales, as measures of its performance. The cost of changing price, which in this case would be the cost of searching for an optimum, would also be introduced into an expanded model. Explicit consideration of this cost should serve to reinforce the conclusion that the firm will stop changing price short of the conventional optimum.

Summary of Our Approach

We see the firm as operating in an environment of uncertainty without the knowledge of its demand and cost curves, which are necessary to select an optimum strategy for maximum profits. Since it is forced to make price, output, advertising, and investment decisions under this set of circumstances, it proceeds in a particular way. The firm gauges its ability to cope with the environment and then sets consistent profit and sales objectives for itself for a limited period in the future. It then utilizes its decision rules and the best internal and environmental information it can get to make price and output decisions.

These decisions result in an interaction with the environment which eventually returns imperfect information to the firm on the quality of its decisions. The firm must then transform this information, and any other it may get through salesmen, industry publications, consultants, etc., into a new set of decisions and actions. These actions may require adaptation of the internal structure of the firm or a modification of decisions (e.g. price changes) that directly affect its interaction with the environment.

The evaluation of the results in a particular instance is made by using the specified goals as a criterion. If these goals are reached or surpassed, the firm views the past decisions as successful and then must decide whether the goals should be raised in the next period.

PART TWO

Models of Market Organisation

7 Perfect Competition, Historically Contemplated

G. J. Stigler

No concept in economics – or elsewhere – is ever defined fully, in the sense that its meaning under every conceivable circumstance is clear. Even a word with a wholly arbitrary meaning in economics, like 'elasticity', raises questions which the person who defined it (in this case, Marshall) never faced: for example, how does the concept apply to finite changes or to discontinuous or stochastic or multiple-valued functions? And of course a word like 'competition', which is shared with the whole population, is even less likely to be loaded with restrictions or elaborations to forestall unfelt ambiguities.

Still, it is a remarkable fact that the concept of competition did not begin to receive explicit and systematic attention in the main stream of economics until 1871. This concept – as pervasive and fundamental as any in the whole structure of classical and neoclassical economic theory – was long treated with the kindly casualness with which one treats of the intuitively obvious. Only slowly did the elaborate and complex concept of perfect competition evolve, and it was not until after the First World War that it was finally received into general theoretical literature. The evolution of the concept and the steps by which it became confused with a perfect market, uniqueness of equilibrium, and stationary conditions are the subject of this essay.

The Classical Economists

'Competition' entered economics from common discourse, and for long it connoted only the independent rivalry of two or more persons. When Adam Smith wished to explain why a

Reprinted from *Journal of Political Economy*, LXV 1 (Feb 1957) 1–17, by kind permission of the author and of the University of Chicago Press.

reduced supply led to a higher price, he referred to the 'competition [which] will immediately begin' among buyers; when the supply is excessive, the price will sink more, the greater 'the competition of the sellers, or according as it happens to be more or less important to them to get immediately rid of the commodity'.[1] It will be noticed that 'competition' is here (and usually) used in the sense of rivalry in a race – a race to get limited supplies or a race to be rid of excess supplies. Competition is a process of responding to a new force and a method of reaching a new equilibrium.

Smith observed that economic rivals were more likely to strive for gain by under- or overbidding one another, the more numerous they were:

> The trades which employ but a small number of hands, run most easily into such combinations.
>
> If this capital [sufficient to trade in a town] is divided between two different grocers, their competition will tend to make both of them sell cheaper, than if it were in the hands of one only; and if it were divided among twenty, their competition would be just so much the greater, and the chance of their combining together, in order to raise the price, just so much the less.[2]

This is all that Smith has to say of the number of rivals.

Of course something more is implicit, and partially explicit, in Smith's treatment of competition, but this 'something more' is not easy to state precisely, for it was not precise in Smith's mind. But the concept of competition seemed to embrace also several other elements:

1. The economic units must possess tolerable knowledge of the conditions of employment of their resources in various industries. 'This equality [of remuneration] can take place only in those employments which are well known, and have been long established in the neighbourhood.'[3] But the necessary information was usually available: 'Secrets . . ., it must be acknowledged, can seldom be long kept; and the extraordinary profit can last very little longer than they are kept.'[4]

2. Competition achieved its results only in the long run: 'This equality in the whole of the advantages and dis-

---

[1] *The Wealth of Nations* (Modern Library ed.) pp. 56–7.
[2] Ibid., pp. 126, 342. [3] Ibid., p. 114. [4] Ibid., p. 60.

advantages of the different employments of labour and stock, can take place only in the ordinary, or what may be called the natural state of those employments.'[5]

3. There must be freedom of trade; the economic unit must be free to enter or leave any trade. The exclusive privileges or corporations which exclude men from trades, and the restrictions imposed on mobility by the settlement provisions of the poor law, are examples of such interferences with 'free competition'.

In sum, then, Smith had five conditions of competition:

1. The rivals must act independently, not collusively.
2. The number of rivals, potential as well as present, must be sufficient to eliminate extraordinary gains.
3. The economic units must possess tolerable knowledge of the market opportunities.
4. There must be freedom (from social restraints) to act on this knowledge.
5. Sufficient time must elapse for resources to flow in the directions and quantities desired by their owners.

The modern economist has a strong tendency to read more into such statements than they meant to Smith and his contemporaries. The fact that he (and many successors) was willing to call the ownership of land a monopoly – although the market in agricultural land met all these conditions – simply because the total supply of land was believed to be fixed is sufficient testimony to the fact that he was not punctilious in his language.[6]

Smith did not state how he was led to these elements of a concept of competition. We may reasonably infer that the conditions of numerous rivals and of independence of action of these rivals were matters of direct observation. Every informed person knew, at least in a general way, what competition was, and the essence of this knowledge was the striving of rivals to gain advantages relative to one another.

The other elements of competition, on the contrary, appear

---

[5] Ibid., p. 115.

[6] Ibid., p. 145. Perhaps this is not the ideal illustration of the laxness of the period in the use of the competitive concept, for several readers of this paper have sympathized with this usage. But, to repeat, competition is consistent with a zero elasticity of supply: the fact of windfall gains from unexpected increases in demand is characteristic of all commodities with less than infinitely elastic supplies.

E

to be the necessary conditions for the validity of a proposition which was to be associated with competition: the equalization of returns in various directions open to an entrepreneur or investor or laborer. If one postulates equality of returns as the equilibrium state under competition, then adequacy of numbers and independence of rivals are not enough for equilibrium. The entrepreneur (or other agents) must know what returns are obtainable in various fields, he must be allowed to enter the fields promising high rates of return, and he must be given time to make his presence felt in these fields. These conditions were thus prerequisites of an analytical theorem, although their reasonableness was no doubt enhanced by the fact that they corresponded more or less closely to observable conditions.

This sketch of a concept of competition was not amplified or challenged in any significant respect for the next three-quarters of a century by any important member of the English school. A close study of the literature, such as I have not made, would no doubt reveal many isolated passages on the formal properties or realism of the concept, especially when the theory was applied to concrete problems. For example, Senior was more interested in methodology than most of his contemporaries, and he commented:

> But though, under free competition, cost of production is the regulator of price, its influence is subject to much occasional interruption. Its operation can be supposed to be perfect only if we suppose that there are no disturbing causes, that capital and labour can be at once transferred, and without loss, from one employment to another, and that every producer has full information of the profit to be derived from every mode of production. But it is obvious that these suppositions have no resemblance to the truth. A large portion of the capital essential to production consists of buildings, machinery, and other implements, the results of much time and labour, and of little service for any except their existing purposes. . . . Few capitalists can estimate, except upon an average of some years, the amounts of their own profits, and still fewer can estimate those of their neighbours.[7]

Senior made no use of the concept of perfect competition hinted at in this passage, and he was wholly promiscuous in his use of the concept of monopoly.

Cairnes, the last important English economist to write in the

[7] N. W. Senior, *Political Economy* (New York, 1939) p. 102.

classical tradition, did break away from the Smithian concept of competition. He defined a state of free competition as one in which commodities exchanged in proportion to the sacrifices (of labor and capital) in their production.[8] This condition was amply fulfilled, he believed, so far as capital was concerned, for there was a large stock of disposable capital which quickly flowed into unusually remunerative fields.[9] The condition was only partly fulfilled in the case of labor, however, for there existed a hierarchy of occupational classes ('non-competing industrial groups') which the laborer found it most difficult to ascend.[10] Even the extra rewards of skill beyond those which paid for the sacrifices in obtaining training were a monopoly return.[11] This approach was not analytically rigorous – Cairnes did not tell how to equate the sacrifices of capitalists and laborers – nor was it empirically fruitful.

Cairnes labeled as 'industrial competition' the force which effects the proportioning of prices to psychological costs which takes the place to the extent that the products are made in one non-competing group, and he called on the reciprocal demand theory of international trade to explain exchanges of products between non-competing groups. Hence we might call industrial competition the competition within non-competing groups, and commercial competition that between non-competing groups. But Sidgwick and Edgeworth attribute the opposite concepts to Cairnes: commercial competition is competition within an industry, and industrial competition requires the ability of resources to flow between industries.[12] Their nomenclature seems more appropriate; I have not been able to find Cairnes's discussion of commercial competition and doubt that it exists.[13]

The Critics of Private Enterprise

The main claims for a private-enterprise system rest upon the workings of competition, and it would not have been unnatural

[8] *Some Leading Principles of Political Economy Newly Expounded* (London, 1874) p. 79.

[9] Ibid., p. 68.   [10] Ibid., p. 72.

[11] Ibid., p. 85. Thus Cairnes tacitly labeled all differences in native ability as 'monopolistic'.

[12] Henry Sidgwick, *Principles of Political Economy* (London, 1883) p. 182; F. Y. Edgeworth, *Papers Relating to Political Economy* (London, 1925) II 280, 311.

[13] Karl Marx once distinguished interindustry from intraindustry competition in *Theorien über den Mehrwert* (Stuttgart, 1905) II, part 2, 14 n.

for critics of this system to focus much attention on the competitive concept. They might have argued that Smith's assumptions were not strong enough to insure optimum results or that, even if perfect competition were formulated as the basis of the theory, certain deviations from optimum results (such as those associated with external economies) could occur. The critics did not make this type of criticism, however, possibly simply because they were not first-class analysts; and for this type of development we must return to the main line of theorists, consisting mostly of politically conservative economists.

Or, at another pole, the critics might simply have denied that competition was the basic form of market organization. In the nineteenth century, however, this was only a minor and sporadic charge.[14] The Marxists did not press this point: both the labor theory of value and the doctrine of equalization of profit rates require competition.[15] The early Fabian essayists were also prepared to make their charges rest upon the deficiencies in the workings of competition rather than its absence.[16] The charge that competition was non-existent or vanishing did not become commonplace until the end of the nineteenth century.

The critics, to the extent that they took account of competition at all, emphasized the evil tendencies which they believed flowed from its workings. It would be interesting to examine their criticisms systematically with a view to their treatment of competition; it is my impression that their most common, and most influential, charge was that competition led to a highly objectionable, and perhaps continuously deteriorating, distri-

---

[14] For example, Leslie repeatedly denied that resource owners possessed sufficient knowledge to effect an equalization of the rates of return (see T. E. Cliffe Leslie, *Essays in Political and Moral Philosophy* (London, 1888) pp. 47, 48, 81, 158–9, 184–5).

[15] See especially vol. III of *Das Kapital* and also F. Engels, *The Condition of the Working-Classes in England*, reprinted in Karl Marx and Friedrich Engels, *On Britain* (London, 1954) pp. 109 ff. The Marxian theory of the increasing concentration of capital was a minor and inconsistent dissent from the main position (see *Capital* (Modern Library ed.) pp. 684 ff.).

[16] See *Fabian Essays* (Jubilee ed., London, 1948), especially those by Shaw and Webb. But the attention devoted to monopoly was increasing, and the essay by Clarke argued that 'combination is absorbing commerce' (ibid., p. 84). A few years later the Webbs used a competitive model in their celebrated discussion of 'higgling in the market' and then went on to describe the formation of monopolistic structures as defences erected against the competitive pressures the Webbs did not quite understand (see *Industrial Democracy* (London, 1920) part III, chap. ii).

bution of income by size.[17] In their explanations of the workings of a competitive economy the most striking deficiency of the classical economists was their failure to work out the theory of the effects of competition on the distribution of income.

The Mathematical School

The first steps in the analytical refinement of the concept of competition were made by the mathematical economists. This stage in the history of the concept is of special interest because it reveals both the types of advances that were achieved by this approach and the manner in which alien elements were introduced into the concept.

When an algebraically inclined economist seeks to maximize the profits of a producer, he is led to write the equation

$$\text{Profits} = \text{Revenue} - \text{Cost}$$

and then to maximize this expression; that is, to set the derivative of profits with respect to output equal to zero. He then faces the question: How does revenue (say, pq) vary with output (q)? The natural answer is to *define* competition as that situation in which p does not vary with q – in which the demand curve facing the firm is horizontal. This is precisely what Cournot did:

> The effects of competition have reached their limit, when each of the partial productions D_k [the output of producer k] is *inappreciable*, not only with reference to the total production $D = F(p)$, but also with reference to the derivative $F'(p)$, so that the partial production D_k could be subtracted from D without any appreciable variation resulting in the price of the commodity.[18]

This definition of competition was especially appropriate in Cournot's system because, according to his theory of oligopoly,

---

[17] A second main criticism became increasingly more prominent in the second half of the nineteenth century: that a private-enterprise system allowed or compelled large fluctuations in employment. For some critics (e.g. Engels), competition was an important cause of these fluctuations.

[18] *Mathematical Principles of the Theory of Wealth* (New York, 1929) p. 90. It is sufficient to assume that D_k is small relative to D if one assumes that the demand function is continuous, for then 'the variations of the demand will be sensibly proportional to the variations in price so long as these last are small fractions of the original price' (ibid., p. 50).

the excess of price over marginal cost approached zero as the number of like producers became large.[19] Cournot believed that this condition of competition was fulfilled 'for a multitude of products, and, among them, for the most important products'.[20]

Cournot's definition was enormously more precise and elegant than Smith's so far as the treatment of numbers was concerned. A market departed from unlimited competition to the extent that price exceeded the marginal cost of the firm, and the difference approached zero as the number of rivals approached infinity. But the refinement was one-sided: Cournot paid no attention to conditions of entry and so his definition of competition held also for industries with numerous firms even though no more firms could enter.

The role of knowledge was made somewhat more prominent in Jevons's exposition. His concept of competition was a part of his concept of a market, and a perfect market was characterized by two conditions:

[1.] A market, then, is theoretically perfect only when all traders have perfect knowledge of the conditions of supply and demand, and the consequent ratio of exchange; . . .

[2.] . . . there must be perfectly free competition, so that anyone will exchange with anyone else upon the slightest advantage appearing. There must be no conspiracies for absorbing and holding supplies to produce unnatural ratios of exchange.[21]

One might interpret this ambiguous second condition in several ways, for the pursuit of advantages is not inconsistent with conspiracies. At a minimum, Jevons assumes complete

---

[19] Let the revenue of the firm be $q_i p$, and let all firms have the same marginal costs, MC. Then the equation for maximum profits for one firm would be

$$p + q_i \frac{dp}{dq} = \text{MC}.$$

The sum of n such equations would be

$$np + q \frac{dp}{dq} = n\text{MC}$$

for $nq_i = q$. This last equation may be written

$$p = \text{MC} - \frac{p}{nE}$$

where E is the elasticity of market demand (ibid., p. 84).

[20] Ibid., p. 90.

[21] *Theory of Political Economy*, 1st ed. (London, 1871) pp. 87, 86.

independence of action by every trader for a corollary of the perfect market in that 'in the same market, at any moment, there cannot be two prices for the same kind of article'.[22] This rule of a single price (it is called the 'law of indifference' in the second edition) excludes price discrimination and probably requires that the market have numerous buyers and sellers, but the condition is not made explicit. The presence of large numbers is clearly implied, however, when we are told that 'a single trader . . . must buy and sell at the current prices, which he cannot in an appreciable degree affect'.[23]

The merging of the concepts of competition and the market was unfortunate, for each deserved a full and separate treatment. A market is an institution for the consummation of transactions. It performs this function efficiently when every buyer who will pay more than the minimum realized price for any class of commodities succeeds in buying the commodity, and every seller who will sell for less than the maximum realized price succeeds in selling the commodity. A market performs these tasks more efficiently if the commodities are well specified and if buyers and sellers are fully informed of their properties and prices. Possibly also a perfect market allows buyers and sellers to act on differing expectations of future prices. A market may be perfect and monopolistic or imperfect and competitive. Jevons's mixture of the two has been widely imitated by successors, of course, so that even today a market is commonly treated as a concept subsidiary to competition.

Edgeworth was the first to attempt a systematic and rigorous definition of perfect competition. His exposition deserves the closest scrutiny in spite of the fact that few economists of his

---

[22] Ibid., p. 92. This is restated as the proposition that the last increments of an act of exchange (i.e. the last exchange in a competitive market) must be proportional to the total quantities exchanged, or that dy exchanges for dx in the same proportion that y exchanges for x, or

$$\frac{dy}{dx} = \frac{y}{x}.$$

It would have been better for Jevons simply to assert that, if x_i exchanges for y_i, then for all i

$$\frac{x_i}{y_i} = \frac{P_y}{P_x}.$$

[23] Ibid., p. 111. In the Preface to the second edition, where on most subjects Jevons was farseeing, the conceptual treatment of competition deteriorated: 'Property is only another name for monopoly. . . . Thus monopoly is limited by competition . . .' (*Theory*, 4th ed., pp. xlvi–xlvii).

time or ours have attempted to disentangle and uncover the theorems and conjectures of the *Mathematical Psychics*, probably the most elusively written book of importance in the history of economics. For his allegations and demonstrations seem to be the parents of widespread beliefs on the nature of perfect competition.

The conditions of perfect competition are stated as follows:

The *field of competition* with reference to a contract, or contracts, under consideration consists of all individuals who are willing and able to recontract about the articles under consideration. . . .

There is free communication throughout a *normal* competitive field. You might suppose the constituent individuals collected at a point, or connected by telephones – an ideal supposition [1881], but sufficiently approximate to existence or tendency for the purposes of abstract science.

A *perfect* field of competition possesses in addition certain properties peculiarly favourable to mathematical calculation; . . . The conditions of a *perfect* field are four; the first pair referable to the heading *multiplicity* or continuity, the second *dividedness* or fluidity.

I. An individual is free to *recontract* with any out of an indefinite number, . . .

II. Any individual is free to *contract* (at the same time) with an indefinite number; . . . This condition combined with the first appears to involve the indefinite divisibility of each *article* of contract (if any X deal with an indefinite number of Ys he must give each an indefinitely small portion of x); which might be erected into a separate condition.

III. Any individual is free to *recontract* with another independently of, *without the consent* being required of, any third party, . . .

IV. Any individual is free to *contract* with another independently of a third party; . . .

The failure of the first [condition] involves the failure of the second, but not *vice versa*; and the third and fourth are similarly related.[24]

The natural question to put to such a list of conditions of competition is: Are the conditions necessary and sufficient to achieve what intuitively or pragmatically seems to be a useful concept of competition? Edgeworth replies, in effect, that the conditions are both necessary and sufficient. More specifically,

[24] *Mathematical Psychics* (London, 1881) pp. 17–19.

competition requires (1) indefinitely large numbers of participants on both sides of the market; (2) complete absence of limitations upon individual self-seeking behavior; and (3) complete divisibility of the commodities traded.[25]

The rationale of the requirement of indefinite numbers is as follows. With bilateral monopoly, the transaction will be indeterminate – equilibrium can be anywhere on the contract curve.[26] If we add a second buyer and seller, it is shown that the range of permissible equilibriums (the length of the tenable contract curve) will shrink.[27] By intuitive induction, with infinitely many traders it will shrink to a single point; a single price must rule in the market.[28]

Before we discuss this argument, we may take account also of the condition that individual traders are free to act independently. Edgeworth shows that combinations reduce the effective number of traders and that 'combiners *stand to gain*'.[29] In effect, then, he must assume that the individual trader not only is free to act independently but will in fact do so.

The proof of the need for indefinite numbers has serious weaknesses. The range of indeterminacy shrinks only because one seller or buyer tries to cut out the other by offering better terms.[30] Edgeworth fails to show that such price competition (which is palpably self-defeating) will occur or that, if it does occur, why the process should stop before the parties reach a unique (competitive) equilibrium. Like all his descendants, he treated the small-numbers case unsatisfactorily.

It is intuitively plausible that with infinite numbers all monopoly power (and indeterminacy) will vanish, and Edgeworth essentially postulates rather than proves this. But a simple demonstration, in case of sellers of equal size, would amount only to showing that

---

[25] Edgeworth's emphasis upon recontract, the institution which allows tentative contracts to be broken without penalty, is motivated by a desire to assure that equilibrium will be achieved and will not be affected by the route by which it is achieved. It will not be examined here.

[26] Ibid., pp. 20 ff.   [27] Ibid., pp. 35 ff.
[28] Ibid., pp. 37–9.   [29] Ibid., p. 43.

[30] '. . . It will in general be possible for *one* of the Y's (without the consent of the other) to *recontract* with the two X's, so that for all these three parties the recontract is more advantageous than the previously existing contract' (ibid., p. 35).

Marginal revenue =

$$\text{Price} + \frac{\text{Price}}{\text{Number of sellers} \times \text{Market elasticity}}$$

and that this last term goes to zero as the number of sellers increases indefinitely.[31] This was implicitly Cournot's argument.

But why do we require divisibility of the traded commodity?

> Suppose a market, consisting of an equal number of masters and servants, offering respectively wages and service; subject to the condition that no man can serve two masters, no master employ more than one man; or suppose equilibrium already established between such parties to be disturbed by any sudden influx of wealth into the hands of the masters. Then there is no *determinate*, and very generally *unique*, arrangement towards which the system tends under the operation of, may we say, a law of Nature, and which would be predictable if we knew beforehand the real requirements of each, or of the average, dealer; . . .[32]

Consider the simple example: a thousand masters will each employ a man at any wage below 100; a thousand laborers will each work for any wage above 50. There will be a single wage rate: knowledge and numbers are sufficient to lead a worker to seek a master paying more than the going rate or a master to seek out a worker receiving less than the market rate. But any rate between 50 and 100 is a possible equilibrium.[33]

It is not the lack of uniqueness that is troublesome, however, for a market can be perfectly competitive even though there be a dozen possible stable equilibrium positions.[34] Rather, the

---

[31] Let one seller dispose of q_i, the other sellers each disposing of q. Then the seller's marginal revenue is

$$\frac{d(pq_i)}{dq_i} = p + q_i \frac{dp}{dQ} \frac{dQ}{dq_i}$$

where Q is total sales, and $dQ/dq_i = 1$. Letting $Q = nq_i = nq$, and writing E for

$$\frac{dQ}{dp} \frac{p}{Q}$$

we obtain the expression in the text.

[32] *Mathematical Psychics*, p. 46.

[33] Of course, let there be one extra worker, and the wage will be 50; one extra master, and it will be 100.

[34] Since chance should operate in the choice of the equilibrium actually attained, it is not proper to say, as Edgeworth does (in a wider context), that the dice will be 'loaded with villainy' (ibid., p. 50).

difficulty arises because the demand (or supply) functions do not possess continuous derivatives: the withdrawal of even one unit will lead to a large change in price, so that the individual trader – even though he has numerous independent rivals – can exert a perceptible influence upon price.

The element of market control arising out of the non-continuity is easily eliminated, of course. If the article which is traded is divisible, then equalities replace inequalities in the conditions of equilibrium: the individual trader can no longer influence the market price. A master may employ a variable amount of labor, and he will therefore bid for additional units so long as the wage rate is below his marginal demand price. A worker may have several employers, and he will therefore supply additional labor so long as any employer will pay more than his marginal supply price. 'If the labour of the assistants can be sold by the hour, or other sort of differential dose, the phenomenon of determinate equilibrium will reappear.'[35] Divisibility was introduced to achieve determinateness, which it fails to do, but it is required to eliminate monopoly power.

Divisibility had a possible second role in the assumptions, which, however, was never made explicit. If there are infinitely many possessors of a commodity, presumably each must have only an infinitesimal quantity of it if the existing total stock is to be finite. But no economist placed emphasis upon the strict mathematical implications of concepts like infinity, and this word was used to convey only the notion of an indefinitely large number of traders.

The remainder of the mathematical economists of the period did not extend, or for that matter even reach, the level of precision of Edgeworth. Walras gave no adequate definition of competition.[36] Pareto noticed the possible effects of social controls over purchases and sales.[37] Henry Moore, in what may

---

[35] *Collected Papers Relating to Political Economy* (London, 1925) i 36. One might also seek to eliminate the indeterminateness by appeal to the varying demand-and-supply prices of individual traders; this is the path chosen by Hicks in 'Edgeworth, Marshall, and the Indeterminateness of Wages', *Economic Journal*, XL (1930) 31–45. This, however, is a complicated solution; one must make special hypotheses about the distribution of these demand-and-supply prices.

[36] *Elements of Pure Economics*, trans. Jaffé (Homewood, Ill., 1954) pp. 83, 185. It is indicative that the word 'competition' is not indexed.

[37] *Cours d'économie politique* (Lausanne, 1896–7) §§ 46, 87, 705, 814; cf. also *Manuel d'économie politique*, 2nd ed. (Paris, 1927) pp. 163, 210, 230.

have been the first article on the formal definition of competition,[38] listed five 'implicit hypotheses' of competition:

I. Each economic factor seeks a maximum net income.

II. There is but one price for commodities of the same quality in the same market.

III. The influence of the product of any one producer upon the price per unit of the total product is negligible.

IV. The output of any one producer is negligible as compared with the total output.

V. Each producer orders the amount of his product without regard to the effect of his act upon the conduct of his competitors.[39]

This list of conditions is noteworthy chiefly because it marked an unsuccessful attempt to revert to the narrower competitive concept of Jevons.

Marshall

Marshall as usual refused to float on the tide of theory, and his treatment of competition was much closer to Adam Smith's than to that of his contemporaries. Indeed, Marshall's exposition was almost as informal and unsystematic as Smith's in this area. His main statement was:

We are investigating the equilibrium of normal demand and normal supply in their most general form: we are neglecting those features which are special to particular parts of economic science, and are confining our attention to those broad relations which are common to nearly the whole of it. Thus we assume that the forces of demand and supply have free play in a perfect market; there is no combination among dealers on either side, but each acts for himself: and there is *free competition*; that is, buyers compete freely with buyers, and sellers compete freely with sellers. But though everyone acts for himself, his knowledge of what others are doing is supposed to be sufficient to prevent him from taking a lower price or paying a higher price than others are doing; . . .[40]

[38] 'Paradoxes of Competition', *Quarterly Journal of Economics*, xx (1905–6) 209–30. Most of the article is concerned with duopoly.

[39] Ibid., pp. 213–14. The fifth statement is held to be a corollary of III and IV; but see p. 123–5 below.

[40] *Principles of Economics*, 1st ed. (London, 1890) p. 402. A comparison with the corresponding passage in the eighth edition (op. cit., p. 341) will reveal the curious changes which were later made in the description of competition.

If this quotation suggests that Marshall was invoking a strict concept of competition, we must remember that he discussed the 'fear of spoiling the market' and the firms with negatively sloping demand curves in the main chapters on competition[41] and that the only time perfect competition was mentioned was when it was expressly spurned.[42]

Soon he yielded a bit to the trend toward refinement of the concept. Beginning with the third (1895) edition, he explicitly introduced the horizontal demand curve for the individual firm as the normal case and gave it the same mathematical formulation as did Cournot.[43] But these were patchwork revisions, and they were not carried over into the many passages where looser concepts of competition had been employed.

Marshall's most significant contribution was indirect: he gave the most powerful analysis up to his time of the relationship of competition to optimum economic organization (book v, chap. xiii, on the doctrine of maximum satisfaction). There he found the competitive results to have not only the well-known qualification that the distribution of resources must be taken as a datum, and the precious exception that only one of several multiple stable equilibriums could be the maximum,[44] but also a new and possibly extremely important exception, arising out of external economies and diseconomies. The doctrine of external economies in effect asserts that in important areas the choices of an individual are governed by only part of the consequences, and inevitably the doctrine opens up a wide range of competitive equilibriums which depart from conventional criteria of optimum arrangement. It was left for Pigou to elaborate, and exaggerate, the importance of this source of disharmonies in *Wealth and Welfare*.

The Complete Formulation: Clark and Knight

Only two new elements needed to be added to the Edgeworth conditions for competition in order to reach the modern concept of perfect competition. They pertained to the mobility of resources and the model of the stationary economy, and both

41 *Principles*, 8th ed. (London, 1929) pp. 374, 458.
42 Ibid., p. 540.   43 Ibid., pp. 517, 849–50.
44 Both of these qualifications were of course recognized by predecessors such as Walras and Edgeworth.

were presented, not first,[45] but most influentially, by John Bates Clark.

Clark, in his well-known development of the concept of a static economy, ascribed all dynamic disturbances to five forces:

1. Population is increasing.
2. Capital is increasing.
3. Methods of production are improving.
4. The forms of industrial establishments are changing: . . .
5. The wants of consumers are multiplying.[46]

The main purpose of his treatise was to analyze the stationary economy in which these forces were suppressed, and for this analysis the assumption of competition was basic:

> There is an ideal arrangement of the elements of society, to which the force of competition, acting on individual men, would make the society conform. The producing mechanism actually shapes itself about this model, and at no time does it vary greatly from it.
>
> We must use assumptions boldly and advisedly, making labor and capital absolutely mobile, and letting competition work in ideal perfection.[47]

Although the concepts of a stationary economy and of competition are completely independent of each other, Clark somehow believed that competition was an element of static analysis:

> The statement made in the foregoing chapter that a static state excludes true entrepreneurs' profits does not deny that a legal monopoly might secure to an entrepreneur a profit that would be permanent as the law that should create it – and that, too, in a social condition which, at first glance, might appear to be static. The agents, labor and capital, would be prevented from moving into the favored industry, though economic forces, if they had been left unhindered, would have caused them to move in. This condition, however, is not a true static state, as it has been defined. . . . Industrial groups are in a truly static state when the industrial agents, labor and capital, show a *perfect mobility, but no motion*. A legal monopoly destroys at a certain point this mobility. . . .[48]

---

[45] In the mathematical exposition of theory it was natural to postulate stable supply and demand functions, and therefore stable technologies and tastes, so one could trace a gradually expanding concept of the stationary economy in Walras, Auspitz and Lieben, and Irving Fisher.

[46] *The Distribution of Wealth* (New York, 1899) p. 56.

[47] Ibid., pp. 68, 71.   [48] Ibid., p. 76; cf. also p. 78.

I shall return to this identification of competition with stationary equilibrium at a later point.

The introduction of perfect mobility of resources as an assumption of competition was new, and Clark offers no real explanation for the assumption. One could simply eliminate his five dynamic influences, and then equilibrium would be reached after a time even with 'friction' (or less than instantaneous mobility). Clark was aware of this possible approach but merely said that 'it is best to assume' that there is no friction.[49] The only gain in his subsequent work, of course, is the avoidance of an occasional 'in the long run'.

Mobility of resources had always been an implicit assumption of competition, and in fact the conditions of adequate knowledge of earning opportunities and absence of contrived barriers to movement were believed to be adequate to insure mobility. But there exist also technological limitations to the rate at which resources can move from one place or industry to another, and these limitations were in fact the basis of Marshall's concept of the short-run normal period. Once this fact was generally recognized, it became inevitable that mobility of resources be given an explicit time dimension, although of course it was highly accidental that instantaneous mobility was postulated.

The concept of perfect competition received its complete formulation in Frank Knight's *Risk, Uncertainty and Profit* (1921). It was the meticulous discussion in this work that did most to drive home to economists generally the austere nature of the rigorously defined concept[50] and so prepared the way for the widespread reaction against it in the 1930s.

Knight sought to establish the precise nature of an economy with complete knowledge as a preliminary step in the analysis of the impact of uncertainty. Clark's procedure of eliminating historical changes was shown to be neither necessary nor sufficient: a stationary economy was not necessary to achieve complete competitive equilibrium if men had complete fore-

---

49 Ibid., p. 81.

50 Although Pigou was not concerned with the formal definition of competition, he must also be accounted an influential figure in the popularization of the concept of perfect competition. In his *Wealth and Welfare* (1912), he devoted individual chapters to the effects of immobility (with incorrect knowledge as one component) and indivisibility upon the ability of a resource to receive an equal rate of return in all cases (ibid., part II, chaps. iv and v).

sight; and it was not sufficient to achieve this equilibrium, because there might still be non-historical fluctuations, owing, for example, to drought or flood, which were imperfectly anticipated.[51] Complete, errorless adjustments required full knowledge of all relevant circumstances, which realistically can be possessed only when these circumstances do not change; that is, when the economy is stationary.

The assumptions necessary to competition are presented as part of a list that describes the pure enterprise economy, and I quote those that are especially germane to competition:

2. We assume that the members of the society act with complete 'rationality'. By this we do not mean that they are to be 'as angels, knowing good from evil'; we assume ordinary human motives . . . ; but they are supposed to 'know what they want' and to seek it 'intelligently'. . . . They are supposed to know absolutely the consequence of their acts when they are performed, and to perform them in the light of the consequences. . . .

4. We must also assume complete absence of physical obstacles to the making, execution, and changing of plans at will; that is, there must be 'perfect mobility' in all economic adjustments, no cost involved in movements or changes. To realize this ideal all the elements entering into economic calculations – effort, commodities, etc. – must be continuously variable, divisible without limit. . . . The exchange of commodities must be virtually instantaneous and costless.

5. It follows as a corollary from number 4 that there is perfect competition. There must be perfect, continuous, costless intercommunication between all individual members of the society. Every potential buyer of a good constantly knows and chooses among the offers of all potential sellers, and conversely. Every commodity, it will be recalled, is divisible into an indefinite number of units which must be separately owned and compete effectually with each other.

6. Every member of the society is to act as an individual only, in entire independence of all other persons. . . . And in exchanges between individuals, no interests of persons not parties to the exchange are to be concerned, either for good or for ill. Individual independence in action excludes all forms of collusion, all degrees of monopoly or tendency to monopoly. . . .

9. All given factors and conditions are for the purposes of this and the following chapter and until notice to the contrary is expressly given, to remain absolutely unchanged. They must be

51 *Risk, Uncertainty and Profit* (New York, 1921) pp. 35–8.

free from periodic or progressive modification as well as irregular fluctuation. The connection between this specification and number 2 (perfect knowledge) is clear. Under static conditions every person would soon find out, if he did not already know, everything in his situation and surroundings which affected his conduct. . . .

The above assumptions, especially the first eight, are idealizations or purifications of tendencies which hold good more or less in reality. They are the conditions necessary to perfect competition. The ninth, as we shall see, is on a somewhat different footing. Only its corollary of perfect knowledge (specification number 2) which may be present even when change takes place is necessary for perfect competition.[52]

This list of requirements of perfect competition is by no means a statement of the *minimum* requirements, and in fact no one is able to state the minimum requirements.

Consider first complete knowledge. If each seller in a market knows any *n* buyers, and each seller knows a different (but overlapping) set of buyers, then there will be perfect competition if the set of *n* buyers is large enough to exclude joint action. Or let there be indefinitely many brokers in any market, and let each broker know many buyers and sellers, and also let each buyer or seller know many brokers – again we have perfect competition. Since entrepreneurs in a stationary economy are essentially brokers between resource owners and consumers, it is sufficient for competition if they meet this condition. That is, resource owners and consumers could dwell in complete ignorance of all save the bids of many entrepreneurs. Hence knowledge possessed by any one trader need not be complete; it is sufficient if the knowledge possessed by the ensemble of individuals in the market is in a sense comprehensive.

And now, mobility. Rigid immobility of every trader is compatible with perfect competition if we wish to have this concept denote only equilibrium which is not affected by the actions of individual traders: large numbers (in any market) and comprehensive knowledge are sufficient to eliminate monopoly power. If we wish perfect competition to denote also that a resource will obtain equal returns in all possible uses, mobility becomes essential, but not for all resources. If one resource were immobile and all others mobile, clearly the returns of all

[52] Ibid., pp. 76-9; cf. also p. 148.

resources in all uses could be equalized. Even if all resources were immobile, under certain conditions free transport of consumers' goods would lead to equalization of returns.[53] Even in the general case in which mobility of resources is required, not all the units of a resource need be mobile. If some units of each resource are mobile, the economic system will display complete mobility for all displacements up to a limit that depends upon the proportion of mobile units and the nature of the displacement.

The condition that there be no costs of movement of resources is not necessary in order to reach maximum output for an economy; under competition only those movements of resources will take place for which the additional return equals or exceeds the cost of movement. But costless movement is necessary if equality is to obtain in the return to a resource in all uses: if the movement between A and B costs $1.00 (per unit of time), the return to a resource at A can vary within $1.00 of either direction of its return at B. Equilibrium could be reached anywhere within these limits (but would be uniquely determined), and this equilibrium would depend upon the historical distribution of resources and consumers.

Next, divisibility. It is not enough to have a large number of informed traders in a market: price must change continuously with quantity if an individual trader is to have only an imperceptible influence upon the market rate, and this will generally require divisibility of the commodity traded. Infinite divisibility, however, is not necessary to eliminate significant control over price by the individual trader, and divisibility of time in the use of a resource is a substitute for divisibility in its quantity. Divisibility, however, is not sufficient to insure uniqueness of equilibriums; even in the simpler problems one must also require that the relevant economic functions display strict monotonicity, but this has nothing to do with competition.

And homogeneity. The formal condition that there be many producers of a commodity assumes homogeneity of this commodity (Knight's assumption 5). Certain forms of heterogeneity are of course unimportant because they are superficial: potatoes need not be of the same size if they are sold by the pound;

---

[53] See P. A. Samuelson, 'International Factor-Price Equalization Once Again', *Economic Journal*, LIX (1949) 181–97; and S. F. James and I. F. Pierce, 'The Factor Price Equalization Myth', *Review of Economic Studies*, XIX (1951–2) 111–22.

laborers do not have to be equally efficient if the differences in their productivity are measurable. As these examples may suggest, heterogeneity can be a substitute for divisibility.

The final assumption, concerning collusion, is especially troublesome. If one merely postulates the absence of collusion, then why not postulate also that even two rivals can behave in such a way as to reach competitive equilibrium? Instead, one usually requires that the number of traders be large enough so that collusion will not appear. To determine this number, one must have a theory of the conditions under which collusion occurs. Economists have generally emphasized two barriers to collusion. The first is imperfect knowledge, especially of the consequences of rivalry and of the policy which would maximize profits for the group, and of course neither of these difficulties would arise in the stationary economy with perfect knowledge. The second barrier is the difficulty of determining the division of profits among colluders, and we simply do not know whether this difficulty would increase with the number of traders under the conditions we are examining. Hence it seems essential to assume the absence of collusion as a supplement to the presence of large numbers: one of the assumptions of perfect competition is the existence of a Sherman Act.

It is therefore no occasion for complaint that Knight did not state the minimum requirements for perfect competition; this statement was impossible in 1921, and it is impossible today. The minimum assumptions for a theoretical model can be stated with precision only when the complete theory of that model is known. The complete theory of competition cannot be known because it is an open-ended theory; it is always possible that a new range of problems will be posed in this framework, and then, no matter how well developed the theory was with respect to the earlier range of problems, it may require extensive elaboration in respects which previously it glossed over or ignored.

The analytical appeal of a definition of competition does not depend upon its economy of assumptions, although gratuitously wide assumptions are objectionable.[54] We wish the definition to

[54] They are objectionable chiefly because they mislead some users or abusers of the concept as to its domain of applicability. That dreadful list of assumptions of perfect competition which textbooks in labor economics so often employ to dismiss the marginal productivity theory is a case in point.

specify with tolerable clarity – with such clarity as the state of the science affords – a model which can be used by practitioners in a great variety of theoretical researches, so that the foundations of the science need not be debated in every extension or application of theory. We wish the definition to capture the essential general content of important markets, so the predictions drawn from the theory will have wide empirical reliability. And we wish a concept with normative properties that will allow us to judge the efficiency of policies. That the concept of perfect competition has served these varied needs as well as it has is providential.

Concluding Reflections

If we were free to redefine competition at this late date, a persuasive case could be made that it should be restricted to meaning the absence of monopoly power in a market. This is an important concept that deserves a name, and 'competition' would be the appropriate name. But it would be idle to propose such a restricted signification for a word which has so long been used in a wide sense, and at best we may hope to denote the narrower concept by a suggestive phrase. I propose that we call this narrow concept *market competition*.

Perfect market competition will prevail when there are indefinitely many traders (no one of which controls an appreciable share of demand or supply) acting independently in a perfect market. A perfect market is one in which the traders have full knowledge of all offer and bid prices. I have already remarked that it was unfortunate that a perfect market was made a subsidiary characteristic of competition, for a perfect market may also exist under monopoly. Indeed, in realistic cases a perfect market may be more likely to exist under monopoly, since complete knowledge is easier to achieve under monopoly.

Market competition can exist even though resources or traders cannot enter or leave the market in question. Hence market competition can rule in an industry which is not in long-run competitive equilibrium and is compatible with the existence of large profits or losses.

It is interesting to note that Chamberlin's definition of 'pure' competition is identical with my definition of market competition: 'competition unalloyed with monopoly elements'.[55] But Chamberlin implied that pure competition could rule in an imperfect market; the only conditions he postulated were large numbers of traders and a standardized commodity. The conditions are incomplete: if one million buyers dealt with one million sellers of a homogeneous product, each pair dealing in ignorance of all others, we should simply have one million instances of bilateral monopoly. Hence pure competition cannot be contrasted with perfect competition, for the former also requires 'perfect' knowledge (subject to qualifications I have previously discussed), and for this reason I prefer the term 'market competition'.

The broad concept of perfect competition is defined by the condition that the rate of return (value of the marginal product) of each resource be equal in all uses. If we wish to distinguish this concept from market competition, we may call it (after the terminology attributed to Cairnes) *industrial competition*. Industrial competition requires (1) that there be market competition within each industry; (2) that owners of resources be informed of the returns obtainable in each industry; and (3) that they be free to enter or leave any industry. In addition, the resources must be infinitely divisible if there is to be strict equality in the rate of return on a resource in all uses.

An industrial competitive equilibrium will obtain continuously if resources are instantaneously mobile or in the long run if they move at a finite time rate. Since the concept of long-run competitive equilibrium is deeply imbedded in modern economic theory, it seems most desirable that we interpret industrial competition as a long-run concept. It may be noticed that a time period did not have to figure explicitly in the pre-Marshallian theory because that theory did not separate and devote special attention to a short-run normal period in which only a portion of the resources were mobile: the basic classical theory was a long-run theory.

The concept of industrial competition has a natural affinity to the static economy even though our definition does not pay any explicit attention to this problem. Rates of return on resources will be equalized only if their owners have complete knowledge of future returns (in the case of durable resources), and it seems improper to assume complete knowledge of the

55 *The Theory of Monopolistic Competition*, 1st ed. (Cambridge, Mass., 1933) p. 6.

future in a changing economy. Not only is it misleading to endow the population with this gift of prophecy but also it would often be inconsistent to have people foresee a future event and still have that event remain in the future.

One method by which we might seek to adapt the definition to a historically evolving economy is to replace the equalization of rates of return by *expected* rates of return. But it is not an irresistibly attractive method. There are troublesome questions of what entrepreneurs seek to maximize under these conditions and of whether risk or uncertainty premiums also enter into their calculations. A more important difficulty is that this formulation implies that the historically evolving industry is in equilibrium in long-run normal periods, and there is no strong reason to believe that such long-run normal periods can be defined for the historically evolving industry. If all economic progress took the form of a secularly smooth development, we could continue to use the Marshallian long-run normal period, and indeed much progress does take this form. But often, and sooner or later always, the historical changes come in vast surges, followed by quiescent periods or worse, and it is harder to assume that the fits and starts can be foreseen with tolerable confidence or that they will come frequently enough to average out within economically relevant time periods.

It seems preferable, therefore, to adapt the concept of competition to changing conditions by another method: to insist only upon the absence of barriers to entry and exit from an industry in the long-run normal period; that is, in the period long enough to allow substantial changes in the quantities of even the most durable and specialized resources. Then we may still expect that some sort of expected return will tend to be equalized under conditions of reasonably steady change, although much work remains to be done before we can specify exactly what this return will be.[56]

The way in which the competitive concept loses precision when historically changing conditions are taken into account is apparent. It is also easily explained: the competitive concept

[56] It is worth noticing that even under static conditions the definition of the return is modified to suit the facts and that mobility of resources is the basic competitive requirement. Thus we say that laborers move so that the net advantages, not the current money return, of various occupations are equalized. The suggestion in the text is essentially that we find the appropriate definition of net advantages for the historically evolving economy.

can be no better than the economic theory with which it is used, and until we have a much better theory of economic development we shall not have a much better theory of competition under conditions of non-repetitive change.

The normative role of the competitive concept arises from the fact that the equality of rate of return on each resource in all uses which defines competition is also the condition for maximum output from given resources. The outputs are measured in market prices, and the maximum is relative to the distribution of ownership of resources. This well-known restriction of the competitive optimum to production, it may be remarked, should be qualified by the fact that the effects of competition on distribution have not been studied. A competitive system affects the distribution of the ownership of resources, and – given a stable distribution of human abilities – a competitive system would probably lead eventually to a stable income distribution whose characteristics are unknown. The theory of this distribution might have substantial normative value.

The vitality of the competitive concept in its normative role has been remarkable. One might have expected that, as economic analysis became more precise and as the range of problems to which it was applied widened, a growing list of disparities between the competitive allocation of resources and the maximum-output allocation would develop. Yet to date there have been only two major criticisms of the norm.[57] The first is that the competitive individual ignores external economies and diseconomies, which – rightly or wrongly – most economists are still content to treat as an exception to be dealt with in individual cases. The second, and more recent, criticism is that the competitive system will not provide the right amount (and possibly not the right types) of economic progress, and this is still an undocumented charge. The time may well come when the competitive concept suitable to positive analysis is not suitable to normative analysis, but it is still in the future.

Finally, we should notice the most common and the most important criticism of the concept of perfect competition – that it is unrealistic. This criticism has been widespread since the

[57] In a wider framework there have of course been criticisms of the competitive norm with respect to (i) the ability of individuals to judge their own interests and (ii) the ability of a competitive system to achieve a continuously high level of employment of resources.

concept was completely formulated and underlies the warm reception which the profession gave to the doctrines of imperfect and monopolistic competition in the 1930s. One could reply to this criticism that all concepts sufficiently general and sufficiently precise to be useful in scientific analysis must be abstract: that, if a science is to deal with a large class of phenomena, clearly it cannot work with concepts that are faithfully descriptive of even one phenomenon, for then they will be grotesquely undescriptive of others. This conventional line of defense for all abstract concepts is completely valid, but there is another defense, or rather another form of this defense, that may be more persuasive.

This second defense is that the concept of perfect competition has defeated its newer rivals in the decisive area: the day-to-day work of the economic theorist. Since the 1930s, when the rival doctrines of imperfect and monopolistic competition were in their heyday, economists have increasingly reverted to the use of the concept of perfect competition as their standard model for analysis. Today the concept of perfect competition is being used more widely by the profession in its theoretical work than at any time in the past. The vitality of the concept is strongly spoken for by this triumph.

Of course, this is not counsel of complacency. I have cited areas in which much work must be done before important aspects of the definition of competition can be clarified. My fundamental thesis, in fact, is that hardly any important improvement in general economic theory can fail to affect the concept of competition. But it has proved to be a tough and resilient concept, and it will stay with us in recognizable form for a long time to come.

8 Monopolistic Competition in Retrospect

G. J. Stigler

Before the Great Depression, that chasm between darkness and light, economists had generally looked upon the economy as a mixture of industries that approximated conditions of perfect competition and industries that were 'monopolies'. The competitive industries, it was believed, were satisfactorily analyzed by the theory of competition, and although the 'monopolies' were diverse in structure and power, they could be informatively analyzed by a discriminating use of the theory of monopoly. Individual economists varied considerably in the relative importance they attached to these two groups of industries, of course, but they varied surprisingly little in the type of analytical system they deemed appropriate to the analysis of economic events. This is not to say that the details of the analytical system were, or were thought to be, definitive: indeed certain portions of the system, such as duopoly, admittedly were (and are) in wretched shape.

Then came the works of Mrs Robinson and Professor Chamberlin, who criticized this viewpoint and demanded a new orientation of our thought. Because of the high quality of their volumes, and because it was the ''thirties', they were enthusiastically received. Then too, their messages seemed to reinforce one another, but this was a confusion that was quickly detected by, and almost only by, Professor Chamberlin.

Of Mrs Robinson's work I need say little. It is amply clear, on a re-reading at this distant date, that her message was in no sense revolutionary, although at times her language was rebellious. Her two basic theses were: (1) that price theory is capable of great improvements in elegance and significant improvements in logic; and (2) that the theory of monopoly is the

Reprinted from G. J. Stigler, *Five Lectures on Economic Principles* (London School of Economics, 1949) by kind permission of the author.

appropriate instrument of analysis of all real situations in which the assumptions of perfect competition are not completely and exactly fulfilled. If she gave no evidence for her second thesis, to which I shall return later, she contributed much to the fulfillment of the first. Her volume marks no break with the tradition of neo-classical economics; indeed it contains, I think, too uncritical an acceptance of the substantive content of orthodoxy.

Professor Chamberlin was a true revolutionary. Instead of assimilating observed market structures into exclusive classes such as competition and monopoly, he told us, we must throw off our theoretical heritage and look at the world with clear and candid eyes. Then we shall find that no simple dichotomy does justice to the rich variety of industrial organization. True, there are (a very few) industries that closely resemble those studied by the economist of perfect competition. True, there are (perhaps more) firms that partake of the nature of monopoly as this concept was used in neo-classical economics. But vastly more often the firm displays a mixture of insulation from other rivals, by means of real or fancied product differences, and of indirect rivalry by way of (1) the willingness of some consumers to shift among products and (2) the ability of firms to change their products. As a result, there are important – in fact, typical – phenomena which cannot be explained, or can be explained only with serious error, if economic reality is forced into the neo-classical categories.

Let us spell out Professor Chamberlin's *Weltanschauung* in a bit more detail. Suppose our primary interest is (or perhaps I should say, begins with) the housing of the people who work in New York City. Even casual observation indicates the prominence of two characteristics in this housing market: (1) a great variety of products; and (2) a certain 'unsystematism' or irregularity or randomness in the interrelationships among these products. (1) The housing facilities range from incredible estates to unbelievable slums. Every unit is unique in a rigorous technological sense and, more relevant, there are thousands of classes of dwellings whose rents need not move in strict proportion on threat of wholesale vacancy or queuing up. Our housing facilities, moreover, roam far afield. They extend to several states directly, and – through summer and winter places and other channels – ultimately to the whole world. They very probably extend also to automobiles, fur coats, and trips abroad, for the competition may well be stronger between these products and various classes of housing than the competition between some classes of housing. (2) Nor is there any systematic arrangement of this assemblage of products. The barriers between products are not of uniform height or thickness, nor is there any discernible order in their occurrence. It is not impossible that apartments A and B do not compete directly and yet are both in close rivalry with automobiles. The existence of many similar and closely situated apartments is compatible with pervasive duopoly.

This picture of economic life was not fundamentally new, but Professor Chamberlin's reaction was. Customarily the picture had led to some sort of 'institutional' economics, that strange mixture of magnificent methodological pronouncements and skinny, *ad hoc* analyses. Chamberlin, however, persevered to construct an analytical system of recognizable type to deal with the picture: the co-ordinates of his diagrams would be price and quantity, not Church and State.

Chamberlin's vision was clearly a legitimate way of looking at economic life. One may even argue that it was more congruent with untutored observation, and in this sense more 'realistic'. But these are points, not of unimportance, but of complete irrelevance, despite the part they played in securing popularity for his theory. There is a question of minor interest: Did Chamberlin develop from this viewpoint a logically consistent theory of economic events? And there is a question of paramount importance: Does a theory incorporating this viewpoint contain more accurate or more compehensive implications than the neoclassical theory? I wish to emphasize this second question because it is not true that a theory which is realistic in its assumptions – if any meaning can be attached to this – is necessarily realistic in its implications, a theme to which I shall return.

But let us return to Chamberlin's picture. How does he reduce this stupendous diversity and complexity to a manageable system without assuming away its essential characteristics?

1. The First Attempt: Chamberlin

One cannot long talk sensibly and simultaneously about a Connecticut estate, a Brooklyn walk-up, and a New Jersey hotel – to say very little of the fur coats and trips to Europe. And so Professor Chamberlin introduced the 'group':

> The group contemplated is one which would *ordinarily* be regarded as composing one imperfectly competitive market: a number of automobile manufacturers, of producers of pots and pans, of magazine publishers, or of retail shoe dealers.[1]

The ambiguity of the concept of a group is not removed by this enumeration or the references to competing monopolists; we are left with the strong impression that the Marshallian industry has reappeared and we do not understand its new rôle, for our new picture is one of diversity. But then our picture is not an analytical system; it is therefore necessary to turn to Chamberlin's use of the concept in order to discover its role in his analytical system.

The subsequent analysis indicates that the group is a collection of (producers of?) fairly close substitutes; and at least once Chamberlin refers to 'groups of products that are close substitutes for each other' (p. 140). More formally, the group may be defined as the collection of firms whose cross-elasticities of demand exceed some pre-assigned value. We must suspend judgment on the usefulness of the concept until we see the results to which it permits Chamberlin to arrive, but several direct implications of the definition should be noticed at once:

1. It is perfectly possible, on Chamberlin's picture of economic life, that the group contain only one firm, or, on the contrary, that it include all of the firms in the economy. This latter possibility can readily follow from the asymmetry of substitution relationships among firms: taking any one product as our point of departure, each substitute has in turn its substitutes, so that the adjacent cross-elasticities may not diminish, and even increase, as we move farther away from the 'base' firm in some technological or geographical sense.

2. The picture of diversity and unsystematism also makes it very likely, if the group contains several firms, that the products be heterogeneous from the technological viewpoint.

---

[1] *Theory of Monopolistic Competition*, 5th ed, p. 81. Our interest at this point is in the early editions, but with two exceptions the quotations are identical in content and pagination in the first and fifth editions. The first exception is in the above quotation: 'ordinarily' is not italicized in the early editions.

3. The picture also dictates that often, and perhaps usually, a large or dominant role is played by firms outside the group in determining prices and profits within the group.

The importance of the group concept for the theory of monopolistic competition must be emphasized. Chamberlin asks the reader: can not the conventional theory of monopoly cope with the problems of monopolistic competition? And he answers: No. 'Monopolistic competition, then, concerns itself not only with the problem of an *individual* equilibrium (the ordinary theory of monopoly), but also with that of a *group* equilibrium (the adjustment of economic forces within a group of competing monopolists, ordinarily regarded merely as a group of competitors)' (p. 69). The group is no mere expedient to get the analysis started, it is the vehicle of Chamberlin's theory of interdependence of products.

What, then, can we say of the (perhaps) 100 products – dwellings and limousines – in the group? Further simplification is obviously necessary, and Chamberlin introduces what he calls the 'uniformity' assumption:

> We therefore proceed under the heroic assumption that both demand and cost curves for all the 'products' are uniform throughout the group. (p. 82)

Again we must pause: the uniformity assumption is only temporary, we are promised, but even a temporary assumption should be meaningful. How can different products have uniform costs and demands? The quantity axes of the various product diagrams are simply not the same: one measures three-room apartments, another four-room houses, and perhaps still another, restaurant meals (an excellent substitute for a kitchen). We cannot translate one into another by the ratio of their prices, for we are constructing the apparatus to explain prices. We do not wish to say that two physically similar apartments are 'really' the same. They are not the same if their prices differ, and perhaps even if they do not differ[2] – this is the fundamental picture. And we do wish to say that restaurant meals plus a bedroom may form a better substitute for a Manhattan apartment than does a Brooklyn apartment – this is also part of the picture.

[2] '. . . general uniformity of price proves nothing as to the freedom of competition from monopoly elements' (p. 88).

And yet, by the uniformity assumption Chamberlin has implicitly defined the group as a collection of physically homogeneous products. The identity of costs and demands is otherwise meaningless, and so also is the demand curve he proceeds to draw for a firm on the assumption that 'competitors' prices are always identical' (p. 90). We simply cannot attach meaning to the statement that physically diverse things have the same price. This physical homogeneity possibly destroys, at least temporarily, Chamberlin's monopolistic competition (except for spatially distributed firms), for he has also assumed that buyers have perfect knowledge (p. 73), in order further to simplify the analysis. With perfect knowledge and homogeneous products, must not the demand curve confronting each firm be infinitely elastic? But the uniformity assumption is only temporary, we recall.

So we have 100 products of various sorts (blinking the inconsistency) or of one sort, but with negatively sloping demand curves (dropping the assumption of perfect knowledge), what then? Our vision tells us that we are unlikely to find symmetry, continuity, or any sort of smoothness in the relationships amonв these products. To meet this problem, Chamberlin introduces what I shall term the 'symmetry' assumption:

> Specifically, we assume for the present that any adjustment of price or of 'product' by a single producer spreads its influence over so many of his competitors that the impact felt by any one is negligible and does not lead him to any readjustment of his own situation. (p. 83)

It is now an anti-climax to notice that Chamberlin further assumes, throughout his entire volume, that (1) the only relationship between products is that of substitution – complementarity 'is beyond the scope of our problem' (p. 39 n.); and (2) the Marshallian cost apparatus is acceptable *in toto*: the vision of diversity and unsystematism does not extend to the resources market.[3]

But now we have utterly abandoned the picture with which our analytical technique was designed to deal: there is no variety and there is only one possible type of interrelationship between products. We probably have a Marshallian industry.

[3] Although, in strict logic, it must: there are no consumer goods that are purchased exclusively by consumers.

We appear also to have negatively sloping demand curves for individual products, because our picture and our group are inconsistent with our uniformity assumption. The tangency of average cost and demand curves which we now deduce is of little importance to us: this familiar result of competitive theory, I will argue later, is not enriched. Possibly of more importance is the finding that even under these extreme conditions our new variable, 'product', cannot be 'measured along an axis' (p. 79) – that is, cannot be measured. Each time 'product' appears in the discussion, we are told to choose it to maximize profits, and nothing more.[4] As a result, for practical purposes the theory of monopolistic competition concerns only consumers moving among products, and ignores products moving among consumers.

We hasten on to the sections in which the uniformity and symmetry assumptions are separately (but, oddly, never jointly) lifted. Oligopoly may, and perhaps usually will, enter if the symmetry assumption fails, and then we are reduced to the familiar uncertainty over assumptions and results (pp. 100–4), from which we salvage only the conclusion that prices may be higher than under competition (p. 104). The effect of diversity of demand and cost conditions is even more devastating: there may be monopoly profits throughout the group at equilibrium – and then again, there may not. Indeed, although Professor Chamberlin does not state the possibility, it is not even clear that equilibrium is attainable: under these vague conditions prices may continue to change, and new firms may continue to enter and old firms continue to leave the 'group'. This indeterminacy is especially likely if we recognize variety through time – the consumers' liking for novelty, which Professor Chamberlin should surely add to his picture. He sums up the effects of diversity:

> To sum up this phase of the matter, our statement of the group problem must be modified by recognizing that the demand curves are not adjusted uniformly to a position tangent to the cost

---

[4] 'The difficulties of representing graphically the variation of "product" render hazardous any attempt to define with precision the exact point of equilibrium. It would seem that the most that can be said is that it will be characterized by (1) the equation of cost and price, and (2) the impossibility of a "product" adjustment by anyone which would increase his profits' (p. 97). This, of course, is a statement of the problem, not of its solution.

curves. In so far as profits are higher than the general competitive level in the field as a whole or in any portion of it, new competitors will, *if possible*, invade the field and reduce them. If this were always possible, as hitherto assumed, the curves would always be tangent and monopoly profits would be eliminated. In fact it is only partially possible. As a result some (or all) of the curves may lie at various distances to the right of the point of tangency, leaving monopoly profits scattered throughout the group – and throughout the price system. (p. 113)

It will be observed that the theory of monopolistic competition now contains no conditions of equilibrium, only a definition of equilibrium.

As a result, in the general case we cannot make a single statement about economic events in the world we sought to analyze. It is true that many such statements are made by Chamberlin, but none follows rigorously from the ambiguous apparatus. All of the definite comparisons with competition, for example, are made when there is uniformity and symmetry.[5] Indeed even these comparisons rest upon the further and technically inadmissible assumption that the cost curves of a firm will be the same under competition and monopolistic competition, although there is no presumption that the size of the 'group' will be the same in the two situations if they really differ.[6]

And so the first attempt has failed.[7] Professor Chamberlin did

[5] This is recognized in a footnote (p. 78 n.), where it is said that if there is not tangency, the monopolistically competitive output of the firm may exceed the competitive output. This is held to be an unimportant exception because of 'considerations introduced below in connection with the group problem'. In the group discussion, under symmetry and uniformity, the footnote is recalled (p. 88) but not elaborated. The exception is forgotten when diversity of costs and demands is reached, although tangency of cost and demand curves has now vanished, and with it the improbability of the exception.

[6] The neglect of cost differences is justified on two grounds. (1) Many industries are constant cost industries – a result borrowed from Marshallian analysis, for which there is no presumption in the Chamberlin group. (2) The belief that even with increasing or decreasing cost industries, 'the divergences from the norms of purely competitive theory are always of the same sort' (p. 87). This belief is without foundation.

[7] I pass over the theory of selling costs because my subject is monopolistic competition, not the economics of Professor Chamberlin. Selling costs played only one role in the discussion that we need notice: their existence was adduced as a criticism of the theory of perfect competition, for none would be needed with perfect knowledge. Professor Chamberlin was right in concluding that perfect competition is a poor instrument in analyzing selling costs. His results might have

not reduce his picture of reality to a manageable analytical system.

2. The Second Attempt: Chamberlin–Triffin

In the course of time and controversy, Professor Chamberlin indicated the probable desirability of abandoning the concept of the group, which in his system was, after all, an anachronistic vestige of neo-classical economics. When discussing the closely related concept of entry of new firms (into a group), he said:

> The upshot of the matter seems to be that the concept is not very useful and is even seriously misleading in connection with monopolistic competition. It is, in reality, a concept usually related to a market for a definite commodity, and the fundamental difficulty is that there is no such commodity under monopolistic competition beyond that produced by an individual firm. (p. 201)

But he does not follow this line of thought to its conclusion:

> It is not meant by this argument to discard completely the concept of an 'industry'. In many connections, it is obviously useful to delimit a portion of the economic system and study it in some degree of isolation from the rest. And if this can be done, although entry is never 'free', it is not wholly without meaning to speak of the *relative* ease with which this particular field may be entered, in the sense of the relative ease with which substitutes for the particular products which compose the 'industry' may be produced. One emerges from any attempt to classify industries, however, with a feeling that it is all exceedingly arbitrary. The 'common sense' definitions of industries in terms of which practical problems are likely to be studied seem to be based much more upon technological criteria than upon the possibility of market substitution. (p. 202 n.)

Except for the last sentence, which is an indirect admission of the entire Marshallian system,[8] the tenor of the argument is that the group must go.

---

been more informative, however, if he had chosen to drop the assumption that the economy was stationary, rather than the assumption that the economy was competitive.

[8] This last sentence is even more remarkable in the original article of which the above quotations are revisions: 'It seems much easier and more defensible to set up classifications based upon technological criteria than upon the possibility of market substitution.' ('Monopolistic or Imperfect Competition?', *Quarterly Journal of Economics*, LI (1937) 568 n.)

This is a most baffling state in which to leave the theory of monopolistic competition, for we recall that the theory differs from that of monopoly only in containing a group equilibrium. 'As for monopoly, *as ordinarily conceived and defined*, monopolistic competition embraces it and takes it as a starting point' (p. 68, not in first edition). But if the group is suspect, if at best it is a notion 'not wholly without meaning', the theory of monopoly seems to be also the final destination.

It was left for an able disciple, Dr Robert Triffin, to carry the purification of the technique a step farther, in his *Monopolistic Competition and General Equilibrium Theory* (1940). He succeeds in making the analytical apparatus portray faithfully the original picture of variety and unsystematism. Costs, demands, and hence profits of each firm are functions of all prices in the economy, i.e. profits of firm $i = \phi$ $(p_1, p_2, \ldots, p_n)$, where n is very large. The firm will maximize profits, subject to the usual uncertainties of oligopolistic situations – that is, it will equate marginal revenue and marginal cost.

And what of the group? It must go, for it is inconsistent with the fundamental vision. 'In the general pure theory of value, the group and the industry are useless concepts' (p. 89). 'Product differentiation robs the concept of industry of both its definiteness and its serviceability' (p. 188). How, then, are we to analyze the inter-relationships among firms? Apparently we cannot; Dr Triffin's chapter (iii) on the theory of external interdependence consists only of an elegant classification of types of interdependence.

Dr Triffin does not fail to draw the conclusion that monopolistic competition has nothing to say of the interdependence of firms; this silence is indeed hailed as an advance over the Marshallian theory (p. 189). The basis for this claim deserves our attention. Dr Triffin visualizes the discipline as composed of two very different types of studies: the 'general pure theory of value'; and the investigation of concrete economic problems – for example, the New York housing problem:

> Is anything gained by limiting the investigation to a group of close competitors, which we would call a group or industry? In an empirical, statistical study, yes: we can, in this way, reduce to a manageable size the research work involved, without any serious loss in precision or exhaustiveness. In the general statement of value theory, no: when competition is discussed in general

abstract terms, we may just as well make the group (or industry) coextensive with the whole economic collectivity. The problems are the same, and the complexity is no greater.

In other words, the value of these groupings is only a concrete, empirical one: it is never useful to speak of 'industries' or 'groups' in a general, abstract way, but it may be very helpful to speak of the oil industry, the coal industry, the steel industry, etc. (p. 88)

And in his conclusion, Dr Triffin goes on:

Instead of drawing its substance from arbitrary assumptions, chosen for their simplicity and unduly extended to the whole field of economic activity, our theory may turn to more pedestrian, but more fruitful methods. It will recognize the richness and variety of all concrete cases, and tackle each problem with due respect for its individual aspects. More advantage will be taken of all relevant factual information, and less reliance will be placed on a mere re-sort to the pass-key of general theoretical assumptions. (p. 189)

I would emphasize the separateness of these two types of economic analysis in Triffin's view of economics: there is neither substitution nor complementarity between the general theory and the specific economic investigation. The theory has nothing to learn from the study of specific problems because these problems are so diverse that no single inductive generalization is possible.[9] Conversely the study of specific problems has nothing to gain from the general theory, for the theory can provide no apparatus to raise relevant questions, to indicate relevant types of facts, or to guide the economist in handling the facts to reach useful conclusions.

This is a fundamentally mistaken role to assign to general theory. The study of economic theory is not defensible on aesthetic grounds – it hardly rivals in elegance the mathematics or physics our sophomores learn. The theory is studied only as an aid in solving real problems, and it is good only in the measure that it performs this function. Dr Trifin's advice is fundamentally to give up theory, 'to tackle each problem with due respect for its individual aspects'. Chamberlin's picture of reality has finally led, when consistently followed, to the familiar reaction: *ad hoc* empiricism.

9 Thus, after Dr Triffin examines freedom of entry, he concludes, 'Which type of entry prevails in any particular case is to be ascertained and "explained" by an investigation of the facts. Analytical reasoning is powerless to deduce the answer from general, universally valid assumptions' (p. 123).

3. The Reasons for Failure

Professor Chamberlin's failure to construct an analytical system capable of dealing informatively with his picture of reality is not hard to explain. The fundamental fact is that, although Chamberlin could throw off the shackles of Marshall's view of economic life, he could not throw off the shackles of Marshall's view of economic analysis. Marshall's technique was appropriate to the problem set to it: it deals informatively and with tolerable logic with the world of competitive industries and monopolies. But it is lost in the sea of diversity and unsystematism, and Chamberlin is lost with it.

Dr Triffin's failure, on the other hand, seems to me attributable to his attempt to make the general theory an accurate description of all reality. It is as if an artist is commissioned to paint the picture of a typical skyscraper: and since skyscrapers are thick and thin, of variable height, of differing colours, with various architectural designs, his painting must be blank because it would violate reality if it contained a single identifiable detail. Dr Triffin should have been warned by the Walrasian theory of general equilibrium he sought to generalize. This theory proved to be relatively uninformative, even when it had as many equations as unknowns; it was not likely to gain in usefulness when the unknowns were multiplied and the equations reduced.

4. Concluding Observations

I wish to close by offering an estimate of the net contribution of the attempt to construct a theory of monopolistic competition. Before undertaking this appraisal, however, it is necessary to set forth certain methodological principles.[10]

The purpose of the study of economics is to permit us to make predictions about the behavior of economic phenomena under specified conditions. The sole test of the usefulness of an economic theory is the concordance between its predictions and the observable course of events. Often a theory is criticized or rejected because its assumptions are 'unrealistic'. Granting for a moment that this charge has meaning, it burdens theory with

[10] The present interpretation of these principles is due to Professor Milton Friedman; see Talcott Parsons, *The Structure of Social Action*.

an additional function, that of description. This is a most unreasonable burden to place upon a theory: the rôle of description is to particularize, while the rôle of theory is to generalize – to disregard an infinite number of differences and capture the important common element in different phenomena.

But this line of argument grants the ungrantable: it is often impossible to determine whether assumption A is more or less realistic than assumption B, except by comparing the agreement between their implications and the observable course of events. One can but show that a theory is unrealistic in essentials by demonstrating that its predictions are wrong.

Should monopoly or competition be used to analyze the New York housing market? The answer is: both. If we are interested in the effects of rent ceilings and inflation, the theory of competition provides informative predictions. If we are interested in why one location rents for more than another, the theory of monopoly may be an informative guide. Different theories, each with its particular assumptions, can be applied to the same phenomena to answer different questions.

These remarks are especially relevant to the theory of monopolistic competition. A good deal of the support for this theory stems from the mistaken demand for correspondence between 'reality' and premises. The theory is further supported by the erroneous view, for which Professor Chamberlin bears some responsibility, that if the premises of competitive theory depart (in a descriptive sense) from the facts, the implications of that theory must be wrong.[11]

This leads me to the specific contribution of the theory of monopolistic competition: the analysis of the many-firm industry producing a single (technological) product under uniformity and symmetry conditions, but with a falling demand curve for each firm. Chamberlin's analysis of this particular situation is essentially correct, and many economists appear to wish to incorporate it into neo-classical theory. It should be incorporated, not if it is a more 'realistic' description of industries, but if it contains different or more accurate predictions (as tested by observation) than the theory of competition. I personally think that the predictions of this standard model of

11 'In all of the fields where individual products have even the slightest element of uniqueness, competition bears but faint resemblance to the pure competition of a highly organized market for a homogeneous product' (p. 9).

monopolistic competition differ only in unimportant respects from those of the theory of competition because the underlying conditions will usually be accompanied by very high demand elasticities for the individual firms. But this is a question of fact, and it must be resolved by empirical tests of the implications of the two theories (a task the supporters of the theory of monopolistic competition have not yet undertaken).

The general contribution of the theory of monopolistic competition, on the other hand, seems to me indisputable: it has led to reorientation and refinement of our thinking on monopoly. We are now more careful to pay attention to the logical niceties of definitions of industries and commodities. We are now more careful to apply monopoly theory where it is appropriate. The importance of the trade mark and of advertising, and the need for study of product structure and evolution, have become more generally recognized. These and other improvements may seem disappointing to the hopeful proposers of a proud new theory, but they should not be. This is the way sciences grow. One of the prominent lessons of the history of human thought is that new ideas do not lead to the abandonment of the previous heritage; the new ideas are swallowed up by the existing corpus, which is thereafter a little different. And sometimes a little better.

9 Chamberlin *versus* Chicago[1]

G. C. Archibald

In the last few years we have had something of a revolution in methodology, and the economists who have advocated the 'new methodology' have found that it gives them a powerful position from which to criticise Professor Chamberlin's theory of Monopolistic Competition.[2] Chamberlin has replied to his critics in an essay called 'The Chicago School'.[3] The object of the present paper is:

(1) to show that, whereas the 'new' or 'Chicago' methodology prescribes that theories be judged by their pre-

[1] I am greatly indebted to R. G. Lipsey for his help with this paper, an earlier draft of which was presented to the Staff Seminar on Methodology, Measurement, and Testing at the London School of Economics. I am indebted to the members of the seminar, and to many other colleagues, for their comments, and particularly to B. A. Corry, K. Klappholz, K. J. Lancaster, E. J. Mishan, Andrew Ozga, M. H. Peston and Peter O. Steiner. I have also been greatly assisted by Miles Kennedy of the Economics Research Division, London School of Economics.

[2] For the 'new methodology' we are, of course, indebted to Professor Friedman ('The Methodology of Positive Economics', in his *Essays in Positive Economics*, Chicago, 1953). Criticisms of monopolistic competition which are based on the new methodology will be found in Friedman, George J. Stigler's 'Monopolistic Competition in Retrospect' (*Five Lectures on Economic Problems*, London, 1949; pp. 131–44 above), and Alfred Sherrard's 'Advertising, Product Variation, and the Limits of Economics', *Journal of Political Economy*, LIX 2 (Apr 1951). For some criticism of Friedman's methodological position, see my 'The State of Economic Science', *British Journal for the Philosophy of Science*, x 37 (May 1959), and a forthcoming article by K. Klappholz and J. Agassi.

[3] *Towards a More General Theory of Value* (New York, 1957). It appears from the last paragraph of his defence (pp. 305–6) that Chamberlin accepts the success of its predictions as the criterion for judging a hypothesis; but he does not himself apply this criterion to monopolistic competition, any more than do his Chicago critics: hence this article. The summary of the Chicago position given here, however, follows closely that of Chamberlin, ibid., pp. 302–3. Chamberlin's reply (pp. 304–5) to the argument that monopolistic competition is peculiarly and fatally *ad hoc* I find so convincing that the question will not be re-opened here.

Reprinted from *Review of Economic Studies*, xxix (Oct 1961) 2–28, by kind permission of the author and of the Managing Editor.

dictions, the Chicago critics of monopolistic competition have in fact attacked its assumptions rather than its predictions;

(2) to find out what predictions monopolistic competition does yield;

(3) since it appears to yield so few as to be virtually empty at the traditional Robbins–Samuelson level of generality, to discover reasons for this failure. The results of this investigation may be briefly summarised: in the case of the individual firm, with advertising and quality variation, the reason is that significant predictions cannot be obtained without more information than is usually assumed or readily available. In the case of the group, even without advertising and quality variation, the reason is that the demand relations of the theory are inadequately specified.

I

The main argument of the Chicago School is roughly as follows:

(a) hypotheses should be judged by the conformity of their predictions to events, rather than by the conformity of their assumptions, in some descriptive sense, to 'reality';

(b) monopolistic competition has been preferred to perfect competition by many economists for the methodologically unsound reason that the assumptions of the former appeared to have greater realism;

(c) if we judge by predictions rather than assumptions, we shall find that perfect competition plus some Marshallian monopoly when required does as well as or better than monopolistic competition, besides saving all the complications and difficulties of the latter.

The argument of (c) really consists of two independent steps:

(1) that we know what monopolistic competition predicts;

(2) that the mixture of perfect competition and Marshallian monopoly theory is a valid construct that predicts at least as successfully as monopolistic competition.

Let us consider these steps in turn:

1. We should expect to find the Chicago critics endeavouring to discover what predictions monopolistic competition yields, comparing the predictions with those of perfect competition and monopoly, and finally addressing themselves to such empirical testing as seemed necessary. But we do not find this at all. Rather we find that much of their argument has the *a priori* character that we would associate with a very different methodological school. When we turn to Chamberlin's defence, we again fail to find any statement of predictions. The Chicago methodologists have somehow failed to make what should have been their most serious criticism of Chamberlin, that he does not state what observable, testable, predictions may be obtained from his theory. Furthermore, they themselves appear to be guilty of judging monopolistic competition, allegedly on the grounds of its predictions, without themselves knowing, or at least stating, what these predictions are. The reasons for this omission appear to be twofold. First, the extension of the theory of the firm 'in isolation' to include advertising and product variation is dismissed as merely 'an extension of Marshallian monopoly'. Perhaps it is; but it was a badly needed extension, and we need to know what predictions, if any, we can get out of it. Second, the theory of the group is supposed to suffer from such fatal defects that no predictions can be got from it. This is in fact true; but not for the reasons advanced by the Chicago School, most of whose arguments appear to be inconsistent with their own methodology (see section II below).

2. Suppose, says Friedman,[4] that the problem was to predict the effect on the price of cigarettes of an increase in the rate of indirect tax, expected to be permanent. Then treating the cigarette industry as though it were perfectly competitive would probably produce broadly correct results. If, on the other hand, the problem was to predict the reactions of cigarette firms to price control during World War II, treating the industry as perfectly competitive would not give correct answers, but '. . . this would doubtless have been recognised before the event'. Stigler takes his example from the New York housing market. If the problem is the effect of rent control, he suggests the use of a perfectly competitive model; if the problem is rent differentials, we may try the monopoly model.[5]

The casual statement that 'this would doubtless have been

---

[4] Op. cit., pp. 36–7.   [5] Op. cit., pp. 132–3 above.

recognised before the event' conceals a matter of major importance. We would normally expect to apply the models of perfect competition and monopoly to different industries, so that the problems would be of the sort 'Is agriculture sufficiently competitive for the competitive model to give good results?' and 'Do Duponts behave like profit-maximising monopolists?' Friedman and Stigler want us to apply both models to the same industry, presuming that we shall know 'before the event' which to use. But *how* are we to know? From a more complete and general theory we might be able to deduce the prediction 'For this change in data, firms will behave as though they were perfectly competitive, for that change as though they were isolated monopolists'; but in the absence of such a theory we can only proceed by the *ad hoc* application of intuition, the antithesis of scientific method. Thus we cannot test the Friedman–Stigler competition–monopoly mixture because we are not given a criterion by which to select the appropriate prediction *ex ante*, i.e. there is no theory susceptible of test.

It actually seems quite likely that, if judicious selection *ex post* from the perfectly competitive and simple monopoly models is permitted, it will be possible to reconcile 'theory' with a large range of events which refute either theory taken separately. The well-known objections to perfect competition are not exclusively concerned with the 'unreality' of its assumptions: many of them are concerned with discrepancies between prediction and observation that have been known for decades. We may recall the most famous discrepancy:[6] a perfectly competitive firm must be producing on a rising part of its marginal cost curve; it is observed that firms often are not,[7] and that businessmen state that they would like to sell more at the

[6] Cf. Piero Sraffa, 'The Laws of Returns under Competitive Conditions', *Economic Journal*, xxxvi (1926).

[7] An example of the tenacity with which Chicago economists cling to perfect competition is provided by Stigler's criticism of statistical cost curves with constant marginal costs in the short-run. He writes: '. . . If marginal costs were constant over a wide range of output and then rose steeply for each firm, the output of the competitive industry would vary in the short-run chiefly through variations in the number of plants in operation and hardly at all through variations in the rate of output of plants that stay in operation. But this is the opposite of the facts' (*The Theory of Price*, rev. ed., 1952, p. 167). Johnston remarks on this passage that the evidence can equally well be interpreted as refuting the hypothesis that the industry in question is perfectly competitive, since, if demand curves are downward sloping, there is no inconsistency (J. Johnston, *Statistical Cost Analysis*, McGraw-Hill, 1960, p. 183).

existing price if only they could. To this we may add the obvious case of advertising. It is well known that a firm in a perfectly competitive market has no occasion to advertise. This is a strong result: it is not merely that advertising is not included as a variable in the perfectly competitive model, but, categorically, that a profit maximiser in a perfectly competitive market will not advertise. But we observe that American cigarette firms do advertise. Are we not compelled to say that this prediction has failed to pass test, and that the hypothesis that American cigarette firms behave as if they were perfectly competitive is therefore refuted? Must we not in fact draw the same conclusion from Friedman's second example (and perhaps Stigler's too)?

Now what are we to make of it when Friedman and Stigler point to the occasions on which perfect competition is *not* refuted, and assure us that 'Different theories, each with its particular assumptions, can be applied to the same phenomena to answer different questions'[8] (so that, presumably, it does not matter if the theory *has* been refuted on other occasions)? It does seem that their position is involved in some difficulty. If we accept the new methodology, and propose to judge a hypothesis by the correspondence of its predictions with facts, and if one (or more) of its predictions does not correspond, can we say anything but 'the hypothesis is refuted'?[9] If, in fact, the Chicago School do not accept that the failure of a prediction to pass test constitutes a refutation of the hypothesis, it seems highly desirable that we should be told what the Chicago criterion for a refutation is. Of course, a hypothesis that makes some wrong predictions (i.e. is refuted) may also make some correct ones, and the correct ones may be useful. Thus, although perfect competition as a hypothesis about business behaviour is refuted, it is useful to know that it gives many correct results. In the same way, Newtonian physics gives many

8 Stigler, op. cit., p. 142 above.

9 '. . . we seek a decision as regards these (and other) derived statements [the predictions deduced from a theory] by comparing them with the results of practical applications and experiments. If the decision is positive, that is, if the singular conclusions turn out to be acceptable, or *verified*, then the theory has, for the time being, passed its test: we have found no reason to discard it. But if the decision is negative, or in other words, if the conclusions have been *falsified*, *then their falsification also falsifies the theory* from which they were logically deduced' (Karl R. Popper, *The Logic of Scientific Discovery*, English ed., London, 1959, p. 33). Italicisation of *verified* and *falsified* his; remainder mine.

correct, and important, results. Both perfect competition and Newtonian physics can be successfully applied to *those practical problems for which it is already known that they give correct results* (if this were not the case, we should never get anywhere, because we should learn nothing useful from hypotheses that got refuted, and we must expect that any hypothesis will be refuted sooner or later). But it is an obvious mistake to infer, from the fact that a refuted hypothesis yields some useful results, that rival hypotheses are not needed. It would be a very dangerous mistake, too: could anything more inhibit progress?

It appears, then, that the Chicago School have muddled two distinct questions. They have asked the practical, engineering question: what do we know? They have neglected to ask the enquiring, scientific question: what don't we know? And they have somehow inferred that, because the answer to the first was 'something', the second could be safely neglected, and that we could accept complacently a hypothesis which we knew could not produce satisfactory answers to all the questions we wanted to ask.

II

We now turn (as briefly as possible, in view of the large literature on the question) to the Chicago argument that monopolistic competition is not worth having because of its difficulties with the concept of a group. I shall argue here that most of the Chicago criticisms of this concept have been inconsistent with Chicago methodology because they depend upon what are essentially matters of fact, which cannot be settled *a priori*, but, according to the methodological precepts of Friedman, should be settled by testing the predictions of the theory. Thus the argument of this paper does not depend upon whether the concept of the group proves to be workable or not: it consists, in this section, of a critique of the critics, and, in section IV below, of an attempt to extract some testable predictions from group theory. I justify the attempt on the grounds that we should see what testable predictions we can get from so famous a theory when we make the best of it, i.e. suspend judgement over difficult assumptions. This justification should commend itself to Chicago methodologists.

The difficulty with the concept of a group was pointed out

by Triffin:[10] it is the difficulty of demarcation if products are not homogeneous. From *a priori* analysis we cannot distinguish between 'large' and 'small' cross-elasticities, therefore theory provides nothing intermediate between the firm and the economy.[11] This is not particularly surprising: it merely suggests that the question of whether or not there are firms that are not perfectly competitive but can usefully be treated in groups is an empirical one. This view seems so obvious, and so much in keeping with the methodology of the Chicago School (according to which we are not to worry too much about the realism of the assumptions of a theory, but to develop and test its predictions), that it is difficult to understand what all the fuss is about. It therefore seems necessary to examine Stigler's arguments with some care.

1. Stigler points out[12] that Chamberlin's original group is apparently a Marshallian industry, composed of producers of fairly close substitutes, and that

(a) the group may be one firm or the whole economy, because of asymmetry in the substitution relationships;

(b) if there are several firms in the group, the products are probably technically heterogeneous;

(c) firms outside the group probably have important effects on prices and products within the group.

These are all matters of fact, and doubtless the facts will be different for different groups. But we may notice at once how conveniently the new methodology accommodates (c). We form the hypothesis that certain firms behave as a monopolistically competitive group. We compare our predictions with

10 Robert Triffin, *Monopolistic Competition and General Equilibrium Theory* (Cambridge, Mass., 1940).

11 It is not clear how the concept of a firm survives unchallenged this attack on the concept of a group. If units of output are heterogeneous (the services of barbers or doctors, and are any two Fords *identical*, anyhow?), what analytical boundary have we between the single unit and the whole economy? This *reductio ad absurdum* may at least suggest that we should not accept too uncritically the notion that groups are impossible if products are not homogeneous. Cf. M. H. Peston, 'A View of the Aggregation Problem', *Review of Economic Studies*, xxvii 1.

12 'Monopolistic Competition in Retrospect', p. 133–4 above. Stigler actually presents the argument historically. The group as a Marshallian industry is 'The First Attempt', and the abandonment of the group, after Triffin, is 'The Second Attempt': both are supposed to be unsuccessful. I obviously agree that the second is unsuccessful, and accordingly concentrate discussion on the first.

observation. If they agree, we conclude that effects from the outside were not *sufficient in magnitude* to matter, and that the hypothesis is therefore the better for having ignored them: if they do not agree, the hypothesis is refuted.[13]

2. Stigler goes on[14] to present what appears to be an extremely damaging argument, that we cannot have downward sloping demand curves *and* the tangency solution together, and that if we drop the former we have perfect competition, while if we lose the latter we lose the equilibrium condition for the group and therefore the ability to do comparative statics. The reason advanced is that the tangency solution in monopolistic competition requires two assumptions, 'uniformity' and 'symmetry', which, Stigler argues, are inconsistent with downward sloping demand curves. 'Uniformity' is Chamberlin's 'heroic assumption' of identical cost and demand curves throughout the group. This, according to Stigler, is meaningless unless the products are homogeneous, in which case we have horizontal demand curves. 'Symmetry' is the assumption that the effects of an adjustment by any one firm are so evenly spread round the group that no single firm need be expected to react. This assumption is held to be inconsistent with marked heterogeneity of products; but, if we drop it, we have oligopoly instead of monopolistic competition.

These arguments appear to be formidable, but let us examine each with care.[15]

(a) The uniformity assumption

(i) Stigler asserts that uniformity requires homogeneity. He writes: 'We simply cannot attach meaning to the statement that physically diverse things have the same price.'[16] This, if it were true, would dispose of much of economics, including the whole idea of opportunity cost. According to Stigler, it is not only meaningless to say 'A theatre ticket and a bottle of

[13] This is what I, at any rate, understand the new methodology to say on a question of this sort. Cf. Friedman's discussion of the 'perfect vacuum' assumption in the hypothesis about falling bodies ('The Methodology of Positive Economics', pp. 16–18).

[14] Op. cit., pp. 137–8 above.

[15] I must confess that I used to think these much more powerful arguments than I do now (my ' "Large" and "Small" Numbers in the Theory of the Firm', *Manchester School*, xxvii 1 (Jan 1959)).

[16] Op. cit., p. 137 above. The argument offered here closely follows Chamberlin's (op. cit., pp. 300–1).

burgundy cost the same. Which shall I have this evening?'; it is even meaningless to say 'A seat at each of these theatres costs the same. To which shall I go?' I assert that it is meaningful to say 'The direct costs of a packet of Camels and a packet of Luckies are equal'. Whether it is true or not is a matter of fact. But suppose that it is not quite true. Do we now give up in despair? Once again, the new methodology[17] provides a solution to our difficulties. There is no *a priori* way of saying whether an inequality of given magnitude matters. The way to proceed is to form the hypothesis, ignore the inequality, and test the predictions. We shall learn from the test if the inequality matters enough to refute the hypothesis.

(ii) The problem of uniformity and homogeneity has already been discussed by Kaldor,[18] who pointed out that identical demand curves are not necessary: if elasticities are different, tangency can occur with different firms selling at different prices. He also argued that identical cost curves need only mean that there is no institutional monopoly, so that each producer *could* produce each product at the same cost. Unfortunately it turns out that institutional monopoly here in-

---

[17] The reader is again referred to Friedman – who, incidentally, agrees with Stigler's anti-group arguments ('The Methodology of Positive Economics', pp. 38–9, and n. 38).

[18] Many of the problems discussed in this section were analysed by Kaldor in the 1930s ('Mrs Robinson's *Economics of Imperfect Competition*', *Economica* (Aug 1934), 'Market Imperfection and Excess Capacity', *Economica* (Feb 1935), and 'Professor Chamberlin on Monopolistic and Imperfect Competition', *Quarterly Journal of Economics* (May 1938), all reprinted in his *Essays on Value and Distribution*, London, 1960, to which I shall refer here). Besides the point quoted above, Kaldor's main arguments were:

(1) An industry can only be defined by gaps in the chain of substitutes. But if substitutes are arranged in a chain or series, some firms within an industry are closer than others, in which case the symmetry assumption will not hold.

(2) Products of the same industry may be imperfect substitutes for three reasons: (*a*) physical differences, (*b*) spatial differences, (*c*) buyers' inertia. (*a*) and (*b*) are probably inconsistent with symmetry; and (*c*) is unlikely to be found alone.

(3) If substitutes are a chain or series, entry will not have symmetrical effects, and, given indivisibilities, entry will not eliminate the monopoly profits of all firms. Thus tangency depends on the unrealistic symmetry assumption.

These are powerful arguments; but what is, of course, not established is whether, in fact, the lack of symmetry in real-world industries is of such significance that the predictions of monopolistic competition will be refuted. The main difference between Kaldor and Chicago on these matters appears to be that, when Kaldor wrote, the 'new methodology' was not current, whereas the Chicago writers are largely responsible for making it current.

cludes patents, copyrights, and trade marks – distinctive features of monopolistic competition. But, once again, this does not establish *a priori* that cost differences are sufficient in magnitude for the predictions of the theory to be refuted.

(iii) In fact the matter of patents, copyrights, brand names, etc., is worth further examination. The income accruing from the ownership of such things is a rent or quasi-rent.[19] Full equilibrium in perfect competition requires that all firms have the same minimum average cost, which involves imputing as rent (an element of fixed cost) the 'profit' accruing from, e.g., unusual entrepreneurial ability. There does not seem to be any reason why the same treatment should not be carried over to rents in monopolistic competition. If this is done, the normal-profit equilibrium condition (tangency solution) is re-established even in the presence of patents, copyrights, and so on. Now abnormal profit is uniquely associated with disequilibrium caused by changes in demand or factor supply. It is not now certain, however, that disequilibrium causes exit or entry: it may merely cause a revaluation of rent-earning factors and an appropriate alteration of fixed cost by the firms in the industry. In the same way, of course, if all land is taken up, and the demand for agricultural produce increases, we predict an increase in rent but no entry, i.e. no increase in the number of farmers. This, however, is an unambiguous prediction based on the fixed supply of land, whereas in the case of monopolistic competition it appears to be an ambiguity: if demand increases, we do not know whether to predict new entry, or merely increased rents for patent-holders, or both. The prediction must, however, depend on whether or not new patents, trade names, etc., which are 'near enough substitutes' can *in fact* be developed. If they can, we have a case of quasi-rent and predict entry; if they cannot, we are dealing with a genuine case of fixity of supply and pure rent: entry is impossible. In the former case, which is the one we are concrned with, there seems to be no insuperable objection to the normal-profit equilibrium condition, and Chamberlin's 'heroic assumptions' do not appear to be strictly necessary.

[19] This point is made by Harrod (Sir R. F. Harrod, 'The Theory of Profit', in *Economic Essays*, 1952).

(b) The symmetry assumption

This, like the uniformity assumption, is really a matter of fact: we can only discover whether there are groups for which our neglect of oligopolistic interdependence is justified by testing predictions.

One is left with the feeling that, in these objections to the concept of a group, Stigler and Friedman are being inconsistent with their own methodological principles. Neither uniformity nor symmetry are descriptively accurate; but we are told by Friedman[20] that we should judge a hypothesis, not by the descriptive accuracy of its assumptions, but by the accuracy of its predictions. Furthermore, Friedman accepts the perfectly competitive group for analysing the behaviour of cigarette manufacturers, and Stigler accepts it for analysing the New York housing market. Why, then, do they experience such difficulty with the unrealistic assumptions of the monopolistically competitive group?

3. Sherrard, the other critic to whom Chamberlin applied the title 'Chicago School', argues for the most part along very much the same lines as Stigler. He does have, however, some novel arguments which we may consider. To the usual *a priori* objections to monopolistic competition, he adds the following: that the analysis of selling costs is bound to fail because the results of advertising are unpredictable, there being no functional relationship between selling costs and sales.[21] This is, of course, a purely *a priori* assertion about a matter of fact. We obviously proceed (as Chamberlin does) by forming a hypothesis which involves a functional relationship between selling costs and sales, and then testing it (which neither Chamberlin nor Sherrard do). Sherrard concludes that monopolistic competition cannot overcome the difficulties presented by product differentiation and selling costs, and suggests that there is a fundamental reason for this. Economics is about scarcity, the relationship between given means and given wants. The effect of product differentiation and advertising is to vary wants: hence the problems of monopolistic competition are outside the scope of economics.[22] If this were true, the reaction of anyone

---

[20] Stigler explicitly states that his general methodological position agrees with Friedman's (op. cit., p. 142 above, n. 10).
[21] Op. cit., pp. 135–6.   [22] Ibid., p. 141.

who wanted to know about the world would be 'so much the worse for economics'; but, fortunately, it is not true. In the first place, *a priori* assertions about the future success of untested hypotheses are not evidence. In the second place, the problem can easily be turned into an ends–means one: the entrepreneur has a limited command over resources (means), his end is profit, and the problem is how he can best deploy the resources to obtain the end. In the third place, variability of wants does not alter the fact of scarcity: it just makes the problems more difficult.

III

We now at last arrive at the enquiry to which the methodology of the Chicago School should have led at once: what testable predictions can we derive from the theory of monopolistic competition? If we want testable predictions, we must know how things change (it is not easy to see how we can hope to observe equilibrium conditions, although there are at least two well-known cases: the refutation of perfect competition by the observation that the rising-marginal-cost condition is not normally fulfilled, and the search for excess capacity in equilibrium). A static theory associates equilibrium values of the variables with given values of the parameters. We therefore attempt to derive predictions about associated changes: 'if this parameter increases (decreases), this variable increases (decreases)'. This is the familiar method of comparative statics.[23] Comparative statics may, however, be carried out at different levels of generality, with or without quantitative information about the functions of the system. The traditional programme of economics, what I call the Robbins–Samuelson[24] programme, is to endeavour to obtain qualitative predictions (direction of change) with only qualitative restrictions upon the functions. Thus we hope to obtain results by qualitative comparative

[23] The empirical testing of a comparative static prediction in general requires that we add a subsidiary dynamic assumption about the speed of response. Testing by trying to observe the fulfilment of equilibrium conditions, however, presents an even worse difficulty: we have to be prepared to say when the unit is in equilibrium.

[24] Samuelson gave this programme formal expression in his *Foundations* (Paul A. Samuelson, *Foundations of Economic Analysis*, Cambridge, Mass., 1947), but it is in the tradition of Marshall, and was given clear verbal expression by Robbins (see, for example, the discussion of statistical and quantitative work in chap. v of L. C. Robbins, *The Nature and Significance of Economic Science*, 2nd ed., London, 1935).

statics, what Samuelson called the 'qualitative calculus'. He wrote:

> The method of *comparative statics* consists of the study of the response of our equilibrium unknowns to designated changes in parameters. . . . *In the absence of complete quantitative information concerning our equilibrium equations, it is hoped to be able to formulate qualitative restrictions on slopes, curvatures, etc., of our equilibrium equations so as to be able to derive definite qualitative restrictions upon the responses of our system to changes in certain parameters.*[25]

The sentence I have italicised in fact describes something narrower than comparative statics: it describes specifically the programme of *qualitative comparative statics*, the hope that it will be possible to predict directions of change without quantitative information. Samuelson further described this programme:

> In cases where the equilibrium values of our variables can be regarded as the solutions of an extremum (maximum or minimum) problem, it is often possible regardless of the number of variables involved to determine unambiguously the qualitative behaviour of our solution values in respect to changes in parameters.[26]

The purpose of this section is to apply the method of comparative statics to the model of a profit-maximising firm 'in isolation', taking advertising and quality variation into consideration, in order to discover whether any *qualitative* predictions can be obtained. The conclusion is that, at this traditional level of generality, the model is almost empty: significant *qualitative* predictions cannot be obtained without *quantitative* information. As far as possible, the reasons for this failure will be explained in the text, but more detailed discussion and proofs must be left to the Mathematical Appendix to this section (pp. 175–82 below). In general, however, it appears that whether or not the qualitative method yields significant results depends upon the structure of the model in question.

Now to explore the qualitative content of Chamberlin's model, we must carry out the comparative static exercises so familiar from the study of perfect competition and Marshallian monopoly: we want to know the effects on price, quantity,

---

25 *Foundations*, p. 20. Italicisation of the second sentence mine.
26 Ibid., p. 21. Italicised in the original.

quality, advertising expenditure, etc., of changes in demand, factor prices, tax rates, and so on. It is indeed surprising that this should be necessary now, about a quarter of a century after *The Theory of Monopolistic Competition* was first published: perhaps the fact that it is is the most serious criticism of both Chamberlin and his Chicago critics. But we cannot find predictions in Chamberlin's book for the simple reason that we cannot find the necessary comparative statics; and, when we try to do comparative statics, we find another handicap. If we want to do comparative static analysis on a system involving three (or more) variables, we must have the equilibrium conditions relating all three at once. But these Chamberlin does not present: instead, he illustrates the relationships between the variables a pair at a time. All we can really get from Chamberlin is that there will be a maximum, and that, at this maximum, all the necessary marginal equalities will hold, i.e.the conditions for a maximum will obtain.[27]

Many of the comparative static exercises presented below have, of course, been done by other writers: it would be ridiculous to pretend that the analysis here is all, or even mostly, original. Yet there has been a general tendency, in the literature on monopolistic competition, to ignore comparative statics, and to concentrate instead on alternative diagrammatic illustrations of familiar equilibrium conditions. There may, however, be a general reason for this: since the theory, broadly speaking, does not yield unambiguous predictions, many economists, concerned with a specific application or problem, and failing to obtain a prediction, may have given up the problem, instead of realising that they had discovered something of general importance. Even Hahn,[28] who has recently

---

[27] This is about all we get from Brems, too (Hans Brems, *Product Equilibrium under Monopolistic Competition*, Cambridge, Mass., 1951). To be told at length that there are equilibria (at which the marginal equalities hold) is not much help when we want testable predictions. Even a full statement of equilibrium conditions is valuable chiefly as a prerequisite to comparative statics.

[28] F. H. Hahn, 'The Theory of Selling Costs', *Economic Journal*, LXIX 274 (June 1959), and 'The Theory of Selling Costs: A Correction', ibid. (Dec 1959). I entirely subscribe to his opening remarks (p. 293): 'The literature on this subject [selling cost, price, and output decisions] is quite large. It appears to suffer from two deficiencies: it has not produced a simple diagrammatic technique to represent the decisions in question and it does not contain an adequate statement of the second-order conditions of a maximum. These two defects are related, since a major part of the writings in this field are "geometrical", and the non-availability of simple diagrams has led to a neglect of second-order conditions. Without these,

made a systematic and most welcome attack on the comparative
static properties of the model, has failed to point out to what
extent his results depend on particular restrictive assumptions
which are not altogether obvious, and he thus failed to point
out that it is nearly impossible to obtain qualitative predictions
from the model without quantitative information. It therefore
seems worthwhile to present the analysis *de novo*; and this has
the additional advantages of autonomy and consistency of
treatment.

In this section I shall attempt the comparative static analysis
for a single profit-maximising firm that advertises and varies
the quality of its output, treating the firm in isolation; in the
next section, I shall investigate the comparative static properties
of Chamberlinian groups. Since there are at least three variables,
price, quantity, and advertising expenditure or quality, the
traditional methods of two-dimensional and verbal analysis are
hardly adequate. I shall do what I can with them in the text,
however, and relegate proofs to a mathematical appendix.

1. Consider first the effects of an increase in demand on a
firm that advertises but does not vary quality. It is well known
that, even in the case of a simple, or Marshallian, monopolist,
who does not advertise, the information that the revenue
function has shifted to the right is insufficient to determine the
direction of the price change. In the two-dimensional case,
total revenue and output will increase,[29] and we may expect
them to in the three-dimensional case as well. None of this is
much help: we do not obtain a testable prediction about price,
and the association of revenue and quantity when demand
changes is likely to be produced by any plausible theory.
Similarly, we cannot say in which direction advertising changes:
if the demand surface shifts out, but we know nothing of the
way in which it has been bent or tilted, we can no more say
how advertising (a way of obtaining revenue) will change than

---

however, the theory cannot be applied to an examination of such questions as the
effects of excise taxes and/or of sales-cost taxes on the decisions of the firm, nor can
the theory be said to be complete.' He therefore sets out to provide a simple
diagrammatic technique, and to examine these questions. If only I found the
diagrammatic technique simple! The second-order conditions here are left to the
Mathematical Appendix.

[29] An increase in output involves an increase in total costs, and is therefore not
worth undertaking unless, as a necessary but not sufficient condition, the increased
output yields an increased total revenue.

we can say how price (another way of obtaining revenue) will change.

2. Still limiting ourselves to the case of advertising without quality variation, let us now consider the effect of variations in factor prices. To do this it is convenient to introduce a new concept, that of a 'factor of revenue'. Since revenue is a function of both the quantity of output and the quantity of advertising, I call both output and advertising 'factors of revenue'. If advertising is held constant, but output increased, revenue is also increased (so long as the demand curve appropriate to the given level of advertising is elastic, as it must be in the neighbourhood of a profit-maximising equilibrium), and if output is held constant, but advertising is increased, revenue is also increased (because the price which will clear the market of a given output is increased). Thus output and advertising may be treated as substitutable factors of revenue, and for any given outlay, which may be devoted to advertising and output in different combinations, there will be a revenue-maximising combination.[30] An increase in a factor price has the effect of making the factor of revenue, output, relatively more expensive; an increase in the price of the advertising medium makes the factor of revenue, advertising, relatively more expensive. There is obviously a close analogy here with the theory of production.[31] We know, however, that, while an increase in the

---

[30] There is an obvious sense in which sales and advertising are complementary: if advertising is increased, sales are. But this involves increased total outlay; the point here is that they are alternative uses for any given total outlay.

[31] I do not rely on the analogy with the theory of production: proofs of the propositions asserted here will be found in the Appendix. A diagrammatic technique may, however, be suggested. If advertising is measured on one axis and output on the other, iso-revenue curves and constant outlay curves may obviously be constructed, and the usual diagrammatic analysis carried out. In this case, however, there are difficulties over both the convexity of the revenue function and the concavity of the outlay function, the former due to what Hicks called the 'cross-effects' (*Value and Capital*, pp. 14–15), and the latter due to the possibility of 'bulk discounts' for advertising, increasing returns, etc. We may expect, and assume, diminishing marginal revenue to both advertising and output, but this is neither necessary nor sufficient for convexity: sufficient (but not necessary) conditions are that an increase in output does not diminish marginal revenue with respect to advertising, and vice versa. We cannot assert *a priori* that the necessary conditions must be satisfied, and thus exclude the possibility of multiple equilibria, but it seems best at this stage to assume a unique and stable equilibrium and see what, if anything, follows. For convexity conditions see R. G. D. Allen, *Mathematical Analysis for Economists* (London, 1938) pp. 340–5, and for the analogous propositions in the theory of production see ibid., pp. 369–74.

price of one factor leads to substitution in favour of the other, there is an 'income effect' against both, so that we cannot say how employment of the relatively cheaper factor changes without further knowledge. Employment of the relatively more expensive factor must fall, but, unless we know what happens to the relatively cheaper factor, we cannot even obtain a prediction about the direction of change in the ratio in which the two factors are combined. In fact, if we neglect 'cross-effects', we can predict that employment of the cheaper factor falls too, but this is still not enough to predict the change in the factor ratio (for which we require the initial proportions, and the relative effects on revenue of a change in each). The effects of an increase in the price of the advertising medium (investigated in the Appendix) are similarly unpredictable. The amount of advertising goes down; the direction of change in the quantity of output is predicted only if 'cross-effects' are neglected; the change in advertising expenditure per unit of output depends on the initial levels of, and changes in, both, and cannot therefore be generally predicted. Furthermore, *in neither case can the direction of change in price be predicted*, even if cross-effects are ignored. The reason is intuitively fairly obvious: a reduction in output, caused by an increase in a factor price, tends to push price up; the associated reduction in advertising tends to push it down; which force proves stronger depends on *relative magnitudes*, and cannot be predicted from purely qualitative considerations. Exactly the same argument applies, *mutatis mutandis*, in the case of an increase in the price of the advertising medium.

3. We now consider the effects of changes in tax rates. A specific indirect tax can be treated as an increase in the cost of the factor of revenue, output (since it varies with the quantity produced and nothing else). It is therefore completely analogous with the case of an increase in a factor price, just discussed, and yields no more results. An *ad valorem* tax is more complicated: it alters the relationship between both factors and revenue. In the two-dimensional, no-advertising case, we analyse it by moving the demand curve inwards and changing its slope. In this case a three-dimensional demand surface is moved inwards and changed in slope. Clearly, unless we know something about the effects on the rate of substitution between the factors advertising and output, and their relative costs (if physical

returns are variable, the relative expensiveness of output and advertising *must* change as the quantity of the former changes), it is going to be difficult to say much. In fact, if we cannot ignore 'cross-effects', we cannot obtain, in this case, any predictions whatever about the direction of change in the variables. Neglecting the cross-effect, then both advertising and output fall, but the change in price is still undetermined. The fall in quantity leads one to expect a higher price, the fall in advertising a lower, and, without knowledge of the relative strengths of their effects on demand and costs, it is impossible to predict the net result.[32]

4. Let us now consider the effects of changes in the data on the choice of product, assuming for simplicity that the firm does not advertise. Unfortunately most of the discussion of product differentiation has been only in terms of 'near' and 'far': it has been argued, for example, that firms will endeavour to create 'private markets', and use all the techniques of product differentiation, branding, and advertising, to separate these markets. An argument of this sort does not, however, constitute a model. If we ask: will a change in demand (or costs, or taxes) cause firms to produce closer or less close substitutes? we are simply not in a position to start to answer it.[33] If an object of monopolistic competition is to handle product differentiation in the sense of 'near' and 'far', it fails. Not only are there no testable implications, there is no theory from which we might try to derive them. Let us see, then, if we can do anything with less ambitious questions by confining ourselves to a model in which we have a continuous index of quality. The necessary assumptions are discussed by Dorfman and Steiner,[34] who consider '. . . a firm which produces a differentiated product whose quality can be measured (e.g. in terms of

---

[32] Hahn, op. cit., p. 307, appears to obtain more definite results. They appear to be due to his assumption (p. 296, n. 3; but see also the 'Correction', which is unfortunately rather obscure) that the 'cross-effects' are negligible. He says that 'the contract effect ["income" effect of the tax] will normally tend to raise prices, but in one instance it will reinforce the substitution effect in lowering prices'. In the next paragraph he speaks of price (and output) as being 'in fact' reduced by the tax. I am in some doubt as to what his conclusion actually is.

[33] Chamberlin suggests (*Towards a More General Theory of Value*, chaps. 3 and 6) that the analysis of spatial competition may provide answers to analogous questions.

[34] Robert Dorfman and Peter O. Steiner, 'Optimal Advertising and Optimal Quality', *American Economic Review*, XLIV 5 (Dec 1954).

horsepower, tensile strength, denier, etc.) and whose rate of sales per unit of time . . . is a continuous and differentiable function of price . . . and a quality index . . .'. They further assume that the cost of production is a continuous and differentiable function of the quality index.[35] This model cannot be used to investigate the effects of changes in factor prices that change the relative costs of different qualities, because they will alter the cost function, but it can be used to investigate the effects of changes, such as indirect taxes, that are independent of quality. (Dorfman and Steiner, following the usual tradition, confined themselves to an elegant investigation of some properties of the equilibrium conditions of the model: they did not enquire into its predictive ability.)

It is intuitively obvious that the comparative static analysis must be very similar to that of advertising: output and quality can be treated as substitutable factors of revenue; and the effect of an indirect tax is to raise the price of the factor output. Consider first a specific indirect tax. In the advertising case, neglecting cross-effects was a sufficient condition for predicting the direction of change in advertising but not in price; in this case, similarly, if we neglect cross-effects, we obtain the prediction that quality deteriorates, but still cannot predict the direction of change in price, which is pushed up by the reduction in output, and down by the deterioration in quality. Consider now an *ad valorem* tax. The intuitive expectation is that an *ad valorem* tax will cause a deterioration in quality (i.e. a concealed price increase), leaving the direction of the price change undetermined (lower quantity – price up; lower quality – price down). Once again, even this result can only be obtained if we ignore cross-effects.[36]

---

[35] Ibid., pp. 831–2.

[36] One other possible way of obtaining a prediction about product changes occurs to me. Suppose that a firm has two varieties of product which are substitutes in demand. Then they will also be substitutes in revenue, and the analysis is again similar to that of advertising. The firm produces all of one or some of both. If a change in the data causes one to become relatively more expensive, then, if both are produced, we expect that relatively less of the now more expensive one will be produced. If only one is produced, then, if any change in produce occurs, it must be in favour of the now relatively cheaper variety. This is an obvious result; but if we cannot also point to changes in the data that will change the relative costs of the varieties, it is trivial too. The result of a change in a specific indirect tax is not certain: it changes the cost of units of both varieties equally. Similarly, the result of a change in an *ad valorem* tax is not certain: its results are unpredictable unless the demand surface is fully specified. All we can say is that, if one variety

5. Finally, consider the case in which we have both advertising and quality variation of the Dorfman–Steiner type. The results are fairly obvious: in the case of a specific tax, quantity falls, but the change in advertising and quality cannot be predicted without ignoring cross-effects; in the case of an *ad valorem* tax we cannot even predict a quantity fall without ignoring cross-effects; in neither case can we predict the direction of change in price without knowing which is stronger, the upward push from the fall in output or the downward push from the fall in advertising and quality.

I think it will be agreed that these results are very meagre. The difficulty with this part of monopolistic competition (or Chamberlin's extension of Marshallian monopoly theory, as we choose to call it) is not that the assumptions are 'wrong', but that, at the traditional level of generality, the implications are few and those few trivial. The implications we have obtained amount to little more than that if quantity, quality, or advertising be made more expensive, there will be less of it! The theory is not totally empty, but very nearly so. (Of course there may be some cases, some parameter shifts, that I have not tried and for which the results are unambiguous. I can offer no 'impossibility theorem': I can only show my own lack of success, and show that there are general reasons for it.) As it stands, however, this model of the firm will not provide an unambiguous answer to such a question as 'In what direction are the variables changed by an increase in a specific indirect tax?' Samuelson remarks that 'it is a poor theory indeed that will not answer so simple a question'.[37]

Before we agree with Samuelson, let us consider the reasons for the failure. The programme of qualitative economics is, in fact, an extremely ambitious one – to deduce directions of change from little more than the traditional assumptions that physical returns must diminish at *some* level of output, that returns to advertising must diminish at *some* level of advertising, and that

---

uses relatively more of a factor than the other, a change in the price of that factor will increase the cost of the first variety relative to the second, and we therefore expect it to diminish the ratio of the output of the first to the second. This result may not be trivial, but it is very obvious. It is the only comparative static result in the field of product differentiation that I have so far found, apart from the meagre results obtained from the Dorfman–Steiner model.

[37] *Foundations*, p. 15.

demand curves slope down. It seems that we might blame the methodology that led us to expect 'something for nothing' (or very nearly nothing) rather than the theory that failed to provide it. All that has happened, after all, is that monopolistic competition has proved to be barren at a level of generality at which perhaps we should not expect much. Of course, the programme has been relatively successful in simple cases – Marshallian monopoly and perfect competition; but in both these cases the number of variables is smaller, and, in the second case, there are particularly convenient restrictions on the demand and cost functions for the individual firm. The qualitative calculus has failed in the Chamberlin case simply because the relations between the variables and the parameters are such that the traditional qualitative restrictions are not sufficient. Samuelson showed how this could happen;[38] and it is familiar from the theories of demand and production – whenever substitution and income effects work in opposite directions, the results depend on relative magnitudes.

It is clear that purely qualitative assumptions may very often prove inadequate, and this has a methodological moral: we must give theory some facts[39] to help it to predict more facts.

[38] Samuelson wrote (*Foundations*, p. 19):

'In general, we should not expect to be able to determine the signs of the rates of change of our variables upon the basis of simple *a priori* qualitative restrictions on our equilibrium equations. . . . [This is because] the restrictions imposed by our hypothesis on our equilibrium conditions (stability and maximum conditions, etc.) are not always sufficient to indicate *definite* restrictions as to algebraic sign of the rates of change of our variables with respect to any parameter.

'Only imagine a change in a parameter which enters into all of a large number of equilibrium equations causing them simultaneously to shift. The resulting net effect upon our variables could only be calculated as a result of balancing the separate effects (regarded as limiting rates of change), and for this purpose detailed quantitative values for all the coefficients involved would have to be known.'

Nonetheless, he expected great things from the qualitative calculus!

[39] In the absence of empirical evidence, restrictions on the functions are sometimes assumed because they are convenient, or 'seem reasonable' (cf. Hahn, op. cit.). The trouble with this procedure is that, if the prediction that follows is then refuted by empirical test, we have no means of telling whether the fault lies with the theory or the particular restriction chosen. Similarly, if a prediction obtained by arbitrarily neglecting 'cross-effects' is refuted, we have no means of telling where the fault lies. Restrictions are also sometimes chosen in order to make the theory predict something already known to be true. Unless there is some means of checking empirically on the restriction chosen, this procedure guarantees the theory against refutation!

A failure of the Robbins–Samuelson programme is not necessarily a disaster: we learn from the analysis how much (or little) qualitative content a theory has, and what sort of empirical work is required to increase its testable content.

IV

The problem of this section is to derive some comparative static predictions from the analysis of the group. This we can attempt without necessarily settling all the difficult questions about symmetry, uniformity, etc. We are simply asking the question: *given* a Chamberlin group, what predictions follow?[40] This seems to be the easiest way of settling the controversy. If no predictions do emerge, we require a new or modified theory; if some are obtained, we have an opportunity of referring the whole matter to the test of fact. As it turns out, we do not obtain any comparative static predictions: we have a failure as complete as that of the last section. The reason is simply that the theory is incomplete: in the absence of a specified relationship between DD' (the 'share-of-the-market' demand curve) and dd' (the 'partial' demand curve), we have not even the minimum of qualitative information necessary for comparative statics. In an attempt to complete the theory I therefore introduce a relationship between DD' and dd' suggested by Kaldor; but even this proves to be insufficient to give the theory comparative static content.

On the assumption that interdependence is ignored, the short-run predictions would be those of the last section – if the last section had yielded any. What we want now is to extend the analysis to the long-run in which the number of firms and the size of plant are allowed to change. It is obvious that the introduction of advertising and product differentiation (remember that we still have no *theory* of product differentiation as a

[40] It has been suggested that, since Chamberlin has apparently 'abandoned' the group, under the influence of Triffin's criticisms, this investigation is unnecessary. I have argued in section II above that many of the criticisms appear to be misdirected; but this is really beside the point: we have the theory of the group (from Mrs Robinson as well as Chamberlin) and we want to know what can be got out of it. It has also been suggested that Harrod's modifications to the theory render this enquiry otiose. But Harrod ('The Theory of Imperfect Competition Revised', in *Economic Essays*) in fact constructed a different model by dropping the assumption of short-run profit maximisation. The comparative static properties of his model might well be investigated; but its existence is irrelevant to the comparative static properties of Chamberlin's model.

form of inter-firm competition) will cause serious analytical difficulties even if they are not actually fatal to the predictive power of the theory. I shall therefore start by attempting to obtain some comparative static results for a group, ignoring advertising and the possibility of product change – that is, by trying to obtain some predictions from the model in the simplest possible case in which the difficulties are minimised.

(1) What we now want is to answer questions of the following sort: when the number of firms is allowed to change, what are the effects on prices, size of plant, etc., of a change in demand? Of a change in costs? Of a change in tax? Remembering our defeat in the last section, where we considered the short-run adjustment of a single firm, let us try the effect of an increase in demand. It is well known that, at full equilibrium, the long-run average cost curve (LRAC) must be downward sloping (because this is tangential to the short-run average cost curve (SRAC) by construction, and the latter must be downward sloping).[41] From this we appear to have two results: first, that, so long as *dd'* curves are downward sloping, we have unexploited economies of scale as well as excess capacity; and, second, that the long-run price must fall with increased demand. The first will be further discussed below; the second Kaldor has already shown to be wrong. The *DD'* curves are moved to the right by the increased demand, and returned to the left by new entry. What happens to size of plant and price depends entirely on what happens to the elasticity of the *dd'* curves as *DD'* moves, i.e. on the effect of changing market size and share on the 'partial' demand curves for the individual firms.[42] Until some restrictions are imposed on the behaviour of *dd'* as *DD'* moves, anything can happen.

Let us now try the effects of a change in costs, taking again the simplest possible case, a specific indirect tax which raises the SRAC curves everywhere by the same amount, as illustrated in Fig. 9.1, where the initial equilibrium is at *Q* and the tax is

---

[41] See Kaldor, 'Market Imperfection and Excess Capacity', in *Essays on Value and Distribution*, p. 63, n. 1, and Harrod, 'Doctrines of Imperfect Competition', in *Economic Essays*, esp. p. 127.

[42] Cf. Kaldor: 'The effect of the entry of new competitors will not necessarily reduce the price of existing products; it may even raise them. The profits which the entrepreneur no longer earns will thus not be passed on to the consumer in the form of lower prices but are mainly absorbed in lower productive efficiency' (op. cit., p. 65).

QM per unit. If we confine ourselves to parallel shifts in *dd'*, as Chamberlin does, tangency will occur at *M*, and the intersection of *dd'* with *DD'* (which is the locus of attainable positions) will occur at a point such as *T*, below the SRAC + *t* curve. Hence no full equilibrium is possible until the number of firms is reduced, and *DD'* shifted to the right. But how far

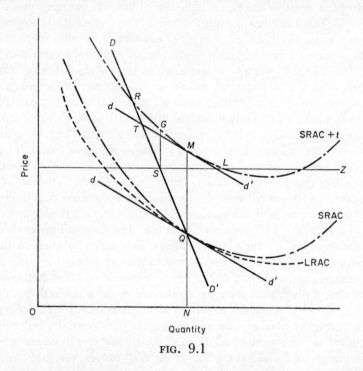

FIG. 9.1

must it shift? What happens to *dd'* as *DD'* shifts? If we retain the parallelism assumption, full equilibrium is only possible at *M*, when the price has risen by the full amount of the tax; but there is no *a priori* reason why we should assume parallelism,[43]

---

[43] We may easily work out the elasticity implications of parallelism. Consider first horizontal displacements of *dd'* caused by shifts in *DD'*: parallelism means that the further to the right is *dd'* (the bigger the firm's market), the lower is its elasticity at any price. Consider now the elasticity of *dd'* as it slides down a given *DD'* curve: parallelism means that the elasticity at the point of intersection with *DD'* is lower the lower is *dd'* (slope unchanged, price lower, quantity greater), i.e. that the elasticity of the particular demand curve is lower the lower the market price. Either or both of these implications may correspond with the facts of a given case; but there is no *a priori* reason for supposing that they must.

and, if we drop it, anything can happen.[44] It is even possible to secure a tangency at *R*, in which case normal profits are still earned, there is no immediate reason for exit, but plants are too large. In general, as *DD'* is moved to the right by the elimination of firms, *dd'* may become flatter, in which case equilibrium will be found to the right of *M*, or steeper, with equilibrium to the left of *M*. Thus the tax may make price increase more or less than the tax in the long and in the short run, and may make plants increase or diminish in size.

From the standpoint of comparative statics, this is a complete failure. The model is empty because it is incomplete: in the absence of a relation between *dd'* and *DD'* anything can happen.

(2) Let us now consider the relationship between the elasticity of the *dd'* curves and the number of firms in the group suggested by Kaldor.[45] Since the theory is empty without such a relationship, it seems to be worth finding out at once whether its addition is sufficient for the theory to yield some results.[46] Kaldor argues that an increase in the number of firms, by increasing the number of products in the group, increases the 'density' of the field of substitutes, and that this must increase the elasticity of demand for each individual product. This does not immediately establish a relationship between *dd'* and *DD'*. If *DD'* moves to the right because of an increase in total market demand, the changes in *dd'* are still unspecified. Now, however, we expect the increased demand to attract new firms, making

[44] See Otto von Mering, *The Shifting and Incidence of Taxation* (Philadelphia, 1942) pp. 71–7, for equally unsuccessful attempts to obtain any predictions from the model in this case, and substantially the same argument that is presented above.

[45] Kaldor, 'Market Imperfection and Excess Capacity', *Economica* (1935) and particularly 'Professor Chamberlin on Monopolistic and Imperfect Competition', *Quarterly Journal of Economics* (1938), both reprinted in the *Essays on Value and Distribution*. I attribute the idea to Kaldor, although it appears from Chamberlin's remarks that it may have been generally current in the 1930s, because it is explicitly set out and easily accessible in his work.

[46] Chamberlin rejects this relation, apparently on the grounds that the size or area of a market cannot be distinguished from the density with which it is populated. See his 'Monopolistic or Imperfect Competition?', *Quarterly Journal of Economics* (1937), which Kaldor criticised in the 1938 article, and his 'Reply' to Kaldor in 1938 (these two papers form the substance of chap. ix of current editions of *The Theory of Monopolistic Competition*). My object here is not to try to settle the argument between Chamberlin and Kaldor (although, in fact, I find Kaldor's arguments most persuasive); it is merely to see if, when a serious deficiency in Chamberlin's theory is filled by Kaldor's relation, any results are then forthcoming.

dd', on Kaldor's argument, more elastic as *DD'* shifts back to
the left. We cannot, of course, tell whether it is more or less
elastic than it originally was because the intermediate shift is
unspecified. Hence, in order to give Kaldor's idea a trial, we
must confine ourselves to cases in which the number of firms
changes while total market demand does not. Then *DD'* is
shifted purely by the changed number of firms: and Kaldor's
relation is that, as *DD'* moves to the right (reduced number of
firms), the *dd'* curves become less elastic.

We now require a case in which the number of firms changes
but total market demand does not, i.e. one in which the change
results from a change in costs. The easiest cost change to handle
is again a specific excise tax. Suppose that we again start from
full equilibrium, at *Q* in Fig. 9.1, and raise the SRAC curve by
the imposition of a specific excise tax. Until and unless the
number of firms changes, the locus of possible positions remains
DD'. Where the new short-run equilibrium occurs depends on
the shape of the family of *dd'* curves: it is *possible* that the new
equilibrium occurs at *R*, in which case normal profits are still
earned. Assume, however, that, whatever does happen, it leads
to subnormal profits, in which case the new short-run equilibrium must lie at a point such as *S*, intermediate between *R* and
Q. At *S* the *dd'* curve must be flatter than is the SRAC + *t*
curve vertically above it at *G* (because, if it were steeper, the
firm would expect a reduction in output to reduce the gap
between average cost and average revenue, and *S* could not be
a position of equilibrium). Now firms leave the industry and
DD' shifts to the right. The reduction in the number of firms
(and products: in this analysis the two must change together),
according to Kaldor's relation, reduces the elasticity of the *dd'*
family. Can we now find a new position of equilibrium on
SRAC + *t*, to the right of the present *DD'* curve, where *dd'* is
less elastic than at *S*, but at the same time tangent to SRAC
+ *t*? This is not difficult. Imagine *dd'* moving to the right
along *SZ*. If it moves with a constant slope, its elasticity falls.
But as we move to the right along SRAC, its slope is diminishing, i.e. changing in the direction of the slope of *dd'*. There does
not, therefore, appear to be any reason why there should not
be a tangency solution to the right of *DD'* consistent with
Kaldor's relation.

Now, have we any comparative static results? Can we say

that the price increase after full adjustment will be greater or less than the short-run price increase, or if the average cost of production will be greater or less than before the tax was imposed? It appears immediately that the second question is unanswerable: the new equilibrium position may lie to the left or to the right of Q (bear in mind that S may lie anywhere on RQ). This can be interpreted as follows: the tax reduces total output but also the number of firms; whether the output of the individual firm rises or falls as a result cannot be predicted, and therefore the direction of change in the least-cost scale of plant, if any, cannot be predicted either. We can answer the first question only if we can exclude equilibria on RL (bear in mind that L may lie on the left or to the right of Q). We already know that we cannot exclude L. Consider now tangency at G. This would require a steeper curve than dd' at S; but, with a higher price, its elasticity could be greater or smaller. But, in any case, we are now comparing elasticities at equal outputs instead of equal prices, and Kaldor's relation does not appear to justify this. The result is that we cannot exclude any point except R itself (trivially excluded by the fact that DD' must shift). Hence, even with Kaldor's relation, we cannot predict how the full-equilibrium values of price, output, and cost of production differ from those of short-run equilibrium. Hence we cannot compare the new full-equilibrium position with the old: the theory is still empty.

(3) Since we have been unable to obtain comparative static results in the simplest possible case, without advertising or quality variation, it is obvious that we shall obtain nothing in more complicated cases with additional variables. We may, however, reconsider the famous excess capacity theorem which has often been regarded as the most significant result obtained by Chamberlin, and the allocative implications of which have undoubtedly been responsible for much of the hostility to his work. In a recent article H. Demsetz has shown that, if advertising is introduced, full equilibrium does not necessarily involve excess capacity.[47] Consider any given level of advertising

---

[47] H. Demsetz, 'The Nature of Equilibrium in Monopolistic Competition', *Journal of Political Economy*, LXVIII 1 (Feb 1959). I am indebted to Mr J. R. Gould for the proof offered here, which I prefer to an earlier proof of my own. Demsetz's proof involves the construction of a '*mutatis mutandis* average revenue curve (M.A.R.)' which relates price to quantity on the understanding that the optimum advertising expenditure is associated with it. Unfortunately this construction is

expenditure, and the demand curve associated with it. The curve of average advertising expenditure is a rectangular hyperbola. Average total cost is obtained by adding this rectangular hyperbola to the curve of average production costs. Tangency between the demand curve and the average total cost curve may occur where the average production cost curve is falling *or rising*, so long as it is not rising fast enough to offset the effect of falling average advertising costs. If this is true for *any* level of advertising expenditure, it is true for the profit-maximising level. Hence, when advertising is introduced, tangency is consistent with production at less than or more than minimum cost of production.[48]

If we introduce quality variation without advertising, we still have the excess capacity result. Consider the curve of average production costs for any given quality, and the demand curve associated with it. Normal profit requires tangency, and, so long as the demand curve is downward sloping, this involves excess capacity. Since this is true for any quality, it is true for the profit-maximising quality. The difference between the two cases is due, of course, simply to the fact that in the advertising case we make the cost function additive, but not in the quality variation case. It is obvious that whenever there are two cost curves to be added together, equilibrium is consistent with production taking place to the left or to the right of the minimum point of either of them considered separately. So long, therefore, as advertising is handled in this way, the model yields no general excess capacity theorem. One result, however,

---

useless for comparative static purposes: the demand conditions for the individual firm are altered by any change in market demand *or* costs (via their influence on the number of firms), so that the M.A.R. curve, like the *dd'* curve, will shift in an unspecified way whenever we try to analyse the results of a change in data.

[48] Demsetz goes on to consider what happens if the minimum points on the curves of average production costs and average advertising costs do not occur at the same output. He suggests that, if selling costs start to rise before production costs, the firm will endeavour to move the selling cost curve by, e.g., acquiring trade names from other firms, while, if production costs rise first, the firm will build smaller plants, or subcontract, while retaining its own market, brand, and curve of selling costs. What this amounts to is the well-known result that there may be economies of 'selling scale' as well as of 'producing scale', that the optimum producing scale may not coincide with the optimum selling scale, and that a system of subsidiaries and subcontracting can be devised to overcome the difficulty. Unfortunately, even if we assume that the *maximum maximorum* has been achieved, we still cannot do comparative statics because the necessary demand relationships are still unspecified.

we still have: if advertising is absent or unimportant, the excess capacity theorem stands, even if quality variation is possible.

It is obviously extremely difficult to prove that a model is empty, and, indeed, this model is not completely empty: all I can claim is that it yields, so far as I can discover, no *qualitative comparative static* predictions, and that this is the consequence of a general defect, the incomplete specification of the demand relationships within the group. I add to this that not even Kaldor's relation appears to fill the gap. Thus the appropriate criticism of monopolistic competition is not that the assumptions about the group are difficult: it is that, making the best of the theory, and assuming groups of the required sort, the theory predicts practically nothing about them, and thus affords inadequate opportunity for testing. This point appears to have escaped both Chamberlin and his methodological critics.[49]

Of course, if the number of variables is restricted, as it may be in some cases of special application, the model may yield some useful results. If, for example, prices are controlled above the equilibrium level, whether by the government, or by some collusive arrangement, we expect supernormal profits and new entry. In the absence of quality variation and advertising, price control and new entry obviously creates additional excess capacity in each firm. If competition is limited to quality variation, excess capacity still follows.[50] But these results, useful as they may be in particular cases, depend upon price being taken as a parameter rather than a variable, and are therefore not counter-examples to the general conclusion that the model is incomplete: if price is taken as a parameter, some additional knowledge about demand is obviously provided.[51] It seems

---

[49] I hope that nothing I have said will be understood to detract from Chamberlin's historical contribution. I have not enlarged upon the importance of *The Theory of Monopolistic Competition* to economic thinking simply because I have been concerned with current controversy and the present state of knowledge. And if I have said little about Mrs Robinson's contribution, it is not for want of appreciation, but because I do not wish to get sidetracked into the 'braces–suspenders' argument.

[50] See Dorfman and Steiner, op. cit., pp. 835–6, for a proof.

[51] The literature is full of examples of specific applications in which some results are obtained because, e.g., price is fixed. Scitovsky, for example, analyses a case in which price is fixed and advertising not even mentioned (Tibor Scitovsky, *Welfare and Competition*, pp. 349–51). He argues that new entry raises demand elasticities (this is Kaldor's relation), but not to infinity, hence there will be excess capacity.

probable, too, that there are other cases of the same type: some results must be forthcoming if, for example, entry is impossible, or advertising is banned and quality subject to regulation. But the model was designed to handle the more general problem, and this it will not do. The limited amount it will do may be seen from the following summary of the results of this section.

(a) Non-perfect competition is not a sufficient condition for monopoly profits, because of entry, and price-fixing will increase the number of firms instead of the profits of existing firms unless entry is controlled.

(b) In a normal-profit equilibrium without advertising, there will be short-run excess capacity and unexploited economies of scale.

(c) With advertising, normal profits are consistent with any position on the cost curves; if prices are fixed, this is still true, but fixed prices, quality variation, and no advertising give excess capacity in full equilibrium.

(d) So long as there are unexploited economies of scale, firms have a motive for trying to integrate, rationalise, or do whatever else may be necessary to make their exploitation profitable.

(e) *We are unable to discover from this model the effects of changes in the data on the equilibrium price or size of plant.*

Obviously if we could specify a demand relationship that completed the model, we should then, when we added advertising and quality variation, still be faced with the inadequacies of qualitative economics discussed in the last section.

V

It only remains to consider how we might proceed further with monopolistic competition. The outstanding implication of the last two sections is that we require more facts, not for their own sake, but in order to put into the theory sufficient content for it to yield significant predictions. Perhaps the most serious criticism of Chamberlin's critics is that they have concentrated upon *a priori* discussion of his assumptions, instead of on discovering what facts were needed to give the theory content, and endeavouring to obtain them so that they might test it. Discussion of the empirical material required is beyond the scope of this paper, but the results of section III are a little discouraging:

we need facts about the demand functions of individual firms (with respect to quality and advertising as well as price) which are likely to be very difficult to get. Hence it may be that, with the observational techniques at our disposal, the theory is not likely, at present, to be very fruitful. As for the theory of the group, it appears that, to proceed further, we require some knowledge of demand relationships within groups. This suggests both theoretical and empirical investigation.

MATHEMATICAL APPENDIX TO SECTION III[52]

This appendix is a somewhat overdue application of the methods of the early chapters of the *Foundations* to some cases that Samuelson did not have occasion to consider there. We have a maximising model in several variables; our problem is to discover if our information is sufficient to determine the direction of change in the variables when a parameter is changed. It is in general obvious that we cannot expect much: the solutions will necessarily involve the second-order partial derivatives, both direct and cross, and, if we have little information about the former, we have less about the latter. We shall, however, at least discover what is the minimum information necessary to determine the direction of change. The main results are:

1. In the case of a specific tax, the direction of change of quantity is unambiguously determined without the need for any additional information.
2. This is not true in any other instance. To determine the direction of change of quality and advertising when tax changes, it is necessary to assume that second-order cross-partial derivatives can be neglected; and this assumption is necessary in the case of an *ad valorem* tax to determine the sign of the quantity change.
3. In no case is the direction of change of price determined, even when cross-effects are ignored. This is because it is determined as a linear combination of the changes in

---

[52] I am greatly indebted to Kelvin Lancaster, George Morton, and John Wise for generous help with this appendix. The responsibility for any errors that remain is entirely mine.

quantity, advertising, and quality, which, in general, have opposite effects upon price.

In what follows, advertising and quality variation are first treated together and then separately. It will be noticed that the only difference between the two follows from the form of the cost functions assumed: in the case of advertising, the costs of production and of advertising are assumed to be independent. It would be possible to treat quality variation in this way, in which case there would be no analytical difference between it and advertising. The treatment offered here is intended to bring out any differences which may follow from the different forms of functions; but the association of one exclusively with advertising and the other exclusively with quality variation is largely a matter of terminological convenience.

1. *The general case: advertising and quality variation*

We assume a single-product profit-maximising firm with demand and cost functions

$$\left.\begin{aligned} p &= \phi(x, q, v) \\ C &= \Psi(x, q) + sv \end{aligned}\right\} \tag{1}$$

where

p = product price
C = total cost
x = quantity of output
q = index of quality
v = quantity of advertising
s = price of a unit of advertising (for convenience this may be assumed constant without loss of generality).

Maximising

$$R - C = x\phi(x, q, v) - \Psi(x, q) - sv \tag{2}$$

yields

$$\left.\begin{aligned} \phi + x\phi_x - \Psi_x &= 0 \quad \text{(i)} \\ x\phi_q - \Psi_q &= 0 \quad \text{(ii)} \\ x\phi_v - s &= 0 \quad \text{(iii)} \end{aligned}\right\} \tag{3}$$

It is now convenient to write

$$a = 2\phi_x + x\phi_{xx} - \Psi_{xx}$$
$$b = x\phi_{qq} - \Psi_{qq}$$
$$c = x\phi_{vv}$$
$$f = x\phi_{qv}$$
$$g = \phi_v + x\phi_{xv}$$
$$h = \phi_q + x\phi_{xq} - \Psi_{xq}.$$

In this notation

$$\left. \begin{aligned} d^2(R - C) &= a\,dx^2 + b\,dq^2 + c\,dv^2 \\ &\qquad + 2f\,dq\,dv + 2d\,dx\,dv + 2h\,dx\,dq. \end{aligned} \right\} \quad (4)$$

For a maximum, (4) must be negative definite, that is

$$a < 0, \qquad \begin{vmatrix} a & h \\ h & b \end{vmatrix} > 0, \qquad \begin{vmatrix} a & h & g \\ h & b & f \\ g & f & c \end{vmatrix} < 0 \qquad (5)$$

and, similarly, the principal minors of corresponding order have the same sign. We shall denote the third-order coefficient matrix of (5) by A.

We now wish to differentiate (3) with respect to the parameters. From inspection, it is obvious that nothing can be said about the effects of an increase in demand unless the changes in ϕ_x, ϕ_q, and ϕ_v are specified. If we wish to consider the effects of a change in costs of production, we must first introduce the production function, and the factor prices as parameters, and solve for the least-cost combination of factors. We may avoid this labour, without loss, by considering the simplest form of an increase in costs, an increase in a specific indirect tax. We shall also be able to compare the results of an increase in s with those of an increase in a tax. We shall finally consider the effects of an increase in an *ad valorem* tax.

Introducing a specific tax at rate t, we merely add the term $-tx$ to (2), and $-t$ to (3) (i). Differentiating (3), thus modified, with respect to t and the variables x, q, and v, we obtain

$$\left. \begin{aligned} a\,dx + h\,dq + g\,dv &= dt \\ h\,dx + b\,dq + f\,dv &= 0 \\ g\,dx + f\,dq + c\,dv &= 0 \end{aligned} \right\} \qquad (6)$$

the matrix of coefficients of the L.H.S. of which is A.

(6) is solved by

$$
\begin{aligned}
\frac{dx}{dt} &= \frac{bc - f^2}{|A|} \\
\frac{dq}{dt} &= \frac{gf - hc}{|A|} \\
\frac{dv}{dt} &= \frac{hf - gb}{|A|} \\
\text{and} \quad \frac{dp}{dt} &= \frac{\phi_x(bc - f^2) + \phi_q(gf - hc) + \phi_v(hf - gb)}{|A|}
\end{aligned}
\tag{7}
$$

(since $dp = \phi_x \, dx + \phi_q \, dq + \phi_v \, dv$).

The solutions (7) constitute the set of consequences predicted by this model to follow from an increase in the tax. The question is whether qualitative knowledge of slopes and curvatures is sufficient to determine the signs of (7), that is, to yield qualitative predictions.

We immediately obtain

$$
\frac{dx}{dt} < 0 \quad \text{since } bc > f^2 \text{ (by (5))}.
$$

This result is perfectly general.[53] *It is, however, the only un-ambiguous result at this level of generality: dq/dt and dv/dt are* unsigned unless the signs of second-order cross-partial derivatives are known; but not even this is sufficient to sign dp/dt, which is a linear combination of the other elements of the solution vector.

If we now arbitrarily assume that all second-order cross-partial derivatives are zero,[54] we may add to (5)

$$
\begin{aligned}
f &= 0 \\
g &= \phi_v > 0 \\
h &= \phi_q > 0
\end{aligned}
$$

which is sufficient to make dq/dt and dv/dt negative. It is not, however, sufficient to sign dp/dt, which is now reduced to

$$
\frac{\phi_x bc - h^2 c - g^2 b}{|A|}
$$

[53] For a far more general proof that does not require the conventional assumptions of convexity and differentiability, see a forthcoming paper by John Wise.

[54] Hahn, who does not consider quality variation, assumes ϕ_{xa} to be negligible (op. cit., p. 296, n. 1; but cf. the subsequent 'Correction'). What he does not do is point out which of his subsequent results depend on this assumption. If the analysis offered here is correct, all save $dx/dt < 0$ must do.

which cannot be signed without knowledge of relative magnitudes. The intuitive explanation is obvious: the reduction in quantity pushes price up, while the reduction in quality and advertising push it down; which is stronger cannot be determined at this level of generality. Qualitative economics fails to predict that a price will be increased by an increase in an indirect tax.

It might now appear unnecessary to continue with the separate investigations of advertising and quality variation. Consider, however, the reasons for the failure. In the first place, unless we are at least prepared to put the cross-partial derivatives equal to zero, we do not even know the signs of all the non-zero coefficients of the system of simultaneous linear equations obtained when the equilibrium system is differentiated with respect to a parameter; but even knowledge of all these signs is not a sufficient condition for determining the signs of the solution vector. The reason for this is intuitively obvious: expansion of the determinants involves subtraction, as well as multiplication and addition, so that signs are bound to depend on relative magnitudes. In the second place, however, we generally have some zero coefficients, and, if we have enough of them in the right places, some parts of the solution may be signed, as was dx/dt above. Thus, given the signs of non-zero coefficients, the extent to which the signs of the solution are unambiguously determined depends on the number and pattern of zero coefficients in the matrix.[55] But the pattern of zero coefficients will depend on the parameter chosen for variation, because the parameters do not, in general, appear symmetrically in all equations (thus compare (16) below with (6)). Hence we cannot say that the qualitative calculus can never obtain results from maximising models in, say, three or more variables: we apparently have to explore each case.

2. *Advertising only*

In the absence of quality variation, the second equation of (3) disappears. (5) is replaced by[56]

[55] For a thorough investigation of these matters, see a forthcoming paper by Kelvin Lancaster, 'The Scope of Qualitative Economics'.

[56] The economic interpretation of these conditions is simple. $a < 0$ is the familiar condition that marginal revenue be falling faster than marginal cost. $c < 0$ is the obviously necessary condition that marginal revenue with respect to advertising is decreasing (cf. Hahn, p. 296 (i)).

*

$$a < 0, \quad \begin{vmatrix} a & g \\ g & c \end{vmatrix} > 0 \quad \text{(we write } B \text{ for } ac - g^2\text{)}$$

and, differentiating with respect to t, we have

$$\left. \begin{aligned} a\,dx + g\,dv &= dt \\ g\,dx + c\,dv &= 0 \end{aligned} \right\} \tag{8}$$

solved by

$$\left. \begin{aligned} \frac{dx}{dt} &= \frac{c}{B} \\ \frac{dv}{dt} &= \frac{-g}{B} \end{aligned} \right\} \tag{9}$$

which give

$$\frac{dp}{dt} = \frac{c\phi_x - g\phi_v}{B}.$$

Once again, dx/dt is immediately negative, dv/dt is unsigned unless the cross-partial, ϕ_{xv}, is ignored, and dp/dt depends upon relative magnitudes.

We may now reconsider the problem of section III(2) above, the effect of a tax change on the ratio of advertising expenditure to quantity produced. Differentiating,

$$\frac{d\left(\dfrac{v}{x}\right)}{dt} = \frac{x\dfrac{dv}{dt} - v\dfrac{dx}{dt}}{x^2}. \tag{10}$$

Plainly, even if dv/dt and dx/dt are signed, (10) is not since dv/dt and dx/dt will have the same sign: (10) depends on the relative magnitudes of these expressions and of x and v. The analogy with the effect on the employment of two substitutable factors of production of a change in the price of one of them is obvious and complete. Thus suppose that we differentiate (i) and (iii) of (3) with respect to s (the price of the advertising medium) instead of t.

We obtain

$$\left. \begin{aligned} \frac{dv}{ds} &= \frac{a}{B} \\ \frac{dx}{ds} &= \frac{-g}{B} \end{aligned} \right\} \tag{11}$$

and

$$\frac{dp}{dt} = \frac{a\phi_v - g\phi_x}{B}$$

Exactly as before, the factor the price of which has risen falls in quantity ($dv/ds < 0$), the substitute falls if cross-effects are ignored, the change in price cannot be predicted, and neither, obviously, can the change in advertising per unit.

3. *Quality variation only*

The third equation of (3) disappears, (5) is reduced to

$$a < 0, \quad \begin{vmatrix} a & h \\ h & b \end{vmatrix} > 0 \quad \text{(we write } D \text{ for } ab - h^2 \text{)}$$

and, differentiating with respect to t and solving, we obtain

$$\left. \begin{aligned} \frac{dx}{dt} &= \frac{b}{D} \\ \frac{dq}{dt} &= \frac{-h}{D} \\ \frac{dp}{dt} &= \frac{b\phi_x - h\phi_q}{D} \end{aligned} \right\} \tag{12}$$

with signs as before. The only difference between (9) or (11) and (12) arises from the fact that advertising is treated as a linear addition to cost, so that the only cross-partial in g is ϕ_{xa}, whereas the sign of dq/dt depends upon h, which includes the cross-partial Ψ_{xq} as well as ϕ_{xq}.

The intuitive interpretation of (12) is clear. A quality reduction can be regarded as a concealed price increase, and therefore as an alternative method of absorbing the tax: quality falls, as does advertising (neglecting cross-effects), but whether it falls enough to offset the forces making for a price increase cannot be determined without quantitative information. In general, however, we might expect that, when the tax is increased, the firm lowers quality, raises price, or both, and that the less it does one the more it does the other. We might also expect that, the more sensitive is demand to quality changes, the less quality will change, because it does not have the effect of a concealed price change. These expectations may be checked by differentiating (12) with respect to ϕ_q (neglecting cross-effects, $\phi_q = h$). This yields

$$\left. \begin{aligned} \frac{\partial(dx/dt)}{\partial h} &= \frac{2hb}{D^2} < 0 \\ \frac{\partial(dq/dt)}{\partial h} &= \frac{-(ab + h^2)}{D^2} < 0 \\ \frac{\partial(dp/dt)}{\partial h} &= \frac{2hb(\phi_x - a)}{D^2}. \end{aligned} \right\} \quad (13)$$

(13) does not fully confirm our expectations. The larger h, the larger the *absolute* change in x *and* q, but the effect on price is still undetermined.

4. *The effect of changing an ad valorem tax*

We cannot now even obtain the direction of change in x without knowledge of the cross-effects. To see this, replace (2) by

$$R - C = x.\phi(x, q, v)(1 - r) - \Psi(x, q) - sv \quad (14)$$

where r is the rate of tax. Now instead of (3) we have

$$\left. \begin{aligned} \phi(1 - r) + x\phi_x(1 - r) - \Psi_x &= 0 \\ x\phi_q(1 - r) - \Psi_q &= 0 \\ x\phi_v(1 - r) - s &= 0 \end{aligned} \right\} \quad (15)$$

and, in place of (6),

$$\left. \begin{aligned} a' \, dx + h' \, dq + g' \, dv &= (\phi + x\phi_x) \, dr \\ h' \, dx + b' \, dq + f' \, dv &= x\phi_q \, dr \\ g' \, dx + f' \, dq + c' \, dv &= x\phi_v \, dr \end{aligned} \right\} \quad (16)$$

where the primes indicate that every demand term in each coefficient is multiplied by $(1 - r)$. Now in (16) two non-zero terms replace the two zeros on the R.H.S. of (6) which were responsible for the numerator-determinant of dx/dt collapsing to a principal minor. Hence every term appears in the expansion of the determinants, so that the signs of every element in the solution vector depend upon relative magnitudes. Putting all cross-effects equal to zero is necessary and sufficient to give

$dx/dr < 0$ $(f' = 0$, g' and $h' > 0)$, as well as dq/dr and $dv/dr < 0$. dq/dr is, of course, undetermined.

The reader may easily check for himself that, in the cases of advertising or quality variation alone, it is also necessary to neglect cross-effects to obtain the sign of dx/dr.

10 Archibald *versus* Chicago

G. J. Stigler

1. G. C. Archibald's attack on Chamberlin's theory of mono-polistic competition proceeds to its goal by way of a detour through Chicago.[1] The detour appears to be dictated by a curious desire to repel the 'Chicago' attacks (my own, by the way, was written at Columbia and launched in London) before presenting his own.

2. I used a method of internal criticism of Chamberlin which was designed to show (1) that his group equilibrium analysis lacked rigor, except under special conditions which led to essentially competitive results, and (2) that his general theory was vacuous. I lamented the absence of equilibrium conditions beyond the empty marginal equalities (read: Archibald's com-parative statics) and said, 'in the general case we cannot make a single statement about the economic events in the world we sought to analyse'.[2] Archibald reproaches us for failing to make the real criticism of Chamberlin, 'that he does not state what observable, testable predictions may be obtained from his theory'.[3] I apologize for having stated this thought in other words.

3. I have no corresponding desire to repel Archibald's attack on Chamberlin. Indeed, I consider it a valuable contribution. One cannot fail, however, to notice the contrast between the generality of Archibald's analysis of the isolated firm, where conventional tools work well, and the primitive and *ad hoc*

---

[1] 'Chamberlin versus Chicago', *Review of Economic Studies* (Oct 1961); pp. 145–83 above.

[2] *Five Lectures on Economic Problems* (1948).

[3] Op. cit., p. 147 above.

Reprinted from *Review of Economic Studies*, xxx (Feb 1963) 64–4, by kind per-mission of the author and of the Managing Editor.

nature of the group analysis. I commend to him the thought that his inability to formulate an interesting general analysis of the group problem arises from exactly those analytical ambiguities in Chamberlin's theory of which I complained. Had Chamberlin been able to devise an analytical characterization of the group, it would have been possible to derive functional relationships between the demand curve of the firm, the number of firms, the amount of advertising, etc.

4. The methodological discussion is a detour on the detour in Archibald's argument; the only purposes for which I invoked the methodological position that assumptions need not be 'realistic' were to explain *why* Chamberlin had not succeeded in constructing a logically valid and empirically meaningful theory, and why he had failed to show the deficiencies of competitive theory. It would have been the height of absurdity to complain of a successful theory that its assumptions were realistic.

5. Chamberlin's theory is not an ideal platform for debating methodology. My views on methodology have undergone some change, but I am duly impressed that these views have a tendency to change much more than my judgment of the quality of specific economic studies. I propose the hypothesis that methodological controversy has never had a marginal product (of scientific progress) above zero. Archibald will surely agree that it would not do for me to provide confirmation of my own predictions.

6. Nevertheless, one final 'methodological' point. Where I am said to deny meaning to the sentence, 'a theatre ticket and a bottle of burgundy cost the same', I would on the contrary say that the meaning is clear: (*a*) there exists a quality of burgundy and size of bottle such that its price in dollars, and possibly even in shillings, equals that of a certain theatre seat, and (*b*) given consumer tastes and income, Archibald cannot find manageable units such that the demand curves for burgundy and tickets are the same. This point occurs in one of several places where Archibald appears to propose the principle: when there are errors and gaps in logic in a formal theoretical solution of a problem, the significance of the logical blemishes is to be judged by recourse to empirical tests of the theory's predictions. This does not strike me as an absurd proposition, mostly because all economists accept it daily when they

use their theories, few of which are perfect. But it surely deserves to be joined with another proposition: the probability that a theory will yield useful predictions is reduced by logical weaknesses in its construction.

11 More on Archibald *versus* Chicago

Milton Friedman

Theorists of monopolistic competition contend that firms have a strong tendency to differentiate their product and that, when there are no 'real' differences, firms will seek to create trivial and 'artificial' differences to establish a separate market. Whatever else Archibald's piece may contribute to monopolistic competition, it is a striking confirmation that these predictions are as applicable to professional writing as to toothpaste.

Archibald's propensity to create apparent differences out of close agreement was first impressed on me by an earlier review of a book by Tjalling Koopmans,[1] in which he discussed at some length an article of mine on methodology.[2] While Archibald makes it clear that his views coincide very closely with mine, he expresses a considerable number of 'criticisms' of my position, almost all of which I found most telling and persuasive. On re-examination of my paper to see how I could have been so misguided, I was surprised to find that I had stated many of the points myself, though sometimes in slightly different words, and that the impression that they constituted 'criticisms' was produced partly by terming them so, partly by selective reference, partly by refusing to regard as relevant to one part of my paper what I had said in another, and partly by assuming that if I had carried my argument farther than in fact I did, I would have said foolish things.

The present article, as Stigler's comment suggests, displays

[1] 'The State of Economic Science', *British Journal for the Philosophy of Science*, x 37 (May 1959) 58–69.
[2] 'The Methodology of Positive Economics', in *Essays in Positive Economics* (Chicago, 1953).

Reprinted from *Review of Economic Studies*, xxx (Feb 1963) 65–7, by kind permission of the author and of the Managing Editor.

Archibald's propensity in much more extreme measure. Archibald refers to an example in which I stated that it would have yielded false predictions to have treated 'cigarette firms . . . as if they were perfect competitors', and in which I noted that 'this would doubtless have been recognized before the event'.[3] Says Archibald, 'the casual statement that "this would doubtless have been recognized before the event" conceals a matter of major importance. . . . Friedman and Stigler want us to apply both models (competitive and monopolistic) to the same industry, presuming that we shall know "before the event" which to use. But *how* are we to know?' I wonder how many readers of Archibald's passage would guess that one of the points my example was intended to illustrate was the importance of specifying 'the circumstances under which the theory holds sufficiently well',[4] that the need for giving explicit attention to this problem and of distinguishing it sharply from the logical validity of a self-contained model was stressed at several places in the paper, or that I devoted the penultimate paragraph of the paper to re-emphasizing the problem, writing, 'In particular, undue emphasis on the descriptive realism of "assumptions" has contributed to neglect of the critical problem of determining the limits of validity of the various hypotheses that together constitute the existing economic theory in these areas. . . . If we are to use effectively . . . abstract models and . . . descriptive material, we must have a comparable exploration of the criteria for determining what abstract model it is best to use for particular kinds of problems, what entities in the abstract model are to be identified with what observable entities, and what features of the problem or of the circumstances have the greatest effect on the accuracy of the predictions yielded by a particular model or theory.'[5]

With respect to Archibald's bald-faced assertions (*a*) that Stigler and I have judged 'monopolistic competition, allegedly on the grounds of its predictions, without [ourselves] knowing, or at least stating, what these predictions are' and (*b*) that we 'are being inconsistent with [our] own methodological prin-

---

[3] Ibid., p. 37. Incidentally, Archibald's imprecision extends even to his paraphrase of my statement. He has me 'treating the industry as perfectly competitive', when I explicitly defined competitive and monopolistic as terms referring to firms, not industries. On my definitions, it is entirely possible for an industry to contain both competitive and oligopolistic firms.

[4] Ibid., p. 36.   [5] Ibid., p. 42.

ciples' because we 'experience such difficulty with the unrealistic assumptions of the monopolistically competitive group',
I can do no better than to quote essentially the whole of what I
said on the subject. I apologize for the length of the quotation
but since my main criticism of Archibald is that he has mis-
represented what Stigler and I have said, it seems fairest to let
the reader judge for himself.

It would be highly desirable to have a more general theory than
Marshall's, one that would cover at the same time both those
cases in which differentiation of product or fewness of numbers
makes an essential difference and those in which it does not. Such
a theory would enable us to handle problems we now cannot and,
in addition, facilitate determination of the range of circumstances under which the simpler theory can be regarded as a good
enough approximation. To perform this function, the more
general theory must have content and substance; it must have
implications susceptible to empirical contradiction and of substantive interest and importance.

The theory of imperfect or monopolistic competition developed
by Chamberlin and Robinson is an attempt to construct such a
more general theory. Unfortunately, it possesses none of the
attributes that would make it a truly useful general theory. Its
contribution has been limited largely to improving the exposition
of the economics of the individual firm and thereby the derivation
of implications of the Marshallian model, refining Marshall's
monopoly analysis, and enriching the vocabulary available for
describing industrial experience.

The deficiencies of the theory are revealed most clearly in its
treatment of, or inability to treat, problems involving groups of
firms – Marshallian 'industries'. So long as it is insisted that
differentiation of product is essential – and it is the distinguishing
feature of the theory that it does insist on this point – the definition
of an industry in terms of firms producing an identical product
cannot be used. By that definition each firm is a separate industry.
Definition in terms of 'close' substitutes or a 'substantial' gap in
cross-elasticities evades the issue, introduces fuzziness and un-
definable terms into the abstract model where they have no place,
and serves only to make the theory analytically meaningless –
'close' and 'substantial' are in the same category as a 'small' air
pressure. In one connection Chamberlin implicitly defines an
industry as a group of firms having identical cost and demand
curves. But this, too, is logically meaningless so long as differentiation of product is, as claimed, essential and not to be put aside.

What does it mean to say that the cost and demand curves of a firm producing bulldozers are identical with those of a firm producing hairpins?[6] And if it is meaningless for bulldozers and hairpins, it is meaningless also for two brands of toothpaste – so long as it is insisted that the difference between the two brands is fundamentally important.

The theory of monopolistic competition offers no tools for the analysis of an industry and so no stopping place between the firm at one extreme and general equilibrium at the other. It is therefore incompetent to contribute to the analysis of a host of important problems: the one extreme is too narrow to be of great interest; the other, too broad to permit meaningful generalizations.

If this passage does not say that the theory has no rigorous implications for 'groups', and hence no 'testable' implications, I am at a loss to know what it does say. And if Archibald can read this passage as implying that the concept of the group is to be rejected because its assumptions are unrealistic, then there is real doubt that any communication between Archibald and me is possible.

Stigler is unduly generous in his evaluation of Archibald's attack on Chamberlin. This attack is seriously marred by Archibald's failure to distinguish between the meaning of the condition 'marginal cost equals marginal revenue' and the condition 'average cost equals average revenue'. The first is a maxim of rational conduct by the firm; it is something the firm seeks to achieve. The second is not. In a world of specialized resources, and certainly in one of monopolies whatever their source, it is either a convention of accounting (total costs equal total receipts) or, if defined to be an equilibrium condition, is imposed on the firm by the capital market via the revaluation of specialized resources. This is what renders the tangency condition irrelevant to productive adjustments and makes the alleged implications about 'excess capacity and unexploited economies of scale' – with or without advertising – highly misleading if not downright wrong.

[6] There always exists a transformation of quantities that will make either the cost curves or the demand curves identical; this transformation need not, however, be linear, in which case it will involve different-sized units of one product at different levels of output. There does not necessarily exist a transformation that will make both pairs of curves identical.' [I have omitted other footnotes in the original source, but included this one, because only this one bears directly on Archibald's commentary.]

A useful concept of 'capacity' should be a technical, production concept, dependent of course on factor prices but not on the state of demand. The definition of capacity as the minimum point of the kind of average cost curve for which tangency is relevant is not such a concept. Let demand rise, but the physical production function and factor prices remain unchanged except that the rents earned by the firm's specialized resources increase, and the minimum point will shift to the right. Does this shift in the minimum point imply a meaningful increase in capacity? Of course not. A useful concept of the capacity of a particular plant is the output at which short-run marginal costs equal long-run marginal costs: if this is the expected output, the plant will be of the right size in the sense that the firm has no incentive to seek either to enlarge it or make it smaller; it is operating at 'capacity'. On this concept of capacity, there is no more reason to expect short-run excess capacity under monopoly than under competition. And this conclusion is of course sensible. Why should a firm's position on product markets have any connection with its incentive to produce whatever output it does produce as cheaply as possible? Similar caveats are in order for alleged unexploited economies of scale.

Because average cost concepts offer such pitfalls to the unsophisticated, I have long felt that it might promote a fuller understanding of economic theory to expunge 'average cost' from the textbooks. Stigler took a large step in that direction in his 1952 revision of his *Theory of Price*, and by doing so, added noticeably to the quality of an already outstanding work. It is too bad that Archibald apparently learned his economic theory from the earlier edition.

12 Reply to Chicago

G. C. Archibald

Stigler

Stigler has raised some interesting points, but he seems to me to be somewhat inconsistent.

1. On the last page of his 'Monopolistic Competition in Retrospect', he assessed '. . . the specific contribution of the theory of monopolistic competition: the analysis of the many-firm industry producing a single (technological) product under uniformity and symmetry conditions, but with a falling demand curve for each firm. Chamberlin's analysis of this particular situation is essentially correct, and many economists appear to wish to incorporate it into neo-classical theory. It should be incorporated, not if it is a more "realistic" description of in-dustries, but if it contains different or more accurate predictions (as tested by observation) than the theory of competition. *I personally think that the predictions of his standard model of imperfect competition differ only in unimportant respects from those of the theory of competition* because the underlying conditions will usually be accompanied by very high demand elasticities for the individual firms. But this is a question of fact, and it must be resolved by empirical tests of the implications of the two theories (a task the supporters of monopolistic competition have not yet under-taken).' (My italics.)

This passage seems to justify my claim that Stigler did not state what, if any, predictions could be got from monopolistic competition. Why write like this if the model is known to be empty?

2. Stigler does also say that the model is empty, on an argument quite different from mine. Mine is that, even if the

Reprinted from *Review of Economic Studies*, xxx (Feb 1963) 68–71, by kind permission of the author and of the Managing Editor.

equilibrium conditions *are* satisfied, we obtain no qualitative predictions because the model is inadequately specified. His is that we do not even have equilibrium conditions unless the uniformity assumption is rigorously adhered to (in which case we apparently get perfect competition on p. 136 but a 'standard model of imperfect competition' on p. 143). I argued that uniformity is not as troublesome as Stigler thought, as follows: (i) it does not, as he asserted, require physical homogeneity; (ii) as Kaldor pointed out, tangency can occur with different firms selling at different prices if their elasticities of demand are different; (iii) earnings due to such things as copyrights and patents – distinctive features of the non-uniform situation that Chamberlin set out to handle – should be imputed as rents or quasi-rents, in which case tangency is possible without uniformity.

Stigler defends his original position on (i) (Friedman discusses (iii)), pointing out that I cannot find manageable units such that the demand curves for burgundy and theatre tickets are the same. True. But I do not think that this justifies the assertion that 'We simply cannot attach meaning to the statement that physically diverse things have the same price', and the conclusion that uniformity therefore requires homogeneity. Different brands of cigarettes do sell for the same price, and may or may not involve the same average direct cost of production – in a meaningful and measurable way.

3. Stigler goes on to chide me for being unduly cavalier about logical defects in theory. I cannot think, though, that in taking the position that the justification of the concept of a group is ultimately an empirical matter, I am in any more *logical* trouble than Stigler, who is prepared on occasion to treat the New York housing market as a competitive industry (group). As Chamberlin remarked, 'People who live in *ad hoc* houses should be more indulgent' (*Towards a More General Theory of Value*, p. 305).

4. Stigler declares that the marginal product of methodological controversy is zero. I submit that, if this is to be taken literally, it is a shocking piece of obscurantism, and an indefensible attempt to close discussion. As Friedman said, 'More than other scientists, social scientists need to be self-conscious about their methodology.' ('Methodology of Positive Economics', p. 40.) But I doubt if it is really meant to be taken

literally. In the context, its meaning is, I suspect, the harmless one that Stigler is not impressed by my methodological remarks, about which, certainly, no more need be said.

Friedman

Friedman's substantive criticisms are three: two charges of misrepresentation, and one that I made a mistake in my criticism of Chamberlin.

1. It is indeed true that Friedman pointed out the necessity of specifying the circumstances in which a theory is to hold. He wrote:

> The important problem in connection with the hypothesis [the falling body example] is to specify the circumstances under which the formula works or, more precisely, the general magnitude of the error in its predictions under various circumstances. Indeed, . . . such a specification is not one thing and the hypothesis another. *The specification is itself an essential part of the hypothesis*, and it is a part that is peculiarly likely to be revised and extended as experience accumulates. [My italics.]

Consider, however, the competition–monopoly mixture that is to be applied to cigarette firms (or the New York housing market). My complaint was precisely that in this case specification is inadequate, i.e. that Friedman's precepts and practice are in this case at variance. He replies by reminding us of his precepts and complaining that I overlooked them.

In fact there is an important issue here which is worth more serious discussion. In general terms, the situation is this: we can successfully predict some of the behaviour of an economic unit from theory A, and some from theory B; where A is right B would be wrong, and vice versa. One way of interpreting the situation is: 'Different theories for different problems.' Another is: 'A and B are both refuted.' How do we now proceed? My view is that the correct predictions of both A and B constitute part of our stock of useful knowledge, available for what I called engineering purposes, but that both A and B are, as scientific hypotheses, refuted. We might now endeavour to construct a more general theory, incorporating A and B. Part of such a theory would be the specification of the circumstances in which each subtheory would hold. Such a theory would be susceptible of refutation, since the specification might be wrong. In the case of the monopoly–competition mixture my complaint is precisely that it is an *ad hoc* mixture and *not* a general theory which includes the appropriate specification, and it is therefore *not* susceptible of refutation.

2. I wrote: '. . . the question of whether or not there are firms that are not perfectly competitive but can usefully be treated in groups is an empirical one. This view seems . . . in keeping with the methodology of the Chicago School . . .', and complained of inconsistency in Friedman and Stigler's dismissal of monopolistic competition on apparently *a priori* grounds. I still think that this position is essentially correct; but I concede that it might have been more carefully expressed. Friedman's crucial objection is that differentiation and uniformity are logically inconsistent. I think that it is a question of 'how much', that it is a matter of fact, rather than a matter of logic, whether, say, two brands of a commodity which differ in the eyes of consumers do or do not differ significantly in their average direct costs of production. Cigarettes will again serve as an example: who wants to put bulldozers and hairpins in the same group? It seems to me that Friedman uses different rules – or different standards of rigour – for judging the perfectly competitive and the monopolistically competitive models. But I do not wish to imply that he rejects monopolistic competition *because* its assumptions are unrealistic.

3. Friedman's third point seems to me to be a most interesting one: in part it actually carries my argument further than I had done. I agree that equality of average cost and average revenue is 'imposed on the firm by the capital market via the revaluation of specialised resources'. This reinforces the argument I used to point out that the tangency solution was possible even in the presence of product differentiation, copyrights, and so on. Now there are two questions: (*a*) does tangency achieved by revaluation constitute an equilibrium condition or a truism of accounting? (*b*) is the minimum point of the resulting average total cost curve a point of any particular interest? Friedman's answer to (*a*) is that, even if it is an equilibrium condition, 'the tangency condition [is] irrelevant to productive adjustments . . .'. This does not seem to be right. The normal profit condition is of course not supposed to have anything to do with the maximising adjustments of the individual firm, but it is

supposed to have something to do with entry and exit, and hence with 'long-run' productive adjustments. Starting from tangency, 'abnormal profit is uniquely associated with disequilibrium caused by changes in demand or factor supply'. It acts as a signal for more capital to enter the industry, and thus make productive adjustments – if, in fact, entry is possible. All this is, of course, completely orthodox, and the difficulty lies not with the tangency condition but with the difficulty of making a judgment as to the possibility of entry independently of whether entry actually occurs.

It is in his answer to (*b*) that Friedman has taken matters further. He points out that the minimum point of the average total cost curve is shifted by the revaluation of specialised factors consequent upon demand changes. Hence tangency to the left of the minimum point has no necessary connection with excess capacity in any technical sense. Hence, even in the absence of advertising, the excess capacity theorem is no use. I think he is quite right. I find that he made essentially this point in his brilliant 'Comment' on the empirical evidence on economies of scale, where he wrote: 'The existence of specialised resources not only complicates the definition of 'optimum' size; even more important, it makes it impossible to define the average cost of a particular firm for different hypothetical outputs independently of conditions of demand. The returns to the specialised factors are now 'rents', at least in part, and, in consequence, do not determine the price, but are determined by it.'[1] This argument applies with equal force, of course, in perfect and monopolistic competition. And if it robs the zero-profit condition of meaning as a long-run equilibrium condition in monopolistic competition, it presumably does in perfect competition too. But I do not think that it does, for the reason explained above. Perhaps, though, it would be better if I had said 'a change in quasi-rents' instead of 'abnormal profit'.[2]

[1] 'Comment' on Caleb A. Smith's 'Survey of the Empirical Evidence on Economies of Scale', in *Business Concentration and Price Policy* (Universities–National Bureau Committee for Economic Research, Princeton, 1955).

[2] I may be permitted to append one further comment. Friedman appears to consider my disagreement with some of his writing as an offence which is the worse because I have expressed agreement with (and acknowledged indebtedness to) so much of it. I find this attitude peculiar.

13 On the Predictive Content of Models of Monopolistic Competition[1]

Josef Hadar

Perhaps the strongest criticism ever directed at the theory of monopolistic competition is the assertion that the theory yields no testable hypotheses, and that therefore it is not a suitable medium through which one can study those market phenomena which cannot be explained by the theories of pure competition and pure monopoly. This position was taken by Stigler [6] twenty years ago. More recently, this theme has been taken up by G. C. Archibald [1, 2] who has amplified it, and given it a more concrete form of expression. Specifically, Archibald has shown that if a shift parameter, such as a tax parameter, is introduced into the model of the monopolistically competitive firm, then those comparative static properties which are typical of monopolistic competition turn out to be indeterminate. In other words, one cannot, in general, predict the effects of a change in the tax on the optimal levels of such decision variables as advertising and price. While Archibald's formal results are correct, there seems to be no compelling reason to subscribe to the view that '. . . the difficulties of the "qualitative calculus" applied to maximising models of the firm are too great to be overcome. . .'.[2] It is the purpose of this paper to suggest one way of surmounting these difficulties – at least partially.

We shall be concerned with a model of the firm which includes three decision variables: price, quantity, and advertising. We investigate the comparative statics of the model mainly with respect to an excise tax and the price of advertising. Our treatment of the problem differs from Archibald's in that we

[1] The author is grateful to William R. Russell and Thomas R. Saving for their helpful comments.

[2] Archibald [2] p. 21.

Reprinted from *Southern Economic Journal*, XXXVI 1 (July 1969) 67–73, by kind permission of the author and of the Associate Editor.

make a more specific assumption about the nature of the effect of advertising on the demand function. The necessity for slightly stronger assumptions than those of the general model emerges, of course, as a corollary of the results obtained by Archibald, but we believe that the formulation presented here is still of sufficient generality to warrant some consideration. The present formulation not only removes a great deal of the indeterminateness from the model, but yields additional hypotheses which, in principle at least, are testable. In section 1 we analyze the case of a single firm, while in section 2 the analysis is extended to a group of firms.

1. Equilibrium of a Single Firm

We begin the analysis with a brief discussion of the circumstances which make advertising a profitable activity. In doing so we shall introduce a concept which plays an important part in the analysis of the main issues of this paper. This introductory discussion is also justified on the grounds that it constitutes a part of the general shut-down condition for a firm in monopolistic competition.

Let $p = h(x, y)$ be the demand function for product x, where p denotes the price of x, and y denotes the amount of advertising. Since we are not interested in drawing a distinction between the different advertising media, the variable y may be considered a composite good (input) the prices of whose components are always proportional to one another. The function h is defined for all nonnegative values of x and y, and is continuously differentiable. It is assumed that $h(x, y) > 0$, $h_x < 0$, and $h_y > 0$ for all x and y, where subscripts attached to functional symbols denote first-order and second-order partial derivatives, respectively.

If $p_0 = h(x_0, y_0)$ and $p_1 = h(x_0, 0)$, then we refer to the quantity $p_0 - p_1$ as the *discount-equivalence* of the advertising ratio y_0/x_0. This terminology has been chosen for the following reason: if the combination p_0 and y_0 generates a demand of x_0 units of x, and the firm reduces its advertising to zero, then it will be able to maintain the level of demand x_0 if it cuts its price by $p_0 - p_1$ dollars.

For simplicity, we refer to a combination such as (x_0, y_0) (and the corresponding output price) as a *production plan*. The price of one unit of advertising will be denoted by α. We say that a production plan with a positive level of advertising is profitable if it yields a level of profit which is higher than the *maximum* profit which can be earned from any feasible production plan with zero advertising. We now state and prove the following theorem:

Theorem

A necessary condition for a production plan (x_0, y_0), $x_0, y_0 > 0$, to be profitable is that the discount-equivalence of y_0/x_0 be greater than $\alpha y_0/x_0$.

Proof

Let $p_0 = h(x_0, y_0)$, x_0, and $y_0(x_0, y_0 > 0)$ be the price, output, and level of advertising, respectively, of the production plan (x_0, y_0), and let $\bar{p} = h(\bar{x}, 0)$ and $\bar{x}$ be the optimal price and output, respectively, given that the firm has decided not to advertise at all. Assuming that the production plan (x_0, y_0) is profitable, we have, by the definition of profitability,

$$h(x_0, y_0)x_0 - f(x_0) - \alpha y_0 > h(\bar{x}, 0)\bar{x} - f(\bar{x}) \qquad (1)$$

where f represents the total cost function. We also have

$$h(\bar{x}, 0)\bar{x} - f(\bar{x}) \geq h(x_0, 0)x_0 - f(x_0) \qquad (2)$$

by virtue of the assumption that $\bar{x}$ is the profit-maximizing output when advertising is zero. From (1) and (2) we get

$$h(x_0, y_0)x_0 - \alpha y_0 > h(x_0, 0)x_0. \qquad (3)$$

Transposing terms, and dividing both sides of the inequality by x_0, yields

$$h(x_0, y_0) - h(x_0, 0) > \frac{\alpha y_0}{x_0} \qquad (4)$$

which proves the theorem.

Briefly, the theorem states that for a positive level of advertising to be profitable the price cut, which upon the elimination of the chosen level of advertising would maintain the firm's current level of demand, must exceed the firm's advertising outlays per unit of output. In some sense, then, a dollar's worth of advertising per unit of output must be more effective than a price cut of one dollar. Note that this is a necessary, but not a sufficient, condition.[3]

It is reasonable to assume that the discount-equivalence of the advertising ratio varies with the level of advertising. Over a fairly wide range we may expect it to increase with average advertising, but after some point its rate of increase is likely to diminish. The relationship between average advertising and its discount-equivalence may conveniently be stated as a formal functional relationship, and we denote this function by $\theta(z)$, where $z = y/x$. In line with the above theorem and general comments about the probable behavior of the discount-equivalence, we make the following assumptions about the function θ:

Given the price of advertising, there exists an interval $[a, b]$ of nonnegative numbers such that $\theta(z) > \alpha z$ (5) whenever $a < z < b$.

$$\theta' > 0 \quad \text{for all } z. \tag{6}$$

There exists a real number c such that $\theta'' < 0$ for $z > c$.   (7)

Primes and double primes denote first and second derivatives, respectively.

Given the definition of discount-equivalence we can write

$$h(x,y) - h(x, 0) = \theta(z) \tag{8A}$$

or equivalently

$$h(x,y) = h(x, 0) + \theta(z). \tag{8B}$$

It will be convenient to replace $h(x, 0)$ by $H(x)$, where the latter represents the ordinary demand function faced by the firm if it never advertises. We assume, of course, that

$$H' < 0 \quad \text{for all } x \tag{9}$$

and write

$$h(x,y) = H(x) + \theta(z). \tag{8C}$$

Our approach to the problem of advertising can now be summarized in terms of the hypothesis embodied in equation (8). This hypothesis says, in effect, that the (maximum) price

---

[3] Dorfman and Steiner ([3] p. 830) state a necessary condition for profitability in terms of the marginal revenue product of advertising, and the price elasticity of the demand function.

which the firm can charge in order to sell the output level x while using y units of advertising is the sum of the following two components: (a) the (maximum) price which the firm can charge in order to sell the output level x without any advertising, and (b) the discount-equivalence of y/x, where the discount-equivalence is a function of z which has the properties given in (5)–(7).

Next, we derive the derivatives of h in terms of the derivatives of H and θ. Upon differentiating (8c), and using (6), (7), and (9) when appropriate, we find

$$h_x = H' - \frac{z}{x}\theta' < 0 \tag{10}$$

$$h_y = \frac{\theta'}{x} > 0 \tag{11}$$

$$h_{xy} = -\frac{1}{x^2}(\theta' + z\theta'') \gtreqless 0 \tag{12}$$

$$h_{yy} = \frac{\theta''}{x^2} < 0 \quad \text{for} \quad z > c. \tag{13}$$

It may be pointed out that the derivatives given in (10), (11), and (13) have the signs that one would normally associate with a demand function which includes output and advertising as arguments, and they are consistent with the general assumptions about the function $h(x, y)$ made earlier in the discussion.

We are now in a position to formulate the firm's profit function. It takes the form

$$\pi = h(x, y)x - f(x) - \alpha y - \beta x \equiv \phi(x, y; \alpha, \beta) \tag{14}$$

where π denotes profit, and β the excise tax. Assuming that the profit function possesses a unique interior maximum for all α and β in some neighborhood, we have the following necessary and sufficient conditions:

$$\phi_x = h(x, y) + xh_x - f' - \beta = 0 \tag{15}$$

$$\phi_y = xh_y - \alpha = 0 \tag{16A}$$

$$\phi_{xx} = 2h_x + xh_{xx} - f'' < 0 \tag{17A}$$

$$\phi_{yy} = xh_{yy} < 0 \tag{17B}$$

$$\begin{vmatrix} \phi_{xx} & \phi_{xy} \\ \phi_{yx} & \phi_{yy} \end{vmatrix} > 0. \tag{18}$$

In addition, we assume that the firm earns enough revenues to pay for all its variable costs. Our assumption about the existence of a unique maximum for all α and β implies, of course, that the two equations (15) and (16A) possess a unique solution for x and y in terms of α and β. This solution can be written as

$$\bar{x} = g(\alpha, \beta) \tag{19}$$
$$\bar{y} = \hat{g}(\alpha, \beta) \tag{20}$$

where bars denote optimal values.

The function g may be interpreted as the firm's supply function of output, and $\hat{g}$ as its demand function for advertising. These functions show how the firm will vary its output and advertising in response to variations in the price of advertising, and the excise tax. It is one of the objectives of this paper to study the effects of such variations, and for this purpose we must determine the signs of the partial derivatives of these functions. But even without evaluating these derivatives formally, we can infer something about the nature of the results from an inspection of condition (16A). The expression xh_y represents the marginal revenue product of the last unit of advertising which, for profit maximization, is required to be equal to the marginal cost of advertising, i.e. α. Substituting for h_y in (16A) from (11) gives

$$\theta' = \alpha. \tag{16B}$$

Condition (16B) says that in order to maximize its profit the firm must choose a value of $z(= y/x)$ at which the slope of the discount-equivalence function is equal to α. But since the function θ has only one argument, namely the ratio y/x, it is clear that the first-order conditions determine a unique level of average advertising which depends only on α. This means that even when the firm finds it optimal to change its price, output, and level of advertising in response to changes in certain parameters such as the excise tax, it will maintain a constant ratio of advertising to output. Or to put it differently, changes in the tax rate (or other parameters which enter the model in a similar fashion) will induce the firm to change its advertising by the *same percentage* as its output.

To derive the comparative static properties formally, we substitute for x and y in the first-order conditions from (19) and

(20), and then differentiate (15) and (16). Differentiating first with respect to the tax rate β we get

$$g_\beta = \frac{\theta''}{xD} < 0 \qquad (21)$$

$$\hat{g}_\beta = \frac{z\theta''}{xD} < 0 \qquad (22)$$

where D is the determinant given in (18). From (21) and (22) we see immediately that

$$\frac{g_\beta}{x} = \frac{\hat{g}_\beta}{y} \qquad (23)$$

which confirms the equality between the percentage rates of change of output and advertising. Differentiating (8c) gives

$$\frac{\partial \hat{p}}{\partial \beta} = H'g_\beta + \theta' \frac{dz}{d\beta} = H'g_\beta > 0 \left(\text{since } \frac{dz}{d\beta} = 0 \right). \qquad (24)$$

Differentiating with respect to α gives

$$g_\alpha = \frac{z\theta''}{xD} < 0 \qquad (25)$$

$$\hat{g}_\alpha = \frac{2h_x + xh_{xx} - f''}{D} < 0. \qquad (26)$$

As in the case of a tax increase, an increase in the price of advertising leads to a reduction in output and advertising, but it is clear from equation (16B) that the ratio y/x must fall (since at the optimal level of z we have $\theta'' < 0$ by (13) and (17B)). Therefore the percentage increase in advertising is smaller than the percentage increase in output. This can easily be verified from (16) which upon differentiation yields

$$\frac{g_\alpha}{x} - \frac{\hat{g}_\alpha}{y} = -\frac{1}{z\theta''} > 0. \qquad (27)$$

However, the change in advertising *expenditure* remains indeterminate since the model places no restrictions on the price elasticity of the function $\hat{g}$. The change in the output price also remains ambiguous as can be seen from (8c) from which we get

$$\frac{\partial \hat{p}}{\partial \alpha} = H'g_\alpha + z\theta' \left(\frac{\hat{g}_\alpha}{y} - \frac{g_\alpha}{x} \right) \qquad (28)$$

which in view of (9), (25), and (27) is of indeterminate sign.

H

It should, of course, not be surprising if the above results did not hold under different sets of assumptions. The fact is, however, that in at least two cases examined, only one property, namely the constancy of the advertising ratio, is affected by changes in some of the assumptions of the model. To save space, we shall only report briefly on the nature of the comparative static properties of two variants of the above model.

The first variant is obtained by replacing the excise tax by an *ad valorem* tax. If the latter is denoted by β, and $\beta < 1$, then instead of (16B) we get

$$\theta' = \frac{\alpha}{1 - \beta}. \tag{16'}$$

Clearly, an increase in the tax (like an increase in the price of advertising) induces the firm to move to a steeper point on the discount-equivalence function, and this brings about a decrease in the advertising ratio. Consequently, the percentage changes in output and advertising are no longer equal. But the absolute changes in the levels of output and advertising remain determinate, both being negative. Thus we see that the effects of a change in an *ad valorem* tax are of the same qualitative nature as those of a change in the price of advertising.

The second variant is constructed by letting the firm be a monopsonistic buyer of advertising. In that case α is replaced by some function, say $\psi(y)$, in which case (16B) becomes

$$\theta' = \psi(y) + y\psi'. \tag{16''}$$

The changes in the advertising ratio can now no longer be predicted since the right-hand side of (16''), the marginal cost of advertising, can be either an increasing, a decreasing, or a constant, function of y. However, as in the first variant, the level of output, as well as the level of advertising, is reduced following an increase in the tax.

Other changes in the assumptions of the basic model are, of course, possible. But the effects of certain types of changes may be inferred from the analysis that has already been presented here. For instance, additional parameters may be introduced in either the function H (the no-advertising demand function), or the cost function. Changes in these parameters have effects similar to those of changes in the excise tax: no change in the advertising ratio, and hence equiproportionate changes in output and advertising. The reason for this is that condition (16) is invariant to the introduction of such parameters into the model. (This will be illustrated in section 2.) On the other hand, if one were to introduce a shift parameter into the function θ itself, representing, for example, the effectiveness of advertising, then the optimal level of average advertising will be adjusted whenever a change in this parameter causes a change in the slope of θ.

2. Group Adjustment and Equilibrium

In this section we extend the analysis to a group of producers who produce differentiated products. If this group represents an industry in a sufficiently narrow sense of the term, then it is reasonable (although not really necessary from a formal point of view) to assume that the products in question are gross substitutes for one another. In order to establish an interrelationship between the various brands of the product we generalize (8c) as follows:

$$h^i(x, y^i) = H^i(x) + \theta^i(z^i) \tag{29}$$
$$i = 1, 2, \ldots, n,$$

where $x = (x^1, x^2, \ldots, x^n)$, and superscripts identify the product (or producer). The function H^i still represents the ordinary (no advertising) demand function of the ith firm, but it now depends on the output levels of all the firms. The levels of advertising of rival firms are not introduced separately, since their effects are transmitted via the changes in the outputs of the corresponding firms. Under these circumstances the profit function and the first-order conditions of each firm depend on the outputs of all firms.

For convenience we shall assume that production plans are made at discrete intervals, and that at each such point in time each firm prepares a plan for one single period. Since each firm has to predict the levels of output that its rivals will sell in the current planning period, some assumption about the formation of these expectations needs to be made. In general, it seems reasonable to assume that such expectations are some function of the levels of output that one's competitors produced in the past, and especially in the preceding period. Since in the present paper we do not intend to study this particular aspect of the problem at the highest level of generality, we shall assume for simplicity that the expectations relationships are of the Cournot variety; in other words, each firm expects its competitors to sell in period t the same output as in period $t-1$.[4] Replacing x_t^j in the profit functions by x^j_{t-1} for all $j, j \neq i$, then the first-order conditions can be stated as

$$h^i(x_t^i, y_t^i, x_{t-1}^{-i}) + x_t^i h_i^i \qquad (30)$$

$$\left. \begin{array}{l} -f^{i\prime} - \beta = 0 \\[2mm] x_t^i h_y^i - \alpha = 0 \end{array} \right\} \; i = 1, 2, \ldots, n, \qquad (31)$$

where x_{t-1}^{-i} is the vector of the n terms x^j_{t-1} without the ith component,

$$h_i^i = \frac{\partial h^i}{\partial x_t^i}, \quad \text{and} \quad h_y^i = \frac{\partial h^i}{\partial y_t^i}.$$

The second-order conditions are essentially the same as those given in (17) and (18), and will not be restated here. We may assume that (30) and (31) have positive solutions for all α, β, and x_{t-1}^{-i} in some neighborhood. These solutions can be written as

$$\bar{x}_t^i = g^i(x_{t-1}^{-i}; \alpha, \beta) \qquad (32)$$

$$\left. \begin{array}{l} \end{array} \right\} i = 1, 2, \ldots, n.$$

$$\bar{y}_t^i = \hat{g}^i(x_{t-1}^{-i}; \alpha, \beta) \qquad (33)$$

The n equations in (32) constitute a system of first-order difference equations which fully describe the time paths of the levels of output of the n firms, given α and β, and a set of initial outputs. The changes over time in the levels of advertising are given by system (33).

Let us now suppose that initially the system is in equilibrium, and the tax rate is increased. Then we know from (21), (22), and (24) that in the period following the tax increase, every firm will cut its output and advertising, and raise its price. In the period following these initial adjustments further changes are made as dictated by the reaction functions in (32) and (33). In order to investigate the nature of these adjustments it is necessary to determine the signs of the derivatives of the func-

---

[4] For some of the implications of modifying the Cournot assumption see, e.g., Hadar [5].

tions g^i and $\hat{g}^i$ with respect to the $x^j{}_{t-1}$. Implicit differentiation of (30) and (31) yields

$$g_j{}^i = \frac{-MR_j{}^i \theta''}{x_t{}^i D}$$ (34)

$$\left. \begin{array}{l} \\ \\ \end{array} \right\} i, j = 1, 2, \ldots, n,$$

$$\hat{g}_j{}^i = \frac{-MR_j{}^i z_t{}^i \theta''}{x_t{}^i D} \left. \right\} i \neq j,$$ (35)

where

$$g_j{}^i = \frac{\partial g^i}{\partial x^j{}_{t-1}}, \quad i \neq j,$$

$$\hat{g}_j{}^i = \frac{\partial \hat{g}^i}{\partial x^j{}_{t-1}}, \quad i \neq j,$$

$$MR_j{}^i = H_j{}^i + x_t{}^i H^i{}_{ij},$$

and

$$z_t{}^i = \frac{y_t{}^i}{x_t{}^i}.$$

Since we are dealing here with substitutes, it follows that $H_j{}^i < 0$ for all i and j. It is, therefore, reasonable to expect that $MR_j{}^i < 0$, and hence $g_j{}^i < 0$ and $\hat{g}_j{}^i < 0$ for all i and j, $i \neq j$. If so, then in the second period following the tax increase firms will raise their levels of output and advertising, in the third period they will lower them again, and so on. We thus see that the adjustments of output and advertising following a change in the tax rate are of an oscillatory nature, but the direction of the changes in each period is the same for all firms. Furthermore, it is clear that $g_j{}^i / x_t{}^i = \hat{g}_j{}^i / y_t{}^i$, so that $z_t{}^i$ remains constant over time. The advertising–output ratio of each firm is, therefore, invariant to changes in both the (excise) tax rate and the outputs of competing firms.

The process defined by (32) may be stable or unstable.[5] If it is stable, the levels of output and advertising will converge to some set of equilibrium values. These can then be expressed as functions of α and β, and differentiation of these functions will indicate whether the (group) equilibrium values of output and advertising will increase or decrease with changes in the parameters. Unfortunately, additional quantitative information is needed in order to determine the signs of these derivatives;

[5] Sufficient conditions for stability of such an adjustment process are given in Hadar [4].

since the levels of output are adjusted in an oscillatory pattern, the equilibrium values depend on the magnitudes of these changes in each period. Hence without additional specifications, the long-run comparative static properties remain indeterminate.

3. Conclusion

The main results of the analysis can be briefly summarized. It was shown that it is possible to specify the nature of the effects of advertising on the demand function of a monopolistically competitive firm in a fashion which leads to meaningful and testable hypotheses. The approach followed in this paper produced a model in which the effects of changes in the shift parameters on the levels of output and advertising are always determinate. Furthermore, we saw that if the firm is a competitive buyer of advertising, then it turns out that the advertising ratio is invariant to changes in parameters belonging to a certain class, an example of which is an excise tax. Changes in parameters in the latter class also result in a predictable change in the price of the firm's output, since the price always moves in a direction opposite to that of the change in output whenever output and advertising change by the same proportion.

When the model is extended to a group of producers, and the assumption is made that expectations are formed in accordance with simple Cournot-type expectations functions, then changes in either the tax or the price of advertising bring about oscillatory adjustments in output and advertising by all firms. However, since all adjustments which occur after the second period following the initial disturbance (e.g. a change in the tax) are made in response to changes in the outputs of one's rivals, and since the latter variables do not appear in equations (16), it follows that the advertising ratio of each firm remains constant during the adjustment process (except possibly in the period following the initial disturbance). Moreover, the invariance of the advertising ratios is independent of the stability properties of the model. If the model is stable, it will move toward a new equilibrium point, but a comparison of the initial and the new group-equilibrium points is not possible in the present model without additional specifications.

REFERENCES

[1] G. C. ARCHIBALD, 'Chamberlin versus Chicago', *Review of Economic Studies*, XXIX (1961) 2–28.

[2] G. C. ARCHIBALD, 'Profit-Maximising and Non-Price Competition', *Economica*, XXXI (1964) 13–22.

[3] R. DORFMAN and P. O. STEINER, 'Optimal Advertising and Optimal Quality', *American Economic Review*, XLIV (1954) 826–36.

[4] J. HADAR, 'Stability of Oligopoly with Product Differentiation', *Review of Economic Studies*, XXXIII (1966) 57–60.

[5] J. HADAR, 'On Expectations and Stability', *Behavioral Science* XIII (1968) 445–54.

[6] G. J. STIGLER, 'Monopolistic Competition in Retrospect', *Five Lectures on Economic Problems* (London: Macmillan, 1949).

14 Imperfect Competition with Unknown Demand[1]

Josef Hadar and Claude Hillinger

The increased attention that has recently been directed at informational aspects of economic models clearly points to the need for a serious re-examination of certain traditional theories. Among those that suggest themselves for such a re-evaluation, theories in the general area of imperfect competition deserve a high priority, primarily because of the fact that firms operating in such markets are normally assumed to have complete knowledge of their demand functions. At the heart of this entire issue is one basic problem which may be stated quite simply by posing the following question: can one construct a meaningful and non-empty theory of imperfect competition without the assumption that firms have complete knowledge of their demand functions? It is the purpose of this paper to show that the answer to this question is in the affirmative. We do this by constructing a model of an imperfectly competitive market in which each firm is assumed to have no information about its demand function (except that it is downward sloping), and we show that this model yields several testable hypotheses that are both interesting and reasonable. We should point out that the basic ideas and methods behind our approach are not entirely novel; efforts in similar directions may be found in the works of Arrow [1], Clower [2], and Day [3].

1. The Pricing Decision

The main components of the model are the demand and cost functions of each firm. These are given by the following equations:

[1] The authors are grateful to Noboru Sakashita for his helpful comments.

Reprinted from *Review of Economic Studies*, xxxvi 4 (Oct 1969) 519–25, by kind permission of the authors and of the Managing Editor.

$$x_t^i = h^i(p_t) \Big] \qquad (1)$$
$$\Big\} \; i = 1, 2, \ldots, n,$$
$$mc_t^i = f^i(x_t^i) \Big] \qquad (2)$$

where x_t^i is the logarithm of the quantity of good i demanded in period t, $p_t = (p_t^1, p_t^2, \ldots, p_t^n)$ is the vector of the logarithms of the market prices in period t, mc_t^i is the logarithm of the marginal cost of the quantity demanded of good i in period t, and n is the number of firms (goods) in the market. Since the slopes of the functions h^i and f^i have the same signs as the slopes of their 'natural' (i.e. non-logarithmic) counterparts, the logarithmic transformations cause no loss of generality. One of the advantages of the present formulation is, of course, that the slopes of the functions h^i and f^i are elasticities, and therefore are independent of the units of measurement. We now state the basic assumptions about the above functions.

A.1(a). There exists a number $a > 0$ such that for all p^t

$$-a \le h_i^i < 0, \qquad i = 1, 2, \ldots, n.$$

A.1(b). $h_j^i \ge 0$ for all p_t, i, and j, $i \ne j$.

A.2. There exists a number $e > 0$ such that for all p_t

$$|h_i^i| - \sum_{\substack{j=1 \\ j \ne i}}^{n} |h_j^i| \ge e \qquad i = 1, 2, \ldots, n.$$

Because of A.1, the above inequalities may also be stated in the equivalent form

$$\sum_{j=1}^{n} h_j^i \le -e \qquad i = 1, 2, \ldots, n.$$

A.3. There exists a number $b \ge 0$ such that for all x_t^i

$$0 \le f^{i\prime} \le b \qquad i = 1, 2, \ldots, n.$$

Assumption A.1(a) requires all own-price elasticities to be negative and bounded from below. While the negativity restriction rules out Giffen goods, the boundedness condition implies that the market demand for every good is always positive. Part (b) of A.1 is the assumption of weak gross substitutability. Assumption A.2 imposes a dominant dgiaonal on

*

the elasticity matrix $[h_j{}^i]$, while A.3 rules out decreasing marginal cost.[2]

Our assumption about the pricing behaviour of firms is that they follow a cost-plus principle; in particular, it is assumed that each firm desires to attain a certain per cent mark-up above marginal cost, and that whenever there appears a discrepancy between desired and realized mark-up, the firm changes its price so as to eliminate, or at least reduce, this gap. This assumption leads to the following price adjustment process:

$$p^i_{t+1} = p_t{}^i + k^i[f^i(x_t{}^i) + \eta^i - p_t{}^i],$$
$$k^i > 0, \quad \eta^i \geq 0, \quad i = 1, 2, \ldots, n, \quad (3)$$

where η^i is the logarithm of the desired ratio of price over marginal cost of firm i.

The η^i may be given an alternative interpretation. We know that under conditions of full information, each firm equates its marginal cost with its marginal revenue; that is, it chooses a price (or output) so as to satisfy the equation $f^i(x_t{}^i) = p_t{}^i + \ln\left(1 + \frac{1}{h_i{}^i}\right)$. Therefore, given the above adjustment process, η^i may also be interpreted as the firm estimate of $\ln\left(1 + \frac{1}{h_i{}^i}\right)$.

It should be pointed out that while the marginal-cost-plus rule (as well as the alternative interpretation) is consistent with the desire to maximize profit, the actual value assigned to η^i may not yield a maximum level of profit. The reason why the firm may not be able to choose an optimal value for η^i is, of course, the fact that it has no information about its demand function, or the actions contemplated by its competitors. One might therefore argue that rather than regard η^i as a fixed parameter, we should allow the firm to change this parameter from time to time, and thus provide the firm with an additional means of improving its profit position. Granting that this argument has some merit, it is nevertheless not unreasonable to assume that over short periods of time the rate of mark-up is

---

[2] Since the dominant diagonal plays a crucial role in our analysis, it is of interest to point out that this dominance can be derived from Assumption A.1, and certain postulates of utility maximization. This derivation is demonstrated in the Appendix.

constant. Furthermore, from a methodological point of view, the constancy of the η^i is necessary to preserve the simplicity as well as the predictive content of the model.[3]

Existence, uniqueness and stability of the equilibrium

It turns out that the above price adjustment process converges to a unique equilibrium under fairly liberal conditions. To show this, we write the adjustment process as a mapping from the positive orthant into itself. Replacing $x_t{}^i$ by $h^i(p_t)$ in (3), we have

$$p^i{}_{t+1} = p_t{}^i + k^i\{f^i[h^i(p_t)] + \eta^i - p_t{}^i\} \equiv g^i(p_t),$$
$$i = 1, 2, \ldots, n. \quad (4)$$

Now, it is well known that a mapping such as the above is a contraction mapping if there exists a number $c < 1$ such that

$$\sum_{j=1}^{n} |g_j{}^i| \leq c \quad \text{for all } p_t \quad i = 1, 2, \ldots, n, \quad (5)$$

where $g_j{}^i = \partial g^i/\partial p_t{}^j$.[4] This condition will be satisfied, provided the adjustment coefficients k^i are sufficiently small; specifically, if

$$0 < k^i < \frac{2}{b(2a - e) + 1} \quad i = 1, 2, \ldots, n, \quad (6)$$

where a, b and e are as defined in Assumptions A.1–A.3, then condition (5) will be satisfied with $c = \max\{1 - k^*, \, \bar{k}[b(2a - e) + 1]\}$, where $k^* = \min k^i$, and $\bar{k} = \max k^i$. Since the contraction property is independent of the initial price vector, the equilibrium vector is globally stable; it is also unique. It is easy to see that when the system is in equilibrium, each firm sells a level of output for which the desired and the realized mark-ups are equal.[5]

Comparative statics

In order to show that the model has empirical content, we investigate the effects on the equilibrium of changes in a shift

[3] Among other things, the introduction of anything like a learning process may make the model unstable. For an example of such an effect see, e.g., Hadar [5].

[4] The essence of the theorem is that according to (5), the mapping g satisfies a Lipschitz condition with a constant less than one, which makes it a contraction. See, e.g., [4].

[5] If the discrete process is replaced by a continuous one, then the model will converge under even weaker conditions. Specifically, convergence will still be ensured if one removes the boundedness conditions, leaving only the sign restrictions, and the dominant diagonal.

parameter – a revenue tax, to be precise. Since in that case each firm will attempt to equate desired mark-up with *net* (after tax) realized mark-up, the price adjustment process takes the form

$$p^i_{t+1} = p_t{}^i + k^i \{ f^i [h^i(p_t) + \eta^i - p_t{}^i - \rho^i \} \equiv g^i(p_t),$$
$$i = 1, 2, \ldots, n, \quad (7)$$

where $\rho^i = \ln(1 - r^i)$, and $r^i (r^i < 1)$ is the tax rate on good i. The equilibrium of the above system is defined by

$$f^i [h^i(\bar{p})] + \eta^i - \bar{p}^i - \rho^i = 0, \qquad i = 1, 2, \ldots, n, \quad (8)$$

where a bar is used to denote equilibrium values. It is clear that the $\bar{p}^i$ depend on the ρ^i, and these relationships (i.e. the solutions of (8) as functions of the ρ^i) can be written as

$$\bar{p}^i = \phi^i(\rho), \qquad i = 1, 2, \ldots, n, \quad (9)$$

where ρ is the vector of the ρ^i. For simplicity, we consider here the effects of changes in the quantity $(1 - r^j)$ – the net revenue of firm j from each dollar of its sales – rather than changes in the r^j themselves. The problem, then, is to obtain conditions (signs, or possibly even magnitudes) on the partial derivatives $\phi_j{}^i = \partial \phi^i / \partial \rho^j$. If we differentiate system (8) with respect to ρ^j, using (9), and then solve for the $\phi_j{}^i$ by means of Cramer's rule, then the following conditions can be shown to hold:

(a) $\phi_j{}^i \leq 0$ all i and j, $\phi_j{}^j < 0$ all j.

When the net revenue of firm j increases, none of the equilibrium prices will rise, but some may fall. The equilibrium price of firm j will necessarily fall.

(b) $|\phi_j{}^j| > |\phi_j{}^i|$ all $j, i \neq j$, $|\phi_j{}^i| \leq 1$ all i and j.

When the net revenue of firm j increases by 1 per cent, the equilibrium price of firm j will fall by a higher percentage than that of the change in the equilibrium price of any other firm in the market. Furthermore, each fall in price (including that of firm j) never exceeds 1 per cent.

(c) $\sum_{j=1}^{n} |\phi_j{}^i| \leq 1$ all i.

When the net revenue of *every* firm is increased by 1 per cent, the equilibrium price of each firm falls, but never by more than 1 per cent. This case also applies to the special situation in which the tax rate (and hence net revenue rate) is the same for every product (firm) in the market.

The effects of a change in ρ^j on the equilibrium levels of demand are given by

$$\frac{\partial \bar{x}^i}{\partial \rho^j} = \frac{\phi_j{}^i}{f^{i\prime}} \leq 0, \qquad i \neq j, \quad \text{and} \quad f^{i\prime} > 0,$$

$$\frac{\partial \bar{x}^i}{\partial \rho^j} = \sum_{\substack{k=1 \\ k \neq i}}^{n} h_k{}^i \phi_j{}^k \leq 0, \qquad i \neq j, \quad \text{and} \quad f^{i\prime} = 0,$$

(10)

indicating that an increase in the net revenue of firm j may either lower, or leave unchanged, the equilibrium levels of demand of those firms whose net revenue rates are not changed. For $i = j$ we have

$$\frac{\partial \bar{x}^j}{\partial \rho^j} = \frac{1 + \phi_j{}^j}{f^{j\prime}} > 0 \text{ for all } j, \text{ and } f^{j\prime} > 0,$$

$$\frac{\partial \bar{x}^j}{\partial \rho^j} = -\left(h_j{}^j - \sum_{\substack{k=1 \\ k \neq j}}^{n} h_k{}^j \phi_j{}^k \right) > 0 \text{ for all } j, \text{ and } f^{j\prime} = 0,$$

(11)

showing that an increase in the net revenue of firm j increases the equilibrium level of demand of that firm.

We see that the qualitative nature of these results is the same as that which characterizes the effects of taxation in full-information models, competitive or otherwise. However, the results obtained here are considerably stronger, not only because we have dispensed with the assumption of full information, but also because some of the results are of a quantitative nature.

2. The Production Decision

Whenever demand is unknown, the firm must not only choose a price, but also a level of production. In fact, since production in any period can exceed demand, the firm may also find itself with an unanticipated inventory. To complete the construction of the model it is necessary to specify the method by which the firm chooses its levels of production and inventory. There exists, of course, a large body of literature dealing with optimal production and inventory decisions under a variety of conditions. We do not intend to make a serious contribution to that literature, but merely to show that one can construct a fairly simple production adjustment process that fits in well with the approach taken in this paper. The variables in this part of the model are defined in natural units (rather than logarithms), and are identified by the following notation:

Y_t^x = production in period t for the purpose of satisfying expected demand in period t,

Y_t^v = production in period t for inventory purposes,

Y_t = total production in period t,

X_t = quantity demanded in period t,

S_t = quantity sold in period t,

V_t = inventory at the end of period t (and beginning of period $t + 1$).

The behavioural assumptions which we are making are:

$$Y_t^x = Y_{t-1}^x + \alpha(X_{t-1} - Y_{t-1}^x), \quad 0 < \alpha < 1, \tag{12}$$

$$Y_t^v = \max\,[-Y_t^x, \quad \beta(\gamma Y_t^x - V_{t-1})], \quad 0 < \beta, \quad \gamma < 1, \tag{13}$$

where the quantity γY_t^x represents desired inventory at the end of period t. We also make use of the following definitional relations:

$$S_t \equiv \min\,(X_t, Y_t + V_{t-1}) \tag{14}$$

$$Y_t \equiv Y_t^x + Y_t^v \tag{15}$$

$$V_t \equiv V_{t-1} + Y_t - S_t. \tag{16}$$

Production to satisfy expected demand is an average of all past demands. As a matter of fact, the present formulation represents a dynamic process of the adaptive expectations variety which is consistent with the minimization of fluctuations in production. Production for inventory is designed to close the gap between desired and realized inventory, and the present formulation is such as to ensure the non-negativity of total production.

The stability proof is somewhat lengthy, and hence is omitted here; but it can be shown that the production model converges. That is, Υ_t^x and S_t converge to the equilibrium level of demand (by virtue of the convergence of X_t, which, in turn, is guaranteed by the convergence of the prices), Υ_t^v converges to zero, and V_t converges to the equilibrium level of desired inventory.

3. Conclusion

We have shown that it is possible to construct a meaningful market model without assuming that the decision-maker possesses information which in most cases he does not in fact have. The marginal-cost-plus policy adopted in this approach is consistent with the desire to maximize profit, and we have shown that the stability of the model can be ensured with a set of conditions that are not unduly restrictive. Moreover, the model yields a number of hypotheses concerning the effects of changes in a shift parameter; while we analysed only the effects of a tax parameter, the results suggest that the effects of other parameter changes will be just as determinate. Finally, one result on which we did not dwell in the text may be stated here as a concluding comment. Since the choices made by each firm under the rules specified in this paper are different from those which the firm would make if it had full information about its demand function, and since under the latter circumstances the profit of each firm would be less than what it could earn under a cartel arrangement, it follows that the actual level of profit earned under conditions of lack of information may be *higher* than that earned under full information. Thus, ignorance is not necessarily the root of all evil.

APPENDIX

In this appendix we specify conditions on individual demand functions which imply that the matrix of market demand elasticities of any given market has a dominant diagonal. It will also be shown that there exists a precise relationship between this dominance condition and gross substitutability. For the purpose of the analysis we think of all the goods as being divided into different groups, each of which consists of a number of differentiated substitutes traded in one 'market'. The set of indices denoting the goods in the product group (i.e. market) under consideration is denoted by I. First, we deal with the elasticity matrix of a typical individual, say, the kth.

Proposition. Suppose that the individual demand functions satisfy the following assumptions:

(a) The quantity demanded of each good in the utility function is strictly positive for all positive prices and income.

(b) All goods are weak gross substitutes; i.e. $h_j{}^{ik} \geq 0$ for all i and j, $i \neq j$, where $h_j{}^{ik}$ denotes the cross-elasticity between goods i and j for individual k.

(c) All goods are strictly superior, i.e. there exists a positive number s^k such that $h_m{}^{ik} \geq s^k$ for all i, where $h_m{}^{ik}$ denotes the income elasticity of individual k's demand for good i.

Then for any product group I there exists a positive number e^k such that

$$\left| h_i{}^{ik} \right| - \sum_{\substack{j \in I \\ j \neq i}} \left| h_j{}^{ik} \right| \geq e^k, \quad \text{where } i \in I. \qquad (A.1)$$

Proof. Since the optimal bundle is strictly positive by Assumption (a), the necessary conditions for utility maximization imply the following conditions on elasticities:[6]

$$\sum_j h_j{}^{ik} = -h_m{}^{ik} \text{ for all } i. \qquad (A.2)$$

But since Assumption (c) rules out Giffen goods, all own-price elasticities are negative, i.e. $h_i{}^{ik} < 0$ for all i. Therefore $(A.2)$ may be rewritten as

$$\left| h_i{}^{ik} \right| - \sum_{\substack{j \in I \\ j \neq i}} h_j{}^{ik} = h_m{}^{ik} + \sum_{j \notin I} h_j{}^{ik} \qquad (A.3\text{A})$$

and since the goods within each product group are substitutes, we can also write

$$\left| h_i{}^{ik} \right| - \sum_{\substack{j \in I \\ j \neq i}} \left| h_j{}^{ik} \right| = h_m{}^{ik} + \sum_{j \notin I} h_j{}^{ik}. \qquad (A.3\text{B})$$

But the relationships between goods in different product groups is also one of weak substitutability by Assumption (b), hence it is clear from $(A.3\text{B})$ and Assumption (c) that condition $(A.1)$ is satisfied with $e^k = s^k$.

---

[6] Samuelson [6].

In fact, it may be noted that the result will hold under slightly weaker conditions. Since all that is required is that the right-hand side of $(A.3B)$ be bounded below by a positive number, a certain degree of complementarity between goods in different product groups may be allowed. Thus, condition $(A.1)$ may hold even if $h_j^{ik} < 0$ for some $j \notin I$, provided h_m^{ik} is of sufficient magnitude.

As for the matrix of market demand elasticities, it is clear that if Assumptions (a)–(c) hold for all individuals, then the market elasticities will satisfy a condition similar to condition $(A.1)$ since market elasticities are simply weighted sums of individual elasticities, the weights being the respective market shares of the individuals.

Finally, a comment on an implication of the above result. We have shown that gross substitutability (and positive income effects) implies a dominant diagonal, and hence stability. The relationship between substitutability and stability has, of course, already been established. Here we have shown that the dominant diagonal of the elasticity matrix is a weaker condition, and that it is a sufficient condition for stability. By imposing the dominant diagonal condition one allows a certain (yet limited) degree of complementarity between goods in different product groups.

REFERENCES

[1] K. J. Arrow, 'Toward a Theory of Price Adjustment', *The Allocation of Economic Resources* (Stanford: Stanford University Press, 1959) pp. 41–51.

[2] R. W. Clower, 'Some Theory of an Ignorant Monopolist', *Economic Journal*, LXIX (1959) 705–16.

[3] R. H. Day, 'Profits, Learning, and the Convergence of Satisficing to Marginalism', *Quarterly Journal of Economics*, LXXXI (1967) 302–11.

[4] L. M. Graves, *Theory of Functions of Real Variables* (New York: McGraw-Hill, 1956) pp. 135–7.

[5] J. Hadar, 'On Expectations and Stability', *Behavioral Science*, XIII (1968) 445–54.

[6] P. A. Samuelson, *Foundations of Economic Analysis* (Cambridge, Mass.: Harvard University Press, 1958) p. 105.

15 On the Theory of Oligopoly[1]

W. J. Baumol

The oligopoly model which is described in this paper does not pretend to generality. It is meant only to describe approximately the current behaviour of a class of firms and there is no doubt that in other times and circumstances the analysis may become totally inapplicable. Nor does it say anything about the strategic give and take which plays so important a part in the theory of games. And in some respects it breaks sharply with received oligopoly theory. But the model seems to accord fairly well with my own rather spotty observation of the behaviour of a number of American business firms. Moreover, it seems to explain several well-known features of business behaviour which have been puzzling, and to carry some concrete implications for welfare economics, taxation theory, development theory and the theory of monetary and fiscal policy in which the place of oligopoly has been somewhat obscure. A few of these applications are described below.

1. The Sales Maximisation Hypothesis

On grounds which I shall only hint at here, I believe that the typical large corporation in the United States seeks to maximise not its profits but its total revenues which the businessman calls his sales. That is, *once his profits exceed some vaguely defined minimum level,* he is prepared to sacrifice further increases in profits if he can thereby obtain larger revenues. This is suggested by his

[1] This paper is taken from a forthcoming book tentatively entitled *Business Behavior, Value and Growth* (to be published by the Macmillan Company in New York). I must express my gratitude to the Guggenheim Foundation for the generous grant which enabled me to complete the manuscript. The paper was delivered as a public lecture at the London School of Economics.

Reprinted from *Economica*, n.s., xxv (Aug 1958) 187–98, by kind permission of the author and of Economica Publishing Office.

readiness to use sales as a criterion of the state of his enterprise (e.g. familiar statements such as 'Business is good – sales are increasing'). More important, it is confirmed by a number of cases where businessmen have rejected opportunities (pointed out to them by consultants) to increase their profits at the expense of sales. If they accepted the consultants' analysis of the facts of the situation, as appears to have been the case, this is the acid test. For them the additional profits (and they were not just short-run profits) were not worth the loss in sales.

My hypothesis, then, is that oligopolists typically seek to maximise their *sales* subject to a minimum profit constraint. The determination of the minimum just acceptable profit level[2] is a major analytical problem and I shall only suggest here that it is determined by long-run considerations. Profits must be high enough to provide the retained earnings needed to finance current expansion plans and dividends sufficient to make future issues of stocks attractive to potential purchasers. In other words, the firm will aim for that stream of profits which allows for the financing of maximum long-run sales. The business jargon for this is that management seeks to retain earnings in sufficient magnitude to take advantage of all reasonably safe opportunities for growth and to provide a fair return to stockholders.

Let us see how the businessman, as a good marginalist, will proceed to set his price and hence his output in order to maximise his sales under the profit constraint.

2. Price–Output Determination: Partial Analysis

Sales maximisation under a profit constraint does not mean an attempt to obtain the largest possible physical volume (which is hardly easy to define in the modern multi-product firm). Rather it refers to maximisation of total revenue (dollar sales) which, to the businessman, is the obvious measure of the amount he has sold.[3] Maximum sales in this sense need not require very large physical outputs. To take an extreme case,

2 More often the profit constraint probably specifies a minimum rate of return on sales or on investment rather than a minimum total profit level. However, it is easily shown that these alternative forms of the profit constraint make no difference to any of the conclusions which follow.

3 We may be tempted to say then that he suffers from money illusion. But this can hardly be taken as a criticism of his rationality – his objectives simply are what they are and there is nothing inherently rational or irrational about them.

at a zero price physical volume may be high but dollar sales volume will be zero. There will normally be a well-determined output level which maximises dollar sales. This level can ordinarily be fixed with the aid of the well-known rule that maximum revenue will be attained only at an output at which the elasticity of demand is unity, i.e. at which marginal revenue is zero.

But this rule does not take into account the profit constraint. That is, if at the revenue-maximising output the firm does in

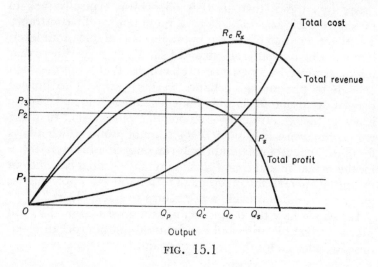

FIG. 15.1

fact earn enough or more than enough profits to meet the competitive requirements, then it will want to produce the sales-maximising quantity. But if at this output profits are too low the firm's output must be changed to a level which, though it fails to maximise sales, does meet the profit requirement.

We see, then, that two types of equilibria appear to be possible: one in which the profit constraint provides no effective barrier to sales maximisation and one in which it does. This is illustrated in Fig. 15.1, which shows the firm's total revenue, cost and profit curves as indicated.

The profit- and sales-maximising outputs are, respectively, OQ_p and OQ_s. Now if, for example, the minimum required profit level is OP_1 then the sales-maximising output OQ_s will provide plenty of profit and that is the amount it will pay the sales maximiser to produce. His selling price will then be set at

$Q_s R_s / O Q_s$. But if the producer's required profit level is $O P_2$, output $O Q_s$ which yields only profit $Q_s P_s$ clearly will not do. Instead, his output will be reduced to level $O Q_c$ which is just compatible with his profit constraint.

I shall argue presently that in fact only equilibrium points in which the constraint is effective ($O Q_c$ rather than $O Q_s$) can normally be expected to occur when other decisions of the firm are taken into account.

The profit-maximising output $O Q_p$ will usually be smaller than the one which yields either type of sales maximum $O Q_s$ or $O Q_c$. For if at the point of maximum profit the firm's marginal costs are positive an increase in output will increase total sales revenue since marginal revenue must at that point be equal to marginal cost and hence it too must be positive. Therefore, if at the point of maximum profit the firm earns more profit than the required minimum,[4] it will pay the sales maximiser to lower his price and increase his physical output.

Suppose now that the total profit curve has a single peak, as in Fig. 15.1, rather than being composed of several hills and valleys. Then a rise in required minimum profits, if it affects output at all, will cause a rise in price and a decrease in the quantity produced. For starting from a sales-maximising output of either variety, an output level which was just shown to be larger than the profit-maximising quantity, any increase in output will only lower profits. Hence if the required minimum profit rises, say, from $O P_2$ to $O P_3$, so that at the initial output $O Q_c$ the profit level is no longer acceptable, the higher required profit level can only be attained by a cut in physical sales (to $O Q_c'$), i.e. by a rise in price.

3. Choice of Input and Output Combinations

The typical oligopolistic firm is a multi-product enterprise (frequently the number of distinct items runs easily into the hundreds) and, of course, it employs a large variety of inputs. In this section I examine briefly the effect of sales (rather than profit) maximisation on the amounts and allocation of the firm's various inputs and outputs.

We obtain the following result which may at first appear

---

[4] If it earns less than the required minimum at this output there is obviously no output which will satisfy the profit constraint.

rather surprising: given the level of expenditure the sales-maximising firm will produce the same quantity of each output, and market it in the same ways as does the profit maximiser. Similarly, given the level of their total revenues, the two types of firm will optimally use the same inputs in identical quantities and will allocate them in exactly the same way. This result may be somewhat implausible because one is tempted to think of some products or some markets as higher profit–lower

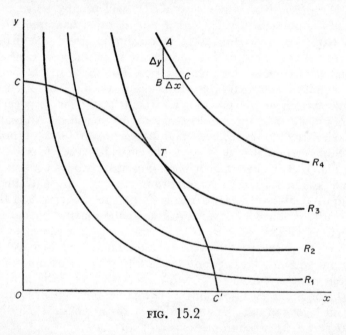

FIG. 15.2

revenue producers than others and one would expect the profit-maximising firm to concentrate more on the one variety and the sales-maximising firm to specialise more in the other. But we shall see in a moment why this is not so, though later I shall show that this view contains an element of truth.

It is easy to illustrate our result geometrically. In Fig. 15.2 let x and y represent the quantities sold of two different products (or sales of one product in two different markets) or the quantities bought of two different inputs. The curves labelled R_1, R_2, etc., are iso-revenue curves, i.e. any such curve is the locus of all combinations of x and y yielding some fixed amount of revenue. Where x and y represent quantities sold if their prices were fixed the R curves would be ordinary straight price lines. Their convexity to the origin represents the diminishing marginal revenues from the sale of x and y as their quantities increase which is the result of their falling prices (negatively sloping demand curves).[5] Similarly, curve CC' represents all combinations of x and y which can be produced with a fixed outlay (total cost). The standard analysis tells us that the point of tangency T, between CC' and one of the R curves, is the point of profit maximisation. But it is also the point of revenue maximisation because it lies on the highest revenue curve attainable with this outlay. This demonstrates our result.

A little reflection should now render the result quite plausible. The point is simply that, *given the level of costs*, since profit equals revenue minus costs, whatever maximises profits must maximise revenues. Hence differences between the profit and the sales maximiser's output composition or resource allocation must be attributed not to a reallocation of a given level of costs (or revenues) but to the larger outputs (and hence total costs and revenues) which, we have seen, are to be expected to accompany sales maximisation.[6]

Explained in the way we have just done our theorem is completely trivial. But when the sales maximiser's profit constraint is taken into account a more interesting but closely related conclusion can be drawn.

We may view the difference between maximum attainable profits and the minimum profit level expected by the sales maximiser as a fund of sacrificeable profits which is to be devoted to increasing revenues as much as possible.[7] Since each

---

[5] The absolute value of the slope of such a line equals the ratio of the marginal revenue of x to that of y. For points A and C represent the same total revenue. Hence the move from A to B represents a loss in revenue ΔR equal to the gain from moving from B to C; i.e. we have $\Delta R = \Delta y$ marginal revenue of y = the marginal revenue of $x . \Delta x$ (approximately) so that $\Delta y/\Delta x = MRx/MRy$. Therefore the falling slope of an R curve as x increases implies a falling marginal revenue of x relative to that of y. A similar discussion applies to the input analysis.

[6] We conclude that when the operations researcher encounters the problem of allocating optimally some *fixed* quantity of a firm's resources, the values of all other decision variables being given, his answer will be exactly the same whether he is dealing with a sales- or a profit-maximising firm.

[7] Provided that sales maximisation does not permit a surplus of profits over the required minimum as would be the case (Fig. 15.1) when required minimum profit is OP_1 so that the sales-maximising output OQ_s is optimal. But as already noted, I shall argue in a later section that this will not normally occur, i.e. that the profit constraint will ordinarily be effective.

output is produced beyond the point of maximum profits its marginal profit yield will, of course, be negative. In other words, each time it increases the output of some product in order to increase its total revenue the firm must use up more of its fund of sacrificeable profits. This fund of sacrificeable profits must be allocated among the different outputs, markets, inputs, etc., in a way which maximises total dollar sales. The usual reasoning indicates that this requires the marginal revenue yield of a dollar of profit sacrificed, e.g. by product x, to be the same as that obtained from a dollar of profit lost to any other product, y. In other words, we must have

$$\frac{\text{Marginal revenue product of } x}{\text{Marginal profit yield of } x} = \frac{\text{Marginal revenue product of } y}{\text{Marginal profit yield of } y}$$

This relationship indicates that, even in the sales-maximising firm, relatively unprofitable inputs and outputs are to be avoided, whatever the level of outlay and total revenue.

4. Advertising and Service Competition

As Professors Chamberlin and Brems have emphasised, firms characteristically compete not only in terms of price. In fact, more typically the oligopolist's competitive strategy is planned in terms of advertising outlay, product modification and special services offered to the buyer. The decision as to how far to carry each of these activities can be influenced profoundly by the firm's choice of objectives – whether it chooses to maximise sales or profits.

I shall discuss explicitly only the decision on the magnitude of the advertising budget because it is so easily quantifiable. However, the analogy with service and product characteristic planning is fairly clear and certainly suggestive.

The relevant diagram for the advertising decision is completely elementary. On the horizontal axis in Fig. 15.3, I represent the magnitude of advertising expenditure and on the vertical axis total sales (revenue) and total profit. In drawing the total revenue curve I assume, as most businessmen seem to do, that increased advertising expenditure can always increase physical volume, though after a point sharply diminishing returns may be expected to set in.[8] This means that total revenue must vary with advertising expenditure in precisely the same manner. For unlike a price reduction a *ceteris paribus* rise in advertising expenditure involves no change in the market value of the items sold. Hence, while an increase in physical volume produced by a price reduction may or may not increase dollar sales, depending on whether demand is elastic or in-

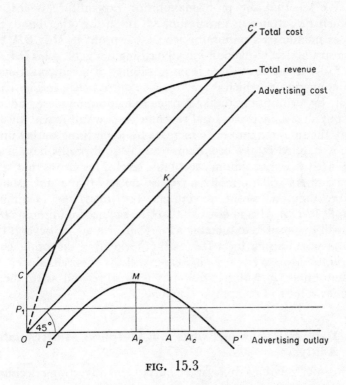

FIG. 15.3

elastic, an increase in volume brought about by added advertising outlay must always be accompanied by a proportionate increase in total revenue.

The 45° line, as usual, is able to transfer data on advertising expenditure from the horizontal to the vertical axis – i.e. advertising outlay *OA* is equal to *AK*. The other costs of the firm (*OC*) are taken to be independent of the level of advertise-

[8] Of course this is not necessarily true – potential customers may perhaps be repelled by excessive advertising.

ment, since it simplifies but does not affect the argument.[9] If these other costs are added (vertically) to the advertising cost curve (45° line) we obtain the line which depicts the firm's total (production, distribution and selling) costs as a function of advertising outlay. Finally, subtracting these total costs from the level of dollar sales at each level of advertising outlay we obtain a total profits curve PP'.

We see that the profit-maximising expenditure is OA_p at which PP' attains its maximum, M. If, on the other hand, the sales maximiser's minimum acceptable profit level is OP_1 the constrained sales-maximising advertising budget level is OA_c. It is to be noted that there is no possibility of an unconstrained sales maximum which is analogous to output OQ_s in Fig. 15.1. For, by assumption, unlike a price reduction, increased advertising always increases total revenue. As a result it will always pay the sales maximiser to increase his advertising outlay until he is stopped by the profit constraint – until profits have been reduced to the minimum acceptable level. This means that sales maximisers will normally advertise no less than, and usually more than, do profit maximisers. For unless the maximum profit level A_pM is no greater than the required minimum OP_1, it will be possible to increase advertising somewhat beyond the profit-maximising level OA_p without violating the profit constraint. Moreover, this increase will be desired since, by assumption, it will increase physical sales, and with them, dollar sales will rise proportionately.

5. Determination of Prices and Outputs: Multivariable Analysis

The inter-relationship between output and advertising decisions now permits us to see the reason for my earlier assertion that an unconstrained sales-maximising output OQ_s (Fig. 15.1) will ordinarily not occur. For if price is set at a level which yields such an output profits will be above their minimum level and it will pay to increase sales by raising expenditure on advertising,

[9] In fact, this assumption is virtually certain to be false for if advertising increases physical sales volume it must surely increase total production and distribution costs. We may prefer to interpret the diagram as a cross-section of three-dimensional revenue and cost functions taken perpendicular to the output axis so that advertising is permitted to increase revenue only by allowing a rise in the price at which the given output is sold.

service or product specifications. This is an immediate implication of the theorem that there will ordinarily be no unconstrained sales-maximising advertising level. Since its marginal revenue is always positive advertising can always be used to increase sales up to a point where profits are driven to their minimum level.

In fact we can strengthen this result and rule out even the possibility that by coincidence the profit constraint will happen to be satisfied exactly at the point of maximum revenue OQ_s so that this point will coincide with OQ_c. For at the point of maximum total revenue the marginal revenue of each output must be zero. On the other hand, the marginal revenue of advertising expenditure is presumably positive. Hence the equilibrium condition (analogous with that of section 3, above)

$$\frac{\text{Marginal revenue of product } x}{\text{Marginal profit yield of product } x} = \frac{\text{Marginal revenue of advertising}}{\text{Marginal profit yield (cost) of advertising}}$$

can never be satisfied at such a point since the *marginal* profit yield of (or loss from) advertising is always finite.

Examining further the multivariable (many products, many types of advertising expenditure) case we shall see that some overall validity remains to two basic results of the earlier part of this article: that the sales-maximising outputs will exceed those which maximise profits and that a reduction in the minimum acceptable profit level will increase both outputs and advertising expenditures. However, these conclusions do require some modification in detail – for there may be some exceptional products or types of advertising expenditure for which they do not hold.

To see the sense in which the results retain their overall validity we note that as the profit requirement is reduced, production, distribution and selling expenditure must be increased in total, so that at least some outputs or some types of advertising activity must have risen. The reason these costs must grow is almost a matter of arithmetic – as the profit constraint is weakened total revenue is permitted to increase. But if revenue grows and profits fall it follows by subtraction that total costs must become larger.[10]

[10] In particular we can conclude that there will be an overall growth in output and advertising in a move from profit to (unconstrained) sales maximisation. For

But while there is necessarily an inverse relationship between the minimum profit requirement and the overall levels of output and advertising this need not be true of every type of product and promotion outlay. For it can be shown that there may be some commodities which are fairly profitable but are inferior revenue producers. These play a role completely analogous with that of inferior goods in the theory of consumer behaviour. When revenues and overall outputs are reduced by stricter profit requirements these inferior outputs and perhaps the funds to be spent advertising them will rise.

6. Some Applications: Pricing and Changes in Overhead Costs

The foregoing analysis has a number of implications for various areas in economic theory, most of which I did not foresee when I first began to work with the sales maximisation hypothesis. First, I shall argue that it can be used to explain some types of business behaviour which have often been observed in practice but which are difficult to rationalise in terms of a profit maximisation objective.

Students consistently find one of the most surprising conclusions of the theory of the firm to be the assertion that overhead costs do not matter. So long as these costs really do not vary with the level of output, and provided that it does not lead the firm to close down altogether, no change in the level of its overhead costs should lead the profit-maximising firm to change either its prices or its outputs. This piece of received doctrine is certainly at variance with business practice where an increase in fixed costs[11] is usually the occasion for serious consideration of a price increase.

---

profit maximisation is equivalent to constrained sales maximisation where nothing less than maximum profit is acceptable while pure sales maximisation is tantamount to an appropriately low (possibly negative) profit requirement. Of course there may be no finite amount of advertisement which yields (unconstrained) maximum sales although here we must probably give up our assumption that advertisement always yields positive marginal revenues. A simple alternative form of the argument employs the notation $P\text{max} = Rp - Cp$ for the profit maximiser's total profits, revenues and costs and $Ps = R\text{max} - Cs$ for those of the sales maximiser. Since $P\text{max} \geq Ps$ and $R\text{max} \geq Rp$, then $Cs = R\text{max} - Ps \geq Rp - P\text{max} = Cp$ so that the sales maximiser's production and advertising outlays will never fall short of those of the profit maximiser.

[11] I use the terms 'fixed costs' and 'overheads' loosely, treating them as synonyms, although this is not standard practice.

It is easy to show, however, that this is precisely the sort of response one would expect of the firm which seeks to maximise sales and treats its profits as a constraint rather than as an ultimate objective. For if, in equilibrium, the firm always earns only enough to satisfy its profit constraint, as I argued in the previous section, then a rise in overhead cost must mean that earnings fall below the acceptable minimum. The result is precisely the same as that of an increase in the minimum profit level; outputs and/or advertising expenditures must be reduced in order to make up the required profits. The purpose of any such decrease in production is, of course, to permit an increase in selling price.

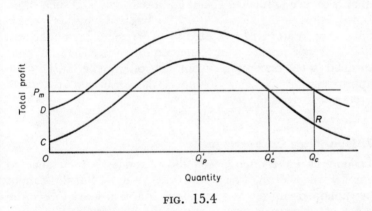

FIG. 15.4

This is very easily related in terms of Fig. 15.4. An increase in overhead costs means, geometrically, a uniform downward shift in the total profit curve by the amount of the overhead expenses. Hence if overheads rise by amount CD output will fall from OQ_c to OQ_c', for at OQ_c profits will now be Q_cR which is less than the minimum acceptable level OP_m. By contrast, the change in overhead costs will leave the profit-maximising output unchanged at OQ_p.

Again, inferior outputs and types of advertising constitute an exception. Sales of these relatively ineffective revenue earners will be increased when increased overheads force the firm to husband its profits more carefully. However, I doubt whether this exception is likely to be very important. Certainly, one would not expect it to loom large in the actual behaviour of business firms whose rough and ready decision-making processes are likely to by-pass the more subtle adjustments called for by optimisation analysis.

In line with this last remark I do not wish to go too far in rationalising the businessman's behaviour with respect to over-head costs. Doubtless, prices are sometimes raised in response to an increase in fixed cost simply because executives are making their pricing decisions in accord with a crude average cost pricing rule of thumb – if costs rise so must prices. And doubt-less average cost pricing is sometimes misused to serve the businessman's interests badly. High prices are charged because costs are high at current low output levels – without considera-tion of the possibility that lower prices can increase volume and so may reduce unit costs. I have come across several such cases. But we must be careful not to sell the businessman short – he is often shrewd and well educated by experience. I really believe that it is not much of an exaggeration to say that the con-strained sales maximum hypothesis often is a fairly close approximation to the rationale of the businessman's use of average cost pricing.

7. Non-Price Competition

Economists have often noted the oligopolist's reluctance to employ price cutting as a competitive weapon. But this cannot be explained entirely as a manifestation of a desire to live the quiet life. For even when competitive activity does become more vigorous it is notorious that this is very likely to take the form of more advertising expenditure or the introduction of new product features some of which are sometimes considered to be little more than frills. It would appear then that the large firm's competitive effort has been channelled away from price policy and into advertising, service and product characteristic modification.

This phenomenon is not a necessary consequence of sales maximisation any more than of profit maximisation. But the sales maximisation hypothesis can certainly help to account for the psychology behind these practices.

To see why this is so we must remember that to the business-man 'sales' mean total revenue, not physical volume. Now a dollar spent on advertising, if it increases physical volume, must necessarily increase total revenue. But a price reduction is a double-edged sword which, while it serves as an influence to increase total revenue in that it usually adds to the number of units which can be sold, simultaneously works in the opposite direction by reducing the revenue on each unit sold. In other words, as the economist knows so well, depending on whether demand is or is not elastic, price cutting is an uncertain means for increasing dollar sales.

True, price cutting is equally undependable as a method of increasing profits – indeed more so, for if it fails to increase total revenue it must almost certainly reduce profits because the resulting increase in outputs must also add to total costs. But, on the other hand, the effect of advertising, improved service, etc., on sales is fairly sure while, very often, their profitability may be quite doubtful. Thus sales maximisation makes far greater the presumption that the businessman will consider non-price competition to be the more advantageous alternative.

8. Implications for Ideal Output Analysis

Because of the theorist's failure to formulate a well-defined theory of oligopoly pricing (even the kinked demand curve analysis indicates why price may tend to stay what it is, and not how it was set in the first place) oligopolistic output has never been subjected to much explicit analysis by welfare economists in their discussions of ideal output. One comes away only with a rather vague general feeling that after all the oligopolist is practically a monopolist and so he is very likely to fall under the same cloud as an output restricter. One suspects that his outputs are smaller than they would be under the full reign of consumer (or rather, public) sovereignty.

The sales maximisation hypothesis does provide us with an analysis of oligopolistic pricing and output determination. Unfortunately it does not seem to open the way to any firm and simple welfare judgments (though what market form *can* be evaluated categorically?). However, some impressionistic conclusions can be drawn.

We recall first that under sales maximisation outputs will tend to be larger, overall, than they would be under profit maximisation. Nevertheless, they may be smaller than those which would result in zero profits, i.e. smaller than the output levels which are often misleadingly called competitive. This

means that in a world where competition was everywhere else
perfect, the allocation of resources to an oligopolistic industry
would probably be too small – though less so than one would
expect of a profit maximisation hypothesis.

But approximations to perfect competition are rare and
marginal cost pricing, if it is to be found at all, is the exception
rather than the rule even in governmentally operated enterprises. Even this weak condemnation of the oligopolistic resource allocation must therefore be considered suspect. Since
other industries also fail to bid for resources with energy as great
as that which is to be expected of perfect competition, there is
no reason to feel that the oligopolistic firm gets less than its
appropriate share. Indeed, if it is true (as is suggested in my
book) that competition sets the level of the minimum profit rate
so that in all firms costs bear a somewhat similar relation to
prices we may surmise that some sort of rough parity is established and that oligopolistic pricing leads to an allocation of
resources which is as close to the optimum as can reasonably be
expected.[12] That is, the distortions may tend roughly to cancel
out.[13]

So much for the judgment of oligopoly in a static context.
When we include in our evaluation the contribution of oligopoly
to economic growth it will be even clearer that the sales maximisation hypothesis sheds a favourable light on the effects of
oligopolistic organisations on the social welfare. Lest this be
taken as apologetics pure and simple, let me add that the
discussion provides no grounds for us to dispense with the
services of a vigorous authority charged with enforcement of the
anti-trust laws in order to prevent the corruption and abuse
which can be, and often have been, the fruits of great concentration of economic power.

The sales maximisation hypothesis has another, rather
disturbing, implication for welfare theory. It means that pre-
fixed lump-sum ('poll') taxes must lose their convenience for

[12] We must be careful, however, and heed Professor McKenzie's warning that
proportionality of prices and marginal costs will not ordinarily produce an optimal
resource allocation. This accounts, in part, for the vague terms in which my present
discussion is couched. See Lionel McKenzie, 'Ideal Output and the Interdependence of Firms', *Economic Journal*, LXI (Dec 1951).

[13] In fact, it is tempting to argue that if oligopolistic profits are kept just high
enough to yield a normal return on stockholders' investment these firms will
actually produce competitive outputs.

discussions of income redistribution. For even these taxes, like other overheads, can and will be shifted, and their imposition will affect incentives and the allocation of resources. They will be shifted because, when they are levied on him, the oligopolist will raise his prices and reduce his selling costs to a point where his profit constraint is once again satisfied. The explanation of the shiftability of this apparently unshiftable tax is simple – the profit non-maximiser has a reserve of unclaimed profits to fall back on when he is driven to do so by what he considers to be an unsupportable increase in his costs, though he can do so only at the sacrifice of sales which mean so much to him. Since no one seems to deny that businessmen do in fact often raise prices when their overheads increase, this point must be accepted even by someone who questions the sales maximisation hypothesis.

In describing the workings and implications of the sales maximisation hypothesis I have given only the barest indications of the grounds on which it is advanced. At best it is just an approximation to a set of complex and variegated facts and there seems to be no way for it to be tested by statistical or other standard techniques of empirical investigation. Nevertheless on the basis of careful examination of a number of cases it appears to represent the facts somewhat better than do some of the more usual models. In addition, as I have just shown, it helps to explain a number of otherwise puzzling features of oligopolistic behaviour. These are surely standard grounds of scientific method for permitting tentatively one hypothesis to supersede another.

16 The Restoration of Pure Monopoly and the Concept of the Industry[1]

Mancur Olson and David McFarland

1. Introduction

This paper is designed to show that the concept of 'pure monopoly' and the concept of 'industry' can be given precise theoretical definitions, and to argue that these concepts, which some modern economists reject, deserve prominent places in the theory of market structure. These concepts have been wrongly rejected, this article argues, because an excessive reliance on elasticity and cross-elasticity of demand has obscured important aspects of market structure theory.

Some theorists have used the following four categories in their analyses of market structure: (1) pure competition, (2) monopolistic competition with the 'large group', (3) oligopoly with a homogeneous product, and (4) oligopoly with a differentiated product. Pure monopoly, evidently at the opposite pole from pure competition, is sometimes either not listed as a market category or is reserved for the completely unrealistic case of a firm that controls the entire supply of *every* product, including leisure.[2]

[1] The authors are indebted to several of their colleagues at Princeton University and at the U.S. Air Force Academy for helpful criticism, especially Professors Jesse Markham, Richard Quandt, Lee Baldwin, Aldrich Finegan, Colonel Wayne Yeoman and Captain Edward Claiborn. None of the critics is responsible for any errors. Both authors are on the faculty of economics at Princeton University, but Lt. Olson is on military leave, stationed at the Department of Economics at the Air Force Academy, which he thanks for generous encouragement of this project. The authors also thank the Princeton University Research Fund for support.

[2] This general approach to market structure stems mainly from Professor Chamberlin, who first restricted the idea of pure monopoly, that is monopoly unmixed with competition, to the case of a firm that controls the output of every economic good. See Edward H. Chamberlin, *The Theory of Monopolistic Competition,*

Reprinted from *Quarterly Journal of Economics*, LXXVI (Nov 1962) 613–31, by kind permission of the authors and of the Acting Editor.

Before the advent of the theory of monopolistic competition many economists thought any firm facing a significantly declining demand curve was a monopolist.[3] The slope of the demand curve alone distinguished monopoly, the unusual, from competition, the usual, type of market structure. Once product differentiation was recognized, the competition faced by a firm with a declining demand curve from firms selling similar, but not identical, products, could no longer be ignored. The pervasiveness of competition among products and therefore of firms with declining demand curves implied that typically firms were in part competitive, in part monopolistic, and that there could be no purely monopolistic pole unless it was the firm with an absolutely inelastic demand curve.[4] But this was immediately recognized as absurd, since a firm, however monopolistic, will always use an elastic part of its demand curve if it maximizes profits.[5] So Professor Chamberlin argued that the idea of pure or traditional monopoly had no counterpart in reality, and that in practice monopoly was always blended with competition.[6] Many other economists have followed him in denying the existence of pure or complete monopoly; Mr Kaldor, for example, claimed that the complete independence of a firm, or pure monopoly, 'is not even conceivable, since it would conflict with our basic assumptions about the nature of human wants'.[7] Though Professor Triffin defines a concept of pure monopoly, he says that the required 'assumptions are totally unrealistic'.[8]

6th ed. (Cambridge, Mass.: Harvard University Press, 1950) pp. 63, 64, 68, 208, and *Towards a More General Theory of Value* (New York: Oxford University Press, 1957) pp. 79–81.

[3] There are some who still regard a monopolist as any firm with a downward sloping demand curve. See, for example, Abba P. Lerner, 'The Concept of Monopoly and the Measurement of Economic Power', *Review of Economic Studies*, I (1934) 157–75, and George Stigler, *Theory of Price* (New York: Macmillan, 1952) p. 206.

[4] Or perhaps a firm with a demand of unit elasticity throughout. This is, however, a dubious definition, since any firm with positive marginal costs will, if it maximizes profits, use a segment of its demand curve which has an elasticity greater than unity.

[5] Nicholas Kaldor, 'Professor Chamberlin on Monopolistic and Imperfect Competition', *Quarterly Journal of Economics*, LII (May 1938) 526–7.

[6] Chamberlin, *Monopolistic Competition*, pp. 63, 64, 68, 208.

[7] Kaldor, op. cit., p. 526.

[8] Robert Triffin, *Monopolistic Competition and General Equilibrium Theory* (Cambridge, Mass.: Harvard University Press, 1940) p. 132.

The usual argument against the real-world existence of pure monopoly rests on the universality of substitution among products; all products have substitutes of some sort, often highly imperfect substitutes to be sure, but practically significant substitutes nonetheless. If the price of any product goes up some buyers will decide to spend their money on other products or substitute leisure for goods, so there will always be some substitution among products. And so long as there is substitution, a firm does not have a pure monopoly unless it controls the supply of all products. Certainly everyone takes it for granted that any firm selling a product for which there is no perfect substitute has some monopoly power, but this element of monopoly, Chamberlin would argue, is blended with and limited by the competition of other products.

The competition among products also makes the concept of the 'industry' theoretically meaningless, according to Chamberlin, Triffin, and many other students of market structure. Just as the product sold by a given firm in monopolistic competition has more or less perfect substitutes, so each of these substitute products also has its substitutes, and so on, with the result that all goods are directly or indirectly connected with one another in an endless chain of substitution. And it seems theoretically arbitrary and unhelpful simply to assume, as Mrs Robinson did, that there are somewhere 'gaps' in this chain of substitution that justify treating the areas between these gaps as separate industries.

Despite the plausibility and popularity of the foregoing objections to the concept of complete or traditional monopoly and the concept of industry, these concepts are nonetheless often used. Economists commonly use the words 'monopoly' and 'industry' without qualification in empirical work. In textbooks and classroom lectures these concepts are often employed, not because they have theoretical validity, but probably because they are convenient, and because it seems esthetically and intuitively natural that there should be a concept of pure monopoly as the polar opposite of pure competition. It is unfortunate that concepts with such general usefulness, both in everyday conversation and in the teaching of economic theory, should have no generally accepted theoretical definition, and should even be thought incapable of being defined in a theoretically meaningful way.[9] Triffin states this view most clearly:

> To summarize, it is now evident that monopolistic competition robs the old concept of industry (and also the Chamberlinian group) of any theoretical significance. . . . The theoretical problem is the problem of general competitiveness between goods. . . . every firm competes with all other firms in the economy, but with different degrees of closeness. . . . When competition is discussed in general abstract terms, we may just as well make the group (or industry) co-extensive with the whole economic collectivity. . . . It is never useful to speak of 'industries' or 'groups' in a general, abstract way. . . . In the general pure theory of value, the group and the industry are useless concepts. The new wine of monopolistic competition should not be poured into the old goatskins of particular equilibrium methodology.[10]

There are no doubt some who would follow Mrs Robinson in assuming that there are always gaps in the chain of substitution, and thus a basis for definitions of 'pure' monopoly and industry. Still others deny that there is any validity in either the theory of imperfect competition or the theory of monopolistic competition, and accept Marshall's explanation of 'industry' and 'monopoly'.

These approaches will not be accepted in this paper. Nothing can be gained by *arbitrarily* assuming gaps in the chain of substitution, nor by denying the ubiquity and importance of substitution among products. Here the usual approach to monopolistic competition will be followed, and there will be an attempt to show that, given the assumptions of that theory, the acceptance of the pure monopoly and industry concepts is logically necessary. These two concepts are not only compatible with the usual modern analysis of market structure, but are logically entailed by that analysis.

The fact that pure monopoly and the industry belong in the theory of monopolistic competition has been overlooked apparently because the concepts of elasticity of demand and cross-elasticity of demand have confused most discussions of market structure. This article will argue that a misplaced emphasis on

9 P. W. S. Andrews, 'Industrial Analysis in Economics – With Especial Reference to Marshallian Doctrine', in *Oxford Studies in the Price Mechanism*, ed. T. Wilson and P. W. S. Andrews (Oxford: Clarendon Press, 1951) pp. 139–40.

10 Triffin, op. cit., pp. 88, 89.

elasticity and cross-elasticity of demand has led to neglect of the traditional interest in the number of firms in the market, and has obscured a necessary distinction between the near or competitive and remote or noncompetitive character of market substitution among the products of different firms, and has thus hidden an important difference between various market structures.

2. The Number of Firms

Whatever else a pure monopoly might involve, it clearly does not involve large numbers. A monopolist is a single seller and is at the opposite pole from an industry with a large number of sellers. It will then be useful to begin by considering the features that distinguish the workings of a market with many firms from a monopoly.

The most important distinguishing feature of a market with a large number of firms, whether there is pure competition or monopolistic competition in the large group, is that the individual firms in such a market have an incentive to act in opposition to the interests of the group or industry, even to the extent that in equilibrium there are no profits. Consider first a purely competitive industry, and assume (if only for the sake of simplicity) that the firms have zero marginal costs.[11] In such a case it would pay each firm to increase its output as long as its elasticity of demand is greater than unity, for when the demand is elastic any increase in output will bring an increase in revenue. Since the elasticity of demand for the firm is always a multiple of the elasticity of demand for the industry, increases in output will continue to be profitable for each individual firm even after the industry is on the inelastic portion of its demand curve, and the total revenue of all firms taken together is decreasing. This process continues until, in equilibrium, there are no profits. If as usual there are positive marginal costs, the price will be greater than zero, but in any event in equilibrium no firm realizes profits.

Thus all of the firms are worse off than if they had not tried to maximize profits by increasing output. There was a time when this was not understood. Some economists seem to have thought that in a situation of the kind described above firms

[11] Assume also that there is no entry or exit of firms.

would not increase output, on the ground that the result of such behavior would be lower profits for all of them, which contradicts the assumption of the rational pursuit of self-interest upon which economic theory rests. J. M. Clark, for instance, said that 'if all the competitors followed suit the moment any [price] cut was made, each would gain his quota of the resulting increase in output, and no one would gain any larger proportion of his previous business than a monopoly would gain by a similar cut in prices. Thus the competitive cutting of prices would naturally stop exactly where it would if there was no competition.'[12] Accordingly, Clark concludes that a competitive market will function properly only if each firm has a very slight degree of monopoly power. As Professor Knight points out, 'there does seem to be a certain Hegelian contradiction in the idea of perfect competition after all'.[13]

This view is now known to be mistaken.[14] It does not follow, because every firm would lose from increasing its output as a result of the fall in price, that no firm would increase its output in a competitive market. For whenever numbers are large each firm is so small that it can ignore the effect of its output on price in the market as a whole. Each firm finds it advantageous to increase output to the point where marginal cost equals price and to ignore the effects of its extra output on price, and therefore on the group interest. True, the net result is that all firms are worse off, but not because any firm has failed to act in its own self-interest. If a firm, foreseeing the fall in price resulting from the increase in industry output, were to restrict its own output, it would lose more than ever, for the price it received would fall quite as much in any case and it would have a smaller output as well. A firm that reduces its output in a market with large numbers gets only a small share of any extra revenue accruing to the industry because of that reduction in output.

The nature of the mistake Clark and other economists apparently made in an earlier day is now widely understood. Economists today recognize that if all of the firms in an industry with a large number of firms are maximizing profits, the profits for the industry as a whole will be less than they could be if the

12 J. M. Clark, *The Economics of Overhead Costs* (Chicago: University of Chicago Press, 1923) p. 417.
13 Frank H. Knight, *Risk, Uncertainty and Profit* (Boston: Houghton Mifflin, 1921) p. 193.
14 See Chamberlin, *Monopolistic Competition*, p. 4.

firms did not individually seek to maximize profits. And all would agree that this theoretical conclusion fits the facts for markets characterized by large numbers.

What we have been saying about pure competition also applies to the 'large group' case in monopolistic competition, where, as is well known, profits are zero in equilibrium and the average cost curve is tangent to the average revenue curve.[15] For in the large group case, by definition, each firm is so small in relation to the group that it can ignore the effects of increases in its own output on the group. Accordingly, it pays each firm to increase its output as much as its own, relatively elastic, demand curve would dictate, and ignore the generally adverse effects its increase in output would have on the group as a whole because of the lower elasticity of the demand curve facing the group as a whole.[16] Since the individual firm would continue to increase output until its marginal revenue equaled marginal cost, and since the elasticity of the demand curve facing the group as a whole is less elastic than that facing a given firm, the marginal revenue to the group as a whole will be less than the marginal cost, and the group as a whole will therefore be worse off when individual firms increase output to the point where individual profits are maximized.[17]

Therefore in any market with large numbers, whether the product be homogeneous or differentiated, whether each firm faces a perfectly elastic or a sloping demand curve, the firms act in opposition to their common interest in higher profits for the group, with the result that in equilibrium there are no profits. This paradoxical consequence comes about because the effects of the individual firm's actions are so small in relation to the market that no one firm in the industry is significantly affected by them.

[15] Of course, entry or exit of firms may be required to achieve an equilibrium with the tangency condition, and Chamberlin's 'uniformity' and 'symmetry' assumptions must also be granted. See *Monopolistic Competition*, pp. 81–100.

[16] This is Chamberlin's 'demand curve for the general class of product', of which his *DD* curve is a 'fractional part' (*Monopolistic Competition*, p. 90). While there are practical objections to the general use of such a demand curve, these objections do not apply to its use for this particular purpose. The point here is simply that the individual firm absorbs only a small part of any loss to the group that results when it increases its output, but gets all of the gain from the extra output.

[17] See William Baumol, *Welfare Economics and the Theory of the State* (Cambridge, Mass.: Harvard University Press, 1952) pp. 108–18.

The very absence of this condition has always been used to describe oligopoly. In an oligopolistic market, by definition, a firm's action will significantly affect competing firms, so a firm has to take other firms' reactions into account in making its own decisions. In an oligopolistic market, as is well known, if one firm increases its output and cuts its price, this will have a noticeable effect on other firms in the group, and may induce them also to cut prices and increase output, leaving all of the firms including the one which first cut its price worse off than before. Foreseeing this, the first firm may not cut price, and the oligopolistic industry may in equilibrium have positive profits because the firms may have an incentive to forego actions not consistent with the interests of the group.

In an oligopolistic market, as in the markets with large numbers, the product may be homogeneous or differentiated. The usual market categories, then, can be distinguished by two criteria: (1) whether any individual firm in the group is large enough to have a perceptible effect on the fortunes of the group as a whole or any other firm in the group, and (2) whether the products sold by the firms in the group are homogeneous or differentiated. The first criterion distinguishes oligopoly from pure competition and monopolistic competition in the large group, both of which we will here describe as types of 'atomistic competition'. The second criterion distinguishes both atomistically competitive and oligopolistic markets into two sub-cases according to whether the product is homogeneous or differentiated. The elasticity and cross-elasticity of demand need not play any role in the derivation of the different types of market structure.

The extent to which a firm must consider the effects of its actions on the state of the market is a much more significant factor in distinguishing types of market structure than the elasticity or cross-elasticity of demand. The analysis in this paper has progressed from the case where the firm's actions have no perceptible effect on the market or on any other firm, to the case where the effects of its actions on the market are great enough so that other firms may react to its changes in output. Why not include the remaining category: the case where the effect of a firm's action on the market is so great that it alone determines the state of the market? That is the case where the 'group' is composed of only one firm, where there is only one

*

seller in the market, where a firm's effect on the market and its effect on itself are exactly the same, and where it alone determines the price. In such a case the firm can ignore the reactions of other firms entirely, not because it is so small that the effects of its actions are not perceived by others, but because the firm is so large that it alone absorbs all of the effects of its actions on the market. Here the firm *is* the group, and there is obviously no possibility that the firm will act in opposition to the group interest. This situation surely should be called 'pure monopoly'.

3. Substitution among Products

Some readers may, at this point, feel that this conclusion is only a verbal illusion, but the following pages will perhaps persuade them that this judgment was premature. The market category of pure monopoly can have empirical content in spite of the ubiquity of substitution of one product for another and of competition among different products. This conception of pure monopoly requires *no assumptions* about the competition among products, and the definition of the market, *that are not also required for models of perfectly competitive markets*. The theory of perfect competition implicitly assumes that, when the price of the product of the perfectly competitive industry changes, there are no reactions from particular firms or groups of firms outside the industry. The simple supply and demand model in perfect competition reveals this most clearly. Suppose that an invention lowers marginal costs in a perfectly competitive industry so that the output of that industry increases and price falls, by amounts that could be computed given the change in marginal costs and the elasticity of demand. If this fall in price perceptibly affects the fortunes of any firms outside of the industry, or any other industry, presumably that firm or industry would have an incentive to change its output and price. Then the industry whose supply curve had shifted in the first place would find that its demand curve had also shifted, thus emasculating supply and demand analysis. Some models of oligopoly with a homogeneous product would face a similar problem. If Cournot's famous mineral springs had produced a product with a close and competitive, but imperfect, substitute, his analysis would be vitiated.

In ordinary Marshallian models of perfect competition, as

well as in many other market models, it is usually assumed that the prices of other, substitute products are constant, and this is possible only if there is no significant interdependence between the demand curve of the firm or the industry considered and any other demand curve. If there is such interdependence and other prices change, the elementary conclusions of supply and demand analysis need not hold. Thus there can be no question but that the ordinary Marshallian supply and demand model assumes that the demand for the product in question is held independent of the price or output of any other single product.[18]

But what is sauce for the perfectly competitive goose is also sauce for the purely monopolistic gander. There is nothing in the order of the universe to suggest that a product produced by one firm alone could not enjoy a demand curve that is unaffected by the price or output of any other product, if a product produced by a small or large number of firms can have such a stable demand curve. The conclusion is that, if the model of perfect competition is to be retained, the category of pure monopoly must be allowed. And surely most economists would concede that the partial equilibrium model of perfect competition is occasionally useful.

Nor is the concept of pure monopoly any less plausible than the concept of the large group in monopolistic competition. It is no more probable that there should be a large number of firms producing goods so similar, yet not identical, that the price–output decision of any one of these firms should have no noticeable affect on *any one* other firm (as is assumed in the large group case), than that a firm should produce a product that had no single close or competitive substitute, so *no one* other firm would react to its price–output decisions (as is assumed in the pure monopoly case). It is no more likely that a firm should find, when it increases its sales, that the extra revenue it acquires should come because consumers spend less on a whole series of similar, competitive products, than that it should find that its increased sales imply that consumers spend less on a whole range of different noncompetitive products.

The contrast between what is usually called monopolistic competition in the large group, and pure monopoly, resolves

[18] Alfred Marshall, *Principles of Economics*, 8th ed. (London: Macmillan, 1920) p. 100.

the paradox between the fact that the substitution among products is always present and important, and the fact that there can be pure monopolies and perfectly competitive industries. For while every economic good shares the consumers' dollars, directly or indirectly, with every other economic good, and every economic good is therefore a possible substitute for every other economic good, it by no means follows that any given good is necessarily a close or competitive substitute for any other particular good, or that the demand for it will be affected by the price of that other good. This does not mean that there are 'arbitrary' gaps in the chain of substitution. Not at all. It is no more arbitrary to assume that a particular firm's product has many distant or noncompetitive substitutes, but no close or competitive substitutes, than it is to assume that it has many close, competitive substitutes, but no identical, perfect substitutes. In the real world presumably particular goods have different types of substitutes. Some have many close substitutes (those produced in the large group of monopolistic competition), some have a few close substitutes (those produced in oligopoly with a differentiated product), some have no close or competitive substitutes (and are produced by perfectly competitive industries or pure monopolists). All goods have substitutes, but some have closer substitutes than others. There is surely nothing 'arbitrary' in this assumption.[19]

When a firm is a pure monopolist, i.e. selling a good that has only distant, noncompetitive substitutes, it can, of course, lower the price of its product without danger of retaliation from any other firm. For though its lower price will bring about the substitution of its product for other products produced in the economy, no *one* other firm will be perceptibly affected by this substitution or find that its subjective demand curve has shifted, so there will be no oligopolistic reaction. This argument is analogous to that of the perfectly competitive model, in which a firm ignores the effect of its output on price and acts as though it faced an infinitely elastic demand curve, because its effect on price is not perceptible to it. It does, however, have an impact on price, just as any action by the pure monopolist has an impact on the rest of the economy. The essential point in both cases is that this impact is diffused over so many firms that

[19] Pure monopoly cannot, of course, be maintained over a long period unless there are obstacles to the entry of new firms.

no one firm perceives it, and accordingly no firm's subjective demand curve is affected.

But if we unearth the concept of pure monopoly, we must also exhume its historic partner, the concept of industry. For the same arguments that have shown the possibility of pure monopoly and pure competition have also shown the possibility of the concept of industry. The concept of industry lost favor because of Chamberlin's insistence that competition among products was ubiquitous, that there was a continuous chain of substitution linking all products. But, as has been shown, the most general view of the process of substitution requires that we do *not* assume that *every* product must necessarily have at the same time *every* type of substitute – very close substitutes and moderately close substitutes, as well as distant, noncompetitive substitutes. That would be arbitrary. Instead it should be assumed that all goods are stretched out along a continuum: some have perfect substitutes, some have many close substitutes, some have a few close substitutes, and some have no close substitutes. Groups of firms that produce a set of products with no close, competitive substitutes have usually been called 'industries'. And that is as it should be. Moreover, there is no more reason to expect that the concept of industry should apply any more to very large groups of firms, as in perfect competition, than to assume that it should apply to small groups of firms, or to a single firm. There is no necessary connection between the number of firms that sell a product and the closeness of the substitutes for the product.

If an invention changed the shape of the cost curves and enabled, say, a half dozen firms to take over what had been a perfectly competitive industry, these six firms would constitute an industry, just as the perfectly competitive firms they replaced had done. If in turn one of these six oligopolistic firms was to take over the other five, and to produce by itself all that the other five, and the perfect competitors that preceded them, had produced, this one firm would be a pure monopolist. It would be the only firm in the industry. A simple example of this kind shows that there is not now, nor was there ever, any reason to assume that the concept of industry was appropriate in pure competition but inappropriate in monopolistic competition. If an economist uses the concept of industry in the study of pure competition, he is by any logical procedure required to allow the concept of industry in the theory of monopolistic competition.

4. Elasticity and Cross-Elasticity of Demand

The confusions in economic writing about the concept of monopoly and the concept of industry probably stem primarily from an excessive concern for the elasticity of the demand curve facing the firm and for the cross-elasticity of demand between firms. The concern with elasticities goes back at least to Sraffa's classic article:

> The extreme case, which may properly be called 'absolute monopoly', is that in which the elasticity of the demand for the products of a firm is equal to unity; in that case, however much the monopolist raises his prices, the sums periodically expended in purchasing his goods are not even partially diverted into different channels of expenditures, and his price policy will not be affected at all by the fear of competition from other sources of supply. So soon as this elasticity increases, competition begins to make itself felt, and becomes ever more intense as the elasticity grows, until to infinite elasticity in the demand for the products of an individual undertaking a state of perfect competition corresponds.[20]

It is in the attempt to understand monopoly or pure monopoly that the elasticity of demand causes the most difficulty. Take for example the following approach, which was suggested (though not finally adopted) by Professor Machlup, and which is implicit in most of the discussions of the degree of monopoly:

> Monopolistic competition would then comprise the cases of closer substitutes and more elastic demand curves, while monopoly would comprise those of remote substitutes and steeper demand curves.[21]

This approach is also basic to most of the literature on the 'degree of monopoly',[22] and is very strong in Mrs Robinson's writing.

[20] Piero Sraffa, 'The Laws of Diminishing Returns under Competitive Conditions', *Economic Journal*, XXXVI (Dec 1926) 545.

[21] Fritz Machlup, 'Monopoly and Competition: A Classification of Market Positions', *American Economic Review*, XXVII (Sep 1937) 448.

[22] For example: K. W. Rothschild, 'The Degree of Monopoly', *Economica*, IX (Feb 1942), and Abba P. Lerner, 'The Concept of Monopoly and the Measurement of Monopoly Power', *Review of Economic Studies*, I (1934).

Competition will be more perfect the smaller is the ratio of the output of one firm to the output of the industry, and more perfect the greater is the elasticity of the total demand curve. At first sight it may appear strange that the degree of competition *within* an industry should be affected by the elasticity of the total demand curve. But after all it is natural that this should be so. For the form of the demand curve represents the degree of competition between the product of this industry and other commodities. The stronger the competition from substitutes for this commodity the smaller the degree of competition within the industry necessary to secure any given elasticity of demand for each separate producer.[23]

Once this focus on the elasticity of demand is accepted, there is no possibility of any but arbitrary designations of the industry or monopoly.[24] Except for the distinction between perfect and 'imperfect' competition, distinctions among market structures are only questions of degree, the degree depending on the elasticity of demand. But the elasticity of demand is ordinarily different for every point on the demand curve, so if cost conditions for a given firm change and the firm charges a different price, the elasticity of demand can change without any necessary change in the number or type of competitors a firm faces. Moreover, the elasticity of demand for a particular good, in some cases, depends on the extent to which leisure would be substituted for that good. Or it might depend partly on the importance of a particular product in the budget of the consumer, and thus the extent to which his income would allow him to purchase a constant amount of that product when its price rises. A fall in the price of a good affects the demand for that good and for other goods by means both of an income effect and a substitution effect.[25] To the extent that the income effect determines the elasticity of demand, it is clear that the elasticity of demand is not a measure of the amount of rivalry or competition among firms or the degree of monopoly. It is not even a measure of how good a substitute one product is for another. It

23 Joan Robinson, 'What is Perfect Competition?', *Quarterly Journal of Economics*, XLIX (Nov 1934) 116.

24 Ralph W. Pfouts and C. E. Ferguson, 'Market Classification Systems in Theory and Policy', *Southern Economic Journal*, XXVI (Oct 1959) 118. These authors state that 'a satisfactory theoretical system cannot be constructed on the basis of demand elasticity coefficients alone'. We would add that neither elasticity nor cross-elasticity is necessary.

25 J. R. Hicks, *Value and Capital* (Oxford: Clarendon Press, 1953) chaps. ii and iii, esp. p. 48.

follows that Mrs Robinson is not correct in saying that 'the form of the demand curve represents the degree of competition between the product of [an] industry and other commodities'.[26] For these reasons, among others, it is evident that there need be little relation between the elasticity of demand for a firm and the number or importance of its rivals or competitors.

The cross-elasticity of demand in turn is in part determined by the elasticity of demand, so the foregoing arguments to a degree also weaken the concept of cross-elasticity of demand as a measure of the amount and kind of competition among firms.

The basic objection to the concept of cross-elasticity, however, is that it causes neglect of the two basic determinants of market structure: the degree of closeness or remoteness of substitution among products and the number of firms in the relevant group or industry. The concept of cross-elasticity, and for that matter the concept of elasticity, lead to neglect of the two elements which this paper argues are fundamental to an understanding of market structure.

The coefficient of cross-elasticity neglects the closeness or remoteness of substitution among products most glaringly when it is used to classify pure competition and pure monopoly. The cross-elasticity of demand between a pure monopolist and any other firm is obviously zero, for the output or price of the pure monopolist will not be noticeably affected by the output or price of any other firm. Similarly, in pure competition, as several previous writers have pointed out,[27] the cross-elasticity of any pure competitor, i, with any other firm, j, will be zero, at least so long as the rising marginal costs essential to pure competition are recognized. The output, q_i, of any firm i in pure competition will not be significantly affected by the price, p_j, of any firm j: in short $p_j \, dq_i / q_i \, dp_j$ is zero. Even if firm j should reduce its prices to deprive other firms of sales, it would because of its rising marginal costs be unable to satisfy the demand at the lower prices, so the sales of firm i would not be

[26] Robinson, op. cit., p. 116.

[27] For example, E. F. Beach, 'Triffin's Classification of Market Positions', *Canadian Journal of Economics and Politics*, IX (Feb 1943) 69–74; William Fellner, *Competition Among the Few* (New York: Knopf, 1949) pp. 50–4; A. G. Papandreou, 'Market Structure and Monopoly Power', *American Economic Review*, XXXIX (Sep 1949) 883–97, esp. 889; Chamberlin, *More General Theory*, pp. 79–81; and William Fellner, 'Comment', *American Economic Review*, XLIII (Dec 1953) 898–910.

perceptibly affected.[28] In pure competition by definition no firm is large enough to influence perceptibly the sales of any other firm.

The cross-elasticity of demand of a pure monopolist is zero because he produces a product that has a great many more or less equally distant, noncompetitive substitutes. Because the number of firms producing distant substitutes is so great, no *one* of them will be noticeably affected when the pure monopolist changes his price or output. When a pure monopolist changes his price–output policy, the aggregate effect on other firms may be sizeable; the total amount of substitution of other products for its product when its price rises may be considerable. But the crucial consideration is that no other one firm perceives this change because the number of firms involved is so large.

The cross-elasticity of a purely competitive firm is also zero because it produces a product that has so many very close or identical substitutes. Because the number of firms producing very close or identical substitutes is so great no *one* of them will be noticeably affected when the pure competitor changes his price or output. If the pure competitor should attempt to raise his price unilaterally, the amount of substitution of the outputs of other firms for his firm's output will be considerable, since these other substitutes are virtually identical. But the crucial consideration is that no other one firm perceives any change because the number of firms involved is so large.

Though the cross-elasticities of demand of the pure competi-

28 There are to be sure some, like Professor Bishop, who argue that the rising marginal cost curves essential to pure competition should not be considered in a discussion of the cross-elasticities of *demand*, and that there is therefore some reason for holding that the cross-elasticity of demand in pure competition is not after all zero. If one perfectly competitive firm shades its price, and there is no limit to the amount it can profitably sell at that lower price, the sales of other firms in the industry at their old price will fall to zero, so the cross-elasticity of demand is allegedly infinite in pure competition. This argument is not however very helpful, for the interest in cross-elasticities is due to the hope that they could help explain how firms act in different situations. How firms act in turn depends upon the effect of alternative courses of action upon their profits, and a firm's profits depend on its cost conditions as well as upon its demand curve. In any penetrating analysis, then, the cost conditions must not be ignored. And if they are not, there can be no question that the relevant cross-elasticity for a pure competitor is zero, just as it is for a pure monopolist. See Robert L. Bishop, 'Elasticities, Cross-Elasticities, and Market Relationships', *American Economic Review*, XLII (Dec 1952) 779–803; William Fellner, 'Comment', Edward H. Chamberlin, 'Comment', and Robert L. Bishop, 'Reply', *American Economic Review*, XLIII (Dec 1953) 898–924.

tor and the pure monopolist are the same, no one suggests that a pure monopolist and a pure competitor are in identical situations. In apparently suggesting that they are, the concept of cross-elasticity shows that it is not an adequate device for distinguishing market structures. The concept gives this misleading result because it ignores the distinction between near or competitive and remote or noncompetitive substitution. It neglects the fact that when the pure monopolist raises his price the consumer has no alternative except to pay that higher price and reduce his consumption of other things, or else spend his money on something quite different and forego the good sold by the pure monopolist. The pure competitor cannot raise his price above the competitive level because many other firms produce competitive substitutes for his product; the pure monopolist can raise his price above the competitive level because the only type of substitution that can take place is distant, noncompetitive substitution. The distinction between competitive and noncompetitive substitution thus accounts for the vast difference between pure monopoly and pure competition which the concept of cross-elasticity neglects.

The basic point of the foregoing analysis does not in fact depend upon the assumption, questioned by some economists,[29] that the cross-elasticity of demand in pure competition is zero and thus the same as that of a pure monopolist. The fundamental point is that the cross-elasticity of demand neglects the fundamental distinction between competitive and noncompetitive substitution, and that point is valid whatever the cross-elasticity of demand in pure competition might be. A comparison of pure or traditional monopoly with the large group in monopolistic competition makes this clear. The cross-elasticity of demand in both cases is everywhere known to be zero. Yet these two market structures are hardly identical. In the case of pure monopoly a firm sells a product that has many remote, noncompetitive substitutes. In the large group in monopolistic competition a firm sells a product that has many close and competitive substitutes. Because the effects of the actions of either a pure monopolist or a monopolistic competitor in the large group are spread out more or less evenly over a large number of firms, so that none will react to those actions, the cross-elasticity of demand in both cases is zero. But this means

---

[29] Triffin is one of these economists: op. cit., pp. 105, 133–41.

only that both the pure monopolist and the monopolistic competitor in the large group have in common nothing more than that neither is the same as oligopoly.

There can be no doubt that the pure monopolist and the monopolistic competitor in the large group are in decidedly different situations. This would be true even if the two had not only the same cross-elasticity of demand but also the same elasticity of demand. These two concepts, even when used together, are not sufficient to distinguish all different market structures. The monopolistic competitor in the large group would often have more reason to emphasize selling costs and product variation than the pure monopolist. Because the monopolistic competitor in the large group has many close, competitive substitutes, and the pure monopolist has none, the former may well gain more by making improvements in his product, or by making customers believe that he has made such improvements, than the latter. The monopolistic competitor in the large group will sometimes also have an incentive to merge with or buy out some of his competitors to increase his market power, but the pure monopolist has no such incentive. The monopolistic competitor struggles against a large group of rival firms, while the pure monopolist is concerned only with the fact that when he raises his price some consumers will decide to forego his product to maintain their purchases of a wide range of much different products. The monopolistic competitor in the large group competes, the pure monopolist does not. All these differences between the monopolistic competitor in the large group and the pure monopolist can exist even when the cross-elasticity of demand and the elasticity of demand are the same for both of them. If these two concepts do not, even when used together, reveal such an important distinction as that between pure monopoly and monopolistic competition in the large group, they surely should be called into question.[30]

[30] Chamberlin has recently, in contrast with his earlier writing, used elasticity and cross-elasticity to classify market structures and has seemingly attempted to put the traditional concept of monopoly inside the large group case in monopolistic competition. By this approach he seems to us to be doing violence to the richness of distinction implicit in his own original contribution. Admittedly most economists, who rely on elasticity and cross-elasticity of demand in their classifications of market structure, are logically required to take their concept of monopoly in hand and follow Chamberlin into the large group. But if this paper is correct, and other criteria for distinguishing market structures are appropriate, a distinction between traditional, complete, pure monopoly and the large group in monopolistic

The concepts of elasticity and cross-elasticity of demand also fail to take account of the decisive importance of the number of firms to the type of market structure, a factor that has been recognized for centuries. It was shown above that there need be no relation between a firm's elasticity of demand and the number or importance of its rivals or competitors. The cross-elasticity of demand can also neglect the relationship between the number of firms and the amount of competition. Consider for example a market in which there is product differentiation and only a relatively small number of firms: a market characterized by oligopoly with a differentiated product. The cross-elasticity of demand of a firm in such a market with any other firm in that market will be finite and greater than zero: the price or output changes of one firm in the group will have some finite impact on the price or output of another firm in that group. Now suppose that new firms enter the market, but that the degree of difference between the products – the degree of product differentiation – remains unchanged. With a larger number of competitors in the market, the influence of any one firm on any one other firm in the group will become less, so the cross-elasticity of demand will become smaller. In short the cross-elasticity of demand will suggest that the amount of competition is becoming less just as the number of competitors in the market and the amount of competition is increasing. The concept of cross-elasticity also obscures the importance of the number of firms to the type and amount of competition by putting pure monopoly, involving only one firm, and monopolistic competition in the large group, involving many firms, into the same category because they both involve zero cross-elasticities.

Thus the concept of cross-elasticity can neglect the importance of the number of firms to the amount and kind of competition in a market. And as earlier sections of this article revealed, the size of the group is decidedly important, particularly in that it determines the relationship between the interest of the individual firm and the interest of the group as a whole.

---

competition must be allowed. For Chamberlin's side of the argument see his *Towards a More General Theory*, pp. 78–84, and his 'Elasticities, Cross-Elasticities, and Market Relationships: Comment', cited above, esp. pp. 911–12.

5. Conclusion

The point then is that the concepts of elasticity and cross-elasticity of demand often lead to the neglect of the two most important factors distinguishing the various market structures: (1) the number of firms in the market, and (2) the closeness or competitiveness and remoteness or noncompetitiveness of the substitution among the products of the different firms in that market. Economists have known since the dawn of economic thought that the number of firms was a determinant of the amount of competition in a market, and they have sensed at least since the early thirties that the closeness or remoteness of the substitution among the products of the different firms in the market also affected the quantity and character of the competition in that market. But an excessive preoccupation with the elasticity and cross-elasticity of demand seems to have led to the neglect of these more obvious and fundamental determinants of market structure. This preoccupation is the more unfortunate because the number of firms and the closeness or remoteness of the substitution among the products they sell are by themselves sufficient to classify the various market structures.

Most important, a consideration of the question of numbers and of the competitiveness or noncompetitiveness of substitution makes it clear that the concept of pure monopoly and the concept of industry can be given the simple and sensible definitions that many economists have denied them. Economists have not infrequently been led by the elasticity and cross-elasticity of demand to neglect the most basic and elementary variables affecting market structure, and from there into denying the practical possibility and theoretical specificity of the industry and pure monopoly. The concept of industry in pure competition, which is everywhere acknowledged, is based on assumptions that are perfectly parallel to those required for the concept of industry in monopolistic competition, which is often denied. Yet the methodological inconsistency in granting the concept in the one case but not the other has not generally been recognized. Similarly, some writers have granted the practical existence of pure monopoly, but denied the practical possibility of the industry anywhere except in pure competition, or vice versa. This again is inconsistent. If there is a pure monopoly, it can control an industry; if there is an industry, it can be held by one firm. A moment's reflection about the two elementary determinants of market structure brought out in this article should make clear that if there can be a large number of purely competitive firms in an industry, it is at least possible that sometime there could be only a few firms, or only one firm, in that industry; and that if the required assumption about the remoteness of the substitutes of a product sold by a perfectly competitive industry can be granted, it is also proper to grant the same assumption about noncompetitive substitutability in monopolistic competition, and therefore to give the pure monopoly and the industry a central place in monopolistic competition. The concept of pure monopoly and the concept of industry in monopolistic competition are accordingly implicit in most modern discussions of market structure.

Notes on Contributors

ARCHIBALD, GEORGE CHRISTOPHER, B.A., M.A., *Cambridge* (1945); B.Sc.(Econ.), *L.S.E.* (1951). Lecturer at the London School of Economics 1956–64; Reader at the University of Essex 1964–7; Professor of Economics at the University of Essex 1967–1970. Since 1970, Professor at University of British Columbia. Archibald is one of the most distinguished economic theorists, with principal interests in the theory of the firm and (more recently) in labour economics and regional economics. He is co-author (with R. G. Lipsey) of an elementary textbook in mathematical economics. He has published extensively in journals such as the *American Economic Review*, the *Review of Economic Studies*, the *Journal of Political Economy*, *Economica*, the *Economic Journal*, *Oxford Economic Papers* and the *Manchester School*.

BAUMOL, WILLIAM JACK, B.S.S., *City College of New York* (1922); Ph.D., *L.S.E.* (1949). Assistant Lecturer at the London School of Economics 1947–9; Assistant and then Associate Professor at Princeton University 1949–54; Professor of Economics at Princeton University since 1954. A fine economic theorist with a gift for clarity of exposition; Baumol's interests are extensive, ranging over such fields as welfare economics, industrial organisation, urban economics and the economics of the performing arts. He is the author of several well-known books, of which *Economic Theory and Operations Analysis* (1961; 2nd ed., 1966) displays his pedagogic talents at their best. He has published widely in the leading economic journals.

CYERT, RICHARD MICHAEL, B.S., *Minnesota* (1943); Ph.D., *Columbia* (1951). Assistant and then Associate Professor of Economics and Industrial Administration at Carnegie Institute of Technology 1949–60; Professor of Economics and Industrial Administration at Carnegie Institute of Technology 1960–2; Dean of the Graduate School of Industrial Administration at Carnegie-Mellon University since 1962. Cyert's contributions are equally notable in economics and in management science and he has contributed significantly to the integration of these disciplines in the study of the firm and of market behaviour. He is the author of several books (perhaps the most distinguished of which is that with J. G. March entitled *A Behavioral Theory of the Firm*, 1963) and of a great many articles which have appeared in the leading professional journals of economics, business, accounting and management science.

FRIEDMAN, MILTON, A.B., *Rutgers* (1932); M.A., *Chicago* (1933); Ph.D., *Columbia* (1946). The Paul Snowden Russell Distinguished Service Professor of Economics at the University of Chicago since 1946. Friedman is one of the world's most distinguished and original economists whose work on methodology has exercised a considerable influence upon the pattern of economic research and whose path-breaking theoretical and empirical work in the field of monetary economics has contributed so much to the downgrading of fiscal policy as an instrument of anti-inflation policy in the United States and the United Kingdom. Friedman is the author of many well-known books and of an impressive range of articles in the professional journals of economics and econometrics. He is possibly the most influential economist since J. M. Keynes.

GABOR, ANDRÉ (a graduate of the Universities of Berlin and London). Lecturer and Senior Lecturer in Economics at the University of Nottingham 1947–67. Gabor is a micro-economic theorist who has made significant contributions both in the theory of the firm and in the theory of consumer behaviour. He is best known for his pioneering research into pricing, the importance of which is internationally recognised. He is the author of many articles which have appeared in the leading economic journals.

HADAR, JOSEF, B.A., *Washington State* (1957); Ph.D., *Minnesota* (1962). Professor of Economics at Case Western Reserve University. Hadar is an economic theorist whose principal interests lie within the fields of micro-economics and of econometrics. He is the author of an undergraduate text in micro-theory and of a graduate text (*Mathematical Theory of Economic Behavior*, 1970), as well as a range of articles in the leading economic journals.

HILLINGER, CLAUDE, B.A., *City College of New York* (1953), M.B.A. (1959); Ph.D., *Chicago* (1963). Assistant Professor of Economics at the Case Western Reserve University since 1966. Hillinger is especially interested in economic theory and econometrics. He has published several articles in the leading economic journals.

KAMIEN, MORTON I. Professor of Economics at the Carnegie-Mellon University. Kamien specialises in the application of mathematical techniques in economic analysis. He has published many articles in leading professional journals.

McFARLAND, DAVID, B.A., *Millsaps College* (1953); Ph.D., *Vanderbilt* (1963). Assistant Professor at Princeton University

1960–4; Associate Professor at the University of North Carolina 1964–9; Professor of Economics and Chairman of the Department at the University of North Carolina since 1969. McFarland specialises in the economics of industrial and commercial organisation and has published several articles in this field.

OLSON, MANCUR LLOYD, B.S., *North Dakota State* (1954); B.A., *Oxford* (1956), M.A. (1960); Ph.D., *Harvard* (1963). Assistant Professor of Economics at Princeton University 1963–7; Deputy Assistant Secretary at the Department of Health, Education and Welfare 1967–9; Professor of Economics at the University of Maryland since 1970. Olson has made distinguished contributions in the economic analysis of political behaviour (most notably *The Logic of Collective Action*, 1965), in public finance and in industrial organisation. He has published in an impressively wide range of disciplines, including politics and sociology as well as economics.

PEARCE, IVOR F., B.A., *Bristol* Ph.D., *Nottingham* (1953). Formerly Professor of Economics at the Australian National University and sometime Visiting Fellow of Nuffield College, Oxford. He is now Professor of Economics at the University of Southampton. He is well known for his contributions both in the theory of international trade and in the theory of consumer demand. He is the author of several books and many articles in the leading economic journals.

STIGLER, GEORGE JOSEPH, B.B.A., *Washington* (1931); M.B.A., *Northwestern* (1932); Ph.D., *Chicago* (1938). Assistant Professor at Iowa State University 1936–8; Associate Professor at the University of Minnesota 1938–45; Professor at Brown University 1945–6; Professor at Columbia University 1946–58; Charles R. Walgreen Distinguished Service Professor of American Social Foundations in the University of Chicago since 1958. Stigler has made outstanding contributions in the theory of price, industrial organisation and the history of economic thought. He is the author of many books (including a leading textbook, *The Theory of Price*) and of a very large volume of articles, many of which are classics. An astute inventor of testable hypotheses working closely within the framework of Chicago methodology, and one of the most readable of economists.

WILLIAMSON, JOHN, B.Sc., *L.S.E.* (1958); Ph.D., *Princeton* (1963). Lecturer and then Reader in the University of York 1963–8; Economic Consultant to the Treasury 1968–70; Professor of Economics at the University of Warwick since 1970. Williamson is a leading British economic theorist who has made important contributions in international economics (most notably he is the originator of the 'crawling peg' concept) and in the theory of the firm. One of the most promising economists of his generation.

WILLIAMSON, OLIVER EATON, S.B., *M.I.T.* (1955); M.B.A., *Stanford* (1960); Ph.D., *Carnegie Institute of Technology* (1963). Assistant Professor at the University of California, Berkeley, 1963–5; Consultant to the Rand Corporation 1964–6; Associate Professor at the University of Pennsylvania 1965–8; Professor of Economics at the University of Pennsylvania since 1968. Williamson is probably the leading specialist in industrial organisation with many important contributions in the theory of the firm (his book *The Economics of Discretionary Behavior* (1964) is a classic), in the theory of peak-load pricing and in the economics of anti-trust. He is the author of several books and a wide range of articles in the leading economic journals.

Index